de Gruyter Studies in Organization 50
Gender, Managers, and Organizations

de Gruyter Studies in Organization

Organizational Theory and Research

This de Gruyter Series aims at publishing theoretical and methodological studies of organizations as well as research findings, which yield insight in and knowledge about organizations. The whole spectrum of perspectives will be considered: organizational analyses rooted in the sociological as well as the economic tradition, from a socio-psychological or a political science angle, mainstream as well as critical or ethnomethodological contributions. Equally, all kinds of organizations will be considered: firms, public agencies, non-profit institutions, voluntary associations, inter-organizational networks, supra-national organizations etc.

Emphasis is on publication of *new* contributions, or significant revisions of existing approaches. However, summaries or critical reflections on current thinking and research will also be considered.

This series represents an effort to advance the social scientific study of organizations across national boundaries and academic disciplines. An Advisory Board consisting of representatives of a variety of perspectives and from different cultural areas is responsible for achieving this task.

This series addresses organization researchers within and outside universities, but also practitioners who have an interest in grounding their work on recent social scientific knowledge and insights.

Editor:

Prof. Dr. Alfred Kieser, Universität Mannheim, Mannheim, Germany

Advisory Board:

Prof. Anna Grandori, CRORA, Università Commerciale Luigi Bocconi, Milano, Italy
Prof. Dr. Cornelis Lammers, FSW Rijksuniversiteit Leiden, Leiden, The Netherlands
Prof. Dr. Marshall W. Meyer, The Wharton School, University of Pennsylvania, Philadelphia, U.S.A.
Prof. Jean-Claude Thoenig, Université de Paris, I, Paris, France
Prof. Dr. Barry A. Turner, Middlesex Business School, London, GB
Prof. Mayer Zald, The University of Michigan, Ann Arbor, U.S.A.

Yvonne Due Billing · Mats Alvesson

Gender, Managers, and Organizations

Walter de Gruyter · Berlin · New York 1994

Yvonne Due Billing, PhD, Associate Professor, Institute for Women's Studies in the Social Sciences, University of Copenhagen, Denmark

Mats Alvesson, PhD, Professor, Dept. of Business Administration, University of Gothenburg, Sweden

∞ Printed on acid-free paper which falls within the guidelines of the ANSI to ensure permanence and durability.

Library of Congress Cataloging-in-Publication Data

Billing, Yvonne Due.
    Gender, managers, and organizations / Yvonne Due Billing, Mats Alvesson.
       p.   cm. − (De Gruyter studies in organization ; 50)
    Includes bibliographical references.
    ISBN 3-11-012984-1
    1. Women executives. 2. Sex role in the work environment.
3. Women executives − Denmark − Case studies. 4. Sex role in the work environment − Denmark − Case studies. I. Alvesson, Mats, 1956−   . II. Title. III. Series.
HD6054.3.B55   1993
331.4′816584−dc20
                                              93-26380

Die Deutsche Bibliothek − Cataloging-in-Publication Data

Billing, Yvonne Due:
Gender, managers, and organizations / Yvonne Due Billing ; Mats Alvesson. − Berlin ; New York : de Gruyter, 1994
    (De Gruyter studies in organization ; 50)
    ISBN 3-11-012984-1
NE: Alvesson, Mats:; GT

Converted by: Knipp Satz und Bild digital, Dortmund − Printing: Druckerei Gerike GmbH, Berlin − Binding: Lüderitz & Bauer-GmbH, Berlin − Cover Design: Johannes Rother, Berlin

Preface

This study was made possible through a research grant from the Danish Council for Scientific Policy and Planning, the Women's Studies Commission and the Danish Social Science Research Council in Denmark. The empirical investigations took place 1987 and 1988. This means that any events, reorganizations, cut-downs, etc., which have taken place since 1989 and might have influenced the three organizations we have studied and the gender relations within these, are only marginally touched upon in the present text.

Besides the two research foundations we want to acknowledge institutional support from Samkvind (the Centre for Women's Studies at the Faculty of Social Sciences), University of Copenhagen. Also we would like to thank the following – who in different ways have contributed with either support, critique, practical help or/and encouragement: Flemming Agersnap and Anne Loft, Copenhagen Business School, Jeff Hearn, University of Bradford, Heather Höpfl, Bolton Business School, and Margareta Samuelsson, Gothenburg University, Gitte Shine and Helen Zienkiewicz.

Finally we would especially like to thank Deborah Kerfoot, University of Leeds, UK and Albert Mills, Athabasca University, Canada, who carefully read and commented on the whole manuscript.

Chapter 11 appeared in a different version in Organization Studies, 13, 1.

Yvonne Due Billing
Centre for Women's Studies
Copenhagen University

Mats Alvesson
Dept. of Business Administration
Gothenburg University

Contents

Part One: Gender Perspectives

1 Introduction

1.1 Introductory reflections

This book is about gender, management and organizations. More specifically, it deals with female and male managers within the context of organizations. Within this broad theme various aspects are dealt with. In particular, our interest is in the social and organizational processes and conditions that normally make it more difficult for, but sometimes can be supportive of, women's recruitment and function in management positions. Our empirical observations, as well as more general considerations and evaluations of contemporary macro-level trends, encourage an approach which takes diversity seriously – not only general patterns or averages – when treating women in relationship to organizations and management jobs. This book thus expresses the idea that an understanding of the processes which create 'women' and 'men' in work and career will benefit from the study of different social contexts (organizations) in which they are embedded. Although we mainly focus on female managers, our interest goes beyond this to a broader concern with the relation between gender and organizations.

We devote the first half of the book, as well as the final chapter, mainly to engaging with the literature, and to discuss/develop theoretical ideas. Further this book draws heavily upon and presents the results from our empirical investigations of gender, managerial jobs and organizations.

In three cases, each a study of a different Scandinavian organization, we investigate a number of aspects of significance for the absence/presence of female managers. The most important aspects are; the nature of work; the sex ratio; the division of labour between the sexes; the educational level and qualification structure in the organization; and the history of and climate within the particular organization. The point is to draw attention to central conditions and processes of relevance for understanding the situation of female and male managers and the gendered nature of management, rather than to strictly demonstrate a number of causal correlations between different factors. We connect to culture and symbolism theory and argue for a differentiated approach to gender and organization which would be sensitive to the variations between organizations, functions and levels when it comes to gender bias, discrimination and contradictions in organizational contexts.

Women are virtually absent from leading positions in most public and private organizations. They are almost totally absent from top positions and strongly underrepresented at the higher middle levels in Scandinavia and in most countries in the Western world.[1] This well-known fact is an important basis for this

investigation. More generally, a focal point of the study is the ever present hierarchical sex segregation within society. This means that men are strongly overrepresented in the decision-making bodies at higher levels and also within the most
influential, prestigious and well-paid occupational groups. The overrepresentation of men is less pronounced in certain political contexts. In the Scandinavian
parliaments, for instance, approximately 35% of the members are women,
whereas the overrepresentation of men is more pronounced in the higher levels
of public administration and, even more so, private enterprises. The percentage
of women at the higher management levels is typically only a few per cent, and
at top level, approximately 1%.[2] The study of female managers may thus be
connected to the hierarchical sex segregation of society as a whole; and its investigation may enable us to evaluate tendencies potentially leading to a 'removal'
of this segregation. Furthermore, all this needs to be set in the context of the
current debate on possible 'similarities' and 'differences' between women and
men in general and specifically how they both affect management positions.

Various points of view have been expressed regarding the relative importance
of differences, if any, between women and men with regard to modern working
life and the possible implications of these for functioning in management positions. Many writers (e.g. Marshall, 1984; Tkach, 1980) have emphasized the
basic similarities between women and men, at least with regard to the aspects
that are relevant in this context. Other writers (Loden, 1986; Grant, 1988) have
emphasized that as a result of different experiences, environment, socialization
and biology, women have in a number of important respects different values,
attitudes and psychological characteristics to those of men. It has often been
claimed, especially during recent years, that this implies that women have a
special (complementary or different) management style, perhaps with special
advantages when compared to the style which is characteristic of the 'typical
male' (Loden, 1986; Schmidt, 1987).

This theme may be rephrased to include the extent to which women tend to
function differently from men in their way of working, and in particular, in their
handling of social relations. Thus, the study of female and male managers may
illuminate dimensions of gender relations of broader significance than those directly coupled to this particular category. When women are recruited to, or act,
in managerial positions, gender stereotypes and conventions held by superiors,
subordinates and colleagues of both sexes may become more salient. A study of
female managers thus can complement the study of women working in less senior positions in organizations and illuminate other aspects of the situation of
women (and thereby of men) at work than those produced by traditional studies
of women as subordinated to men. Consequently, the theme of this book can be
seen also as an entrance or 'clue' to understanding broader gender relations in
organizations.

Even though we focus on female managers and a gender perspective on management, our interest goes beyond this to a broader concern with the relation between gender and organization.

More specifically, we will concentrate on female and male managers at the middle level. Even though we take an equal interest in top managers, a number of whom are referred to in the empirical data, the relative absence of women at this level means that our study invariably comes to focus on the middle level. This also implies that the lower managerial level will be touched upon only marginally in the investigation. Group managers, supervisors, etc. are thereby excluded. Often it is difficult to delineate clearly the various levels of management, in particular within private enterprises. Here the job of the middle (and upwards) management level that we are concerned with can be described as; firstly, having subordinates; secondly generally presupposing higher education and/or qualified job experience before taking over the management position; thirdly, having a high degree of responsibility; fourthly, the person in general works more than a normal working week; and lastly, receives a salary within the higher income bracket. We have also interviewed other employees, especially some who have qualifications and/or background experiences relevant for managerial positions. This is partly in order to illustrate the nature of the organizations studied in more detail, but also to obtain an idea of the obstacles, if any, to women reaching management positions as well as the reactions of those who have not (yet) overcome these obstacles.

In order to understand the social conditions and processes which have resulted in the absence, but in recent years, the modest presence, of women in management positions, a wide range of factors must be taken into consideration (see Chapter 3 for an examination of these). In this work, we concentrate on the organizational level. Rather than presenting finished models, we have attempted to be open to a broad spectrum of various factors within different organizations that are important in this context. Existing literature scarcely deals with these issues. Very few studies of women in management and organization take the organizational level and variations between organizations seriously. At the same time, most organizational studies neglect the gender dimension (Hearn & Parkin, 1983; Mills, 1988). According to Burrell & Hearn (1989:10), "gender has either been ignored, treated implicitly as male, considered an organizational 'variable', reduced to relative stereotypes, or been analysed in a blatantly sexist way". On the other hand, within the category of gender/organization studies, very few studies deal with managers. Also in literature on gender/management, organizational differences are often ignored. Thus we see our contribution as being unusual in that we combine the themes of gender, management and organizations, and consider both general patterns and variations from them.

1.2   Objectives of the study

Why be concerned with female managers?[3] Many different reasons may be given depending on the social categories that are regarded as important and also on one's view on human nature and society. The gender dimension may be taken as the centre of interest, or the management aspect may be emphasized; the theme may be seen primarily or exclusively as concerning actual or potential female managers. It could also be seen in relation to a human resource management (HRM) perspective concerning effective utilization of qualified personnel. However, as already mentioned, the theme of female managers may also be related to a more complex theme concerned with the relations between the sexes and gender equality.

Roughly, three general types of answer may be given to the above question. The first can be said to be technocratic/meritocratic and concerns effective utilization of personnel. In this context female *managers* become an aspect of the well-functioning human resource management. A precondition for this situation is that the enterprises and other organizations should be capable of attracting, keeping and developing not only suitable male, but also female employees for positions at higher levels. The low representation of the latter in leading positions in the great majority of enterprises thus constitutes a management problem in that it indicates a lack of ability to handle the potential which exists in the female work force.

The second type of answer is based instead on the group which is directly affected in this context, i.e. actual and potential *female* managers. In this case the reason for taking an interest in female managers is thus an interest in justice, equality and beneficial career prospects for a specific group of people rather than a general interest in management and effectiveness for its own sake. What is involved is essentially a combination of ethical motives, political ideals and the special interests of a specific group. This perspective focuses narrowly on the situation of a specific group, i.e. career-oriented women predominantly from the upper social classes, and their obstacles and prospects. It either downplays, or scarcely deals at all, with broader social and political problems. These two types of answer dominate most literature on the subject (e.g. Loden, 1986; Grant 1988) the majority of which is American.

The third type of answer, which is represented only rarely, emphasizes a *combination* of the *female managers* theme and *broader social*, political and organizational *issues*. If we use female managers as a basis and an example, then knowledge of central organizational aspects and of general conditions of influence and power may be generated with regard to the dimension of women and gender. For instance, the intention may be to develop a gender-oriented and sensitive organization theory (cf. Mills & Tancred, 1992) which takes the dimension of gender seriously, including the division of labour between the sexes and other factors which result in women and men acting differently at the place of work and having different prospects with regard to influence, career, etc.. In this way, the study of female managers can be related to another broader orientation that focuses upon a wider set of gender issues, and also upon potentially wider aspects of organizational life (Hearn & Parkin, 1983; Knights & Willmott, 1986; Mills, 1988). In some parts of the literature within this orientation, an interest is expressed in all social groups in terms of gender. The ambition is not to connect gender analysis just to groups of women and men i.e. people with a certain biological 'equipment' and the social, cultural and ideological attributes which are commonly believed to accompany that equipment but also to look for the gendered connotations of deeper, cultural layers as well as the gendered bias of ideas, social arrangements and practices of organizations (e.g. Ferguson, 1984; Mills, 1988; Calás & Smircich, 1992a, 1992b; Mills & Tancred, 1992).

The theme of female managers exposes not only certain aspects of the human resource management of enterprises and other organizations, together with the obstacles and problems with regard to the career prospects of a specific group, but also more general dimensions of the situation of women and men within organizations, working life and society. Clearly, it is unreasonable to generalize from the specific group of female managers to women in general, or even women in wage work. Nevertheless, once a study of female managers is undertaken, it can have the effect that dimensions, structures and mechanisms of a more general relevance for an understanding of working, organizational and social life are also brought to attention. This broad perspective should be borne in mind for the remainder of the text.

The three answers to the question "Why study female managers?" are not mutually exclusive: a certain overlap cannot be avoided. However, it is difficult in an investigation to provide three equally adequate answers to the question. Also there may be other responses to the question of why we take an interest in female managers.

We are first and foremost concerned with the last approach, i.e. we deal with female managers from a broad perspective. One reason that we do not take up the two aspects mentioned first is that these are well represented in the rapidly increasing literature on the subject. We also think that the 'technocratic' and 'career-oriented' literature is too pragmatic and asks questions that are too narrow as it is only concerned with the limited group of female managers and their particular interests. On the whole other groups of women (and men) are neglected and existing social conditions are more or less taken for granted (Hearn & Parkin, 1986/87). The relationship between women in management positions on the one hand and a more extensive perspective of equality, as well as an understanding of the gender dimension within organizations on the other, has hardly been taken up. Gender-related research within organizations is limited and, moreover, any such research is only rarely concerned with management questions per se.

What then can be our motives for taking an interest in female managers at all?

Do we take up this theme only to illustrate more comprehensive issues or do we take an interest also in female managers as such? As stated above, the core of the study is the social mechanisms and culture dimensions that make it either more difficult or easier for women to become influential and be employed in leading positions within enterprises and other organizations, and also the social conditions which influence the way in which women function in these jobs.

Some of our motives for focusing on female managers are:

– The importance of the role of managers and management within organizations, shown directly by the way in which working life functions, and indirectly by the way in which society manifests itself. Even though the scope of action of managers and the possibilities of their exercising influence are often strongly limited by various external restrictions, managers are still the focal point in the consciousness of those surrounding them, thus they play an important symbolic role (Pfeffer, 1977a, 1981). It is important who holds the leading positions within organizations. The distribution of the sexes can play a major role in this context.

– The importance of the way in which recruitment for management positions takes place and the manner in which management is exercised with regard to gender both as an expression of the underlying gender pattern within organizations, and as a determining factor behind this pattern. The choice of one or other sex of manager has an indirect effect on the composition of the sexes and the division of labour. Thus a 'dialectic' view of organizations may be achieved that is based on a gender perspective.

– The manner in which the presence of women in management positions can put many important dimensions of gender relations into close focus; the traditional subordination of women to men being removed, or even reversed. Women in leading positions may be assumed to expose a gender pattern in society which is different from just looking at equality of the sexes.

– The manner in which women in management positions can illustrate the situation of women when shifting roles have reached a phase where demanding, career-oriented jobs are available to them, i.e. work which plays a dominant position in the life of the individual. There exists a very clear distinction between '9-5 jobs' which may also require high qualifications and jobs which definitely require a commitment far beyond this. Family problems, in particular with small children, may be assumed to become especially difficult when the woman has a job making heavy qualitative demands on her, and quantitative demands greatly exceeding the normal working week.[4] This is well illustrated by the category which includes management positions of the middle level and upwards (other jobs are those of medical practitioners, research workers, etc.).

1.3   Discussion of various motives for the growing interest in the subject

Female managers have become a sociological field of interest. This can be seen clearly from the quantity of literature that has been produced on the subject in Scandinavia since the middle of the 1980's and in the USA since the beginning of the 1970's, some of which is quoted in the bibliography. What is interesting, among other things, about a sociological problem is the process preceding the acknowledgement of the phenomenon as a social problem at all and in this context who first defines the problem and what aspects of it are studied. An examination of literature about women in management indicates that various aims and considerations inspire research projects and writings. Here the various schools of thought within the literature are illustrated as well as our own view point.[5]

A central distinction can be made between normative and non-normative texts. Normative literature in this context means literature which uses problems and anomalies as a basis, and has the direct objective of procuring knowledge that may be used to achieve a specific end regarding these difficulties. The non-normative literature, on the other hand, endeavours to investigate various conditions without making any effort to indicate in what way the problems may be dealt with. This, however, does not mean that the latter type of writing is value neutral, or at least no more or less than is social science in general.

Normative intentions are usually expressed in one or both of the ways mentioned below. First we have *edification*. This means that the idea is to promote, support and/or morally encourage a certain course of action. The intention is often to reinforce the belief in women's competence as managers, and in their right to make a career either under the same conditions as men, or taking into account the specific preconditions of women. Somewhat ironically, texts which emphasize the support and encouragement of women may be regarded as ego-supporting therapy or pep-talk. This edification may be either the central theme of an article, or it may constitute an objective that supplements another, more dominating, objective. The latter can be non-normative. Writing in which edification is a central element are normally popular. The characteristics, experience and capabilities of women are often described in positive but vague phrases. This applies not only to literature about (becoming) female managers. A very large part of literature on management in general is characterized by such ego-reinforcing and ideological touches (cf. Alvesson, 1987; Laurent, 1978).

The same is true for literature in which a major objective is to *elicit propaganda* for female managers within a market which could be imagined to have a demand for these, viz. senior executives and headhunters. As the target group is not the actual and potential female managers themselves, but those who 'purchase' this labour, this type of writing becomes a kind of advertisement. The point is to persuade. Undoubtedly, the objective of advertising may be combined with other objectives, for instance academic ones (see e.g. Grant, 1988).

In literature where the normative intentions are not decisive, the element of edification may have some impact without being a dominating theme. This can result in theses which go far in advocating that more women should apply for and get additional management positions, theses that strongly emphasize the similarities between the sexes, or theses that interpret the differences between the sexes as being an advantage to women and organizations in that female managers can do something special, etc.. The possibility that women often do not give high priority to a career at the expense of other values is not touched upon or is strongly toned down.[6]

Another normative intention in writing is an *instrumental* one. In this case it is a question of investigating the conditions necessary for obtaining management positions for women, and increasing the number of female managers; and, on the basis of these conditions, indicating the means for realizing the objective. This wish can be expressed in writing in the form of manuals and these will concern personal and/or organizational strategies and tactics for achieving the objective. In particular American writers have found a market here. The instrumental objective is, however, also the governing factor in many academic studies. Some examples are studies of obstacles to the effective utilization of personnel and the recruitment of female managers, the consequences of female managers at the place of work, etc.. Research in which the instrumental ambition is predominant is normally followed by discussions or recommendations of policies or such like. "Implications for Management" is generally the heading of such a section or chapter (e.g. Powell, 1988).

Within the non-normative sphere we have strictly descriptive studies and those which test a hypothesis. There are also more discursive studies. The *descriptive* type of research is mostly done by American studies based on questionnaires. Experiments are also carried out, generally in artificial situations with college students as subjects, where different variables are used and correlated with each other (Rosen & Jerdee, 1973; Carbonell, 1984). In spite of the intention to be 'objective' and value neutral, these studies will almost invariably, like other writings within the field, incorporate various kinds of bias and prejudice in their attitudes to the sexes (see Riger & Galligan, 1980).

Descriptive studies are often characterized by purely empirical methods and theoretical reasoning that is in close accordance with these methods. As a consequence, their contribution is limited, tending to be unimaginative and atheoretical. Often, those investigations most concerned with exact measurement are characterized by the lack of a 'theoretical touch'. More is achieved within a broader field in a number of other instances where the investigations are based on both empirical method and a more ambitious level of reasoning, a good example of which is Kanter (1977).

In conclusion, we can speak of a 'purer' *discursive* type of knowledge objective which aims at clarifying various concepts and viewpoints. Empirically well-founded expressions such as 'reality' are not conspicuous here, the main emphasis being on concepts and ideologies. The writing may consist of a critical examination of various theories and not only of research carried out, but also of research themes which are neglected. Also in this category are comprehensive examinations of various complex problems which cannot be dealt with in simple empirical studies owing to their comprehensive nature, and studies with a pure theoretical focus. Unfortunately, there have been only few studies of the discursive type within the field of research into women and management. A good example, however, is Hearn & Parkin (1986/87). Most texts contain non-trivial elements of more than one of the four objectives mentioned the edifying, the instrumental, the descriptive and the discursive.

It is interesting to explore what motives have been guiding specific studies and to consider their relative importance. Certainly, first and foremost this should be clear to the author but also to the reader. After all, what is the point of a certain text? In the present investigation we feel that the normative intentions are not conspicuous. As we see it, our task is not to provide knowledge that can be used to remedy the present unequal distribution of women/men in management positions. Rather our concern is to give an account of social conditions relating to gender, organization and management. We concentrate on reaching an understanding rather than on promoting change.

A considerable part of this book consists of the reporting of three case studies. Although this empirical material is important, there are two main reasons why it is not enough to use this material strictly as a basis for reaching conclusions. The first reason relates to the general proposition that it is difficult or impossible, to complete a purely or strongly 'empirical' project. Notoriously, data is not as reliable as it seems in the first instance, but must be considered in terms of construction and interpretations. Both the paradigm and the theoretical framework adopted, the prior knowledge and the 'subjectivity' of the researcher have effect on how the research object is constructed. What is seen as the research object or parts of it, a segment of 'objective social reality', is better perceived as an interactive effect between certain social phenomena ('out there') and the more or less conscious choices and perceptions of the researcher, partly determined by paradigmatic commitments. What emerges as a research object or data mirroring it is hardly a simple reflection of an objective reality, but a construction of it produced by a researcher and his or her community, in turn heavily influenced by expectations, values, taken-for-granted ideas, biases and so forth (Deetz, 1992; Morgan, 1983; Steier, 1991). The nature of this study makes it extremely difficult to let 'data speak' in an uncomplicated way. Few themes are less suited to strict, neutral, objective analyses and more open to misapprehensions than that of gender and management. The sexes, and preconceived notions about the sexes, concern everyone and it is extremely difficult to be objective and neutral about this topic. In addition to this, it is important to become aware of subtleties and 'invisible' factors. The scope for prejudice, bias, wishful-thinking and misunderstanding is particularly wide here (see also Chapter 6). Naturally, we are no more able than other writers to avoid such sources of 'error'.

The second reason for feeling that empirical studies are of limited value is related to the extent of the complexity of problems in both time and in space. It is important not to restrict the objective of the research to the very narrow sphere that can be dealt with empirically. Not even using a qualitative method, as is used here, is it possible to investigate empirically all aspects that determine the relationship between women and their management jobs. The social and cultural conditions affecting organizations and human beings as regards gender, career and organization are very complex. So are the socialization processes that precede the entry into and the developments which continue at the place of work of those concerned. This problem is exaggerated by the fact that those interviewed are only to a very limited extent aware of the effect of conceptions regarding the sexes and the effect of socialization. All this means that only limited aspects can be mapped out empirically within the framework of an investigation of this nature. Therefore other studies, theories and various kinds of analyses and reasoning must fill the gap which the purely empirical study cannot fill. It follows that we attach relatively great importance to the discursive, reasoning side of the study. The wider literature on the social construction of gender is also examined with the objective of reminding the reader of central dimensions that should be kept in mind when evaluating actual problems.

1.4   Structure and content of the book

The book is divided into three main parts. Part One (Chapters 1-6) provides a general introduction to the subject as well as overviews and critical discussions of research within the field. The most important issue here is why there is an uneven distribution of women and men in management positions. In order to examine this, we have first investigated whether there is any potential for females to obtain management positions. Chapter 2 deals with the percentage of women in the labour force and women's position within the labour market. We discuss division of labour on the basis of sex, education, training and profession. Whilst we focus on the situation in Denmark, comparisons are also made with other countries. It is obvious that many of the factors dealt with in this chapter result in there being fewer female than male managers. However, they only partially explain the extremely small number of female managers.

Other explanatory models are incorporated in Chapter 3, which concerns the social construction of gender, or how we 'become' women and men in a social context with, among other things, different social position, power and influence. Thus, we examine various concepts and theories as to how economic, social, cultural and psychological circumstances and processes shape women and men, and how they give rise to more or less marked differences and inequalities between the sexes at various levels extending from their position on the labour market to their personality differences.

Chapter 3 deals with issues at a general level in relation to the major question of women as managers. It includes the different general explanations that are given when one wants to understand the various kinds of inequalities between the sexes. Some of these explanations are at the macro level; marxist and patriarchy theories fall into this category. Other explanations may be defined as middle range and micro theories, such as structural explanations and role theories. Finally, there are those which cannot be placed in one or the other category: theories of power and of socialization.

After this introduction, which sets out various explanations as to why women and men are 'different' (at levels other than the biological) and why they have an unequal position in society, we go on in Chapter 4 to look at differences between female and male managers as described in particular in Anglo-Saxon literature.

In Chapter 5 the question as to whether the discrimination described earlier, in Chapter 3, makes itself felt within organizations is dealt with. Are sex stereotypes possibly transferred into organizations and in what way is sexuality constructed in organizations? Does discrimination play a role in connection with assessment of personnel? Are female managers discriminated against? Chapter 6 describes some of the most common prejudices and arguments against women as management potential. At the same time, Chapter 6 contains a critical discussion of trends within literature which try to highlight circumstances which, for one thing, can make it more difficult for women to be regarded as potential managers and, for another, can make many women give a career at management level low priority.

After this comprehensive examination and critical review of relevant material within the area of gender, management and organization, Part Two of the book (Chapters 7-9) concentrates on empirical investigations of conditions within three different Scandinavian organizations; the Danish National Board of Social Welfare, Scandinavian Airline Systems and the Danish Ministry of Foreign Affairs. For each of these organizations we describe the composition of the sexes at lower staff level and at management level. We describe the field of work, general personnel matters, career patterns, possible obstacles to women, management behaviour and whether the organization in question expresses gender neutral or biased cultural understandings and attitudes.

As already mentioned, we deal with three different organizations. As a result the issues that have been central have to some extent differed for each of the three cases. Indeed they have been chosen in order to illustrate the question of gender and management as broadly as possible. The studies of the three organizations are presented in three separate chapters and may be read independently of each other.

Part Three (Chapters 10-11) contains a comparison of the three organizations as well as the development of new theoretical ideas on gender and organzation. First, a brief summary is given. We discuss the barriers we have observed and, finally, we discuss the differences and similarities that we believe we have found that occur between women and men. We point to a number of social and organizational changes which we have considered essential if there is to be an understanding as to why the number of female managers is so small.

In Chapter 11, as in Chapter 10, we go beyond the case studies and try to develop a more general theoretical understanding of gender and organizations, partly inspired by the differences in the situation of female managers that we have discovered in the empirical material. We stress the gender symbolism permeating organizational life as a core aspect for understanding the (re)construction of gender at work and the (re)production of gendered hierarchical and vertical division of labour. We also draw attention to gender symbolism varying with the sociocultural context and the actions of organizational participants, and thus argue for a differentiated approach to gender and organization in which the average conditions receive less attention than heterogeneity and diversity of gender relations at workplaces.

Notes

1 Our more general comments, i.e. where the scope of the object is not specified, refer to the most 'modernized' countries in the Western world (as regards gender equality) such as the Scandinavian countries. One sign of this is women's share of seats in parlament. In the Scandinavian Countries it ranges from 33% (Denmark, 1990), 35,6% (Norway, 1989) to 38,1% (Sweden, 1988) whereas in the UK it is 5,6% (1988), in France 5,7% (1988) and in Germany women's share of seats in parlament is 20,5% (1990).

2 In some statistics, especially from the USA, the part of female managers is considerably higher. Without further explanations it is claimed that one third of all "managers" are women (Powell, 1988:13). This can be an effect of a specially broad definition of managers which even includes those employed at lower levels. In some statistics only the two categories managers and workers are included, the first one being defined as "engaged in other than shopfloor or performance-level job". In this way it is possible to reach the conclusion that more than half of the total work force in the USA are managers (e.g. Melin, 1990:221). The term manager thus becomes a 'catch-all' word, which hardly tells you anything at all. We are using the concept as a much narrower category, which is specified later in Chapter 1.

3 This book deals also with male managers in organizations but females are more salient.

4 It is not inevitable of course that women take the main responsibility for small children, which this statement presupposes.

5 For a further discussion of various positions in relation to the theme of women in management at a basic level see Billing & Alvesson (1989).

6 An example of this viewpoint is Marshall (1984). See further details in Chapter 6.

2 Women in the labour market and in management positions

2.1 Introduction

The purpose of this chapter is to provide a statistical illustration of the position of women in the labour market in general, and also as far as management positions are concerned, both in Denmark and in a number of comparable countries. It is taken for granted that, in general, women hold a very small percentage of leading positions. In this chapter we will include a number of important factors relating to employment conditions, position in the labour market and educational background all of which may provide an explanation to this question. Other factors concerning female managers will be taken up in Chapter 4.

It is evident that one cannot expect a large percentage of women to be found in leading positions if women are only a small percentage of the total labour force. It is also true that the chances of attaining a managerial position are small if women are mainly employed on a part-time basis, held to be incompatible with most management positions (as well as with a career route to these). At any rate, part-time employment arguably is not a place from which to 'launch' a career in management.

Finally, one cannot expect a large number of females to become managers if these women have to a great extent received education or training within areas from which managers are not typically recruited. The latter point is questionable, however, as at the present time when management is a subject of much debate, it seems difficult to define the specific qualifications (including educational qualifications) which should be relevant to the job. Naturally, demand for qualifications may also vary from one organization to another.

Below we examine the percentage of women in the labour force, in part-time/full-time work and we assess the division of labour on the basis of sex, both within the labour market and in relation to choice of education/training or choice of profession.

2.2 Women in the labour market

Women are to be found in the labour market on a large scale. In Scandinavia, women constitute almost half of the labour force: the highest figure ever recorded. It corresponds to a participation rate for women of 69.4% of all women between the age of 15 to 74 (Danmarks Statistik, 1990). For men the participation rate is 80.8%. Thus, a smaller percentage of women are on the labour market than the percentage of men.

Of these 69.4% of women 38.4% are in part-time employment as compared with 10.4% of the men (Danmarks Statistik, 1990). 10.9% of these women are unemployed as compared with 7.9% of the men.

The recruitment potential among women thus appears lower than among men for leading positions. What is important here is that so many women are part-time workers. (We will not discuss why so many women choose or find it necessary to work part-time.) One could imagine that those considered suitable for managerial jobs and being career orientated are not randomly distributed within these following four categories: non-wage-earners (voluntary), unemployed, part-time workers and full-time workers, but are mainly to be found in the last group. This would then mean that the somewhat lower percentage of women in full-time jobs does not to any major extent explain the low percentage of female managers.

In many western countries, the percentage of women in the labour force is almost the same as in Denmark, e.g. in the UK 45% (Bradley, 1989). The percentage of married women (aged 25-49) in employment in 1988 was 72% in the UK, in France 68% and in Germany 58% (Lane, 1992). The employment status is however different. According to Lane (1992) the part-time employment figure is 43.8% for British women, 30.6% for German and 23.8% for French women. The proportion of all female part-timers who worked less than 15 hours per week was 34.7% in the UK, compared to 13.8% in Germany. Moreover, a considerable proportion of the part-timers fall outside employment protection law (Lane, 1992). We shall not dwell upon the reasons for the significant differences in employment status between British, German and French women – suffice to note that state policies are important in shaping women's employment pattern differently. In the Scandinavian countries, the supply of child care is more generous than in many other western countries, and today hardly any women with young childen work part-time. Indeed the part-timers (38%) are older women whose involvement in childcare is decreased.

The percentage of women holding leading positions shows a rather consistent figure of 4-5% (e.g. Canada: 4.2%, France: 5.4% [Symons, 1986/87]), so even though one out of two in the labour market is a woman, only one out of 20 at the higher managerial levels is female. At top levels the figure is even smaller, with around 2% women top executives in the USA (Powell, 1988). In Denmark the figure is 2.5% in the public sector, and 4.9% in the private sector (Statistical Inf. 1989).[1]

Even though the potential for women to achieve leading positions is in general less than that of men, there is, after all, a very large number of women on the labour market in full-time employment. We are therefore a long way from explaining why so few of them actually obtain a senior position. This is so, even though we are fully aware that historically, the number of women on the labour market and in full-time employment has been lower than it is now, and that there is a time lag between an increase in the number of women and women's break-through to the management level. As a rule, management positions do not become relevant until 5 to 15 years after entry onto the labour market. As women have to a very great extent been on the labour market for more than 20 years, this time effect can only very marginally explain why almost 1 out of 2 on the labour market is a woman, whereas less than 1 out of 20 at the higher management level is a woman.

Below we will discuss in detail the position of the sexes in the work hierarchy, and the possible implications of this for career prospects.

2.3 The gendered division of labour

Most (industrialized) countries have a labour market that is divided into sectors according to sex. Women play a dominant role within the social security, health and service sector and in the field of teaching and retail trade while men play a dominant role, for instance, within technical fields, within trade and administration (skilled workers, leading positions), national defense, etc. (Reskin, 1984; Bradley, 1989).

The labour market and the educational system is often said to be divided into two parts, one for women and one for men. An ordinary criterion for the division of labour according to sex is whether one sex constitutes more than 60% of the total (and the other consequently less than 40%). As an example only 25 out of 282 job areas in Sweden had a division of labour according to sex within the interval 40:60 (Persson-Tanimura, 1987). The same picture is found in Finland where only 5% work in fields with an almost equal number of women and men. Of the labour force 90% are employed in fields with a one-sided gender structure (i.e. in which over 60% of those within a field are of the same sex) (Peltonen, 1987). Data from other industrialized societies indicate similar patterns of segregation; women's employment is more concentrated than men's however, for example, among non-manual women in the UK, 91% are in the following three broad categories: selling, clerical work or professional work in education, welfare and health (Cockburn, 1985).

As compared to men, women have jobs with less possibility of advancing up the hierarchy to management positions at middle and higher levels (e.g. nursing, education, service). Women tend to become concentrated either within women's 'domains' or in other low pay areas (Crompton, 1986). The gendered division of labour cannot be seen in isolation, however, but must be seen in relation to choice of profession/trade and education.

2.4   Choice of profession/trade and education

The gendered division of labour is reflected in the choice of profession/trade and education. Even though in Denmark the percentage of women within almost all professions/trades and all fields of education/training has increased during the past 10 years, the choice of education/training is still within the framework of the labour market divided according to sex.

During the past 25 years a steadily increasing number of students from within their age group have completed a Higher Preparatory Examination or an upper-secondary school-leaving examination (7% in 1960 and approximately 40% in the 1980's), whilst during the past 15 years, girls have constituted around half of the upper-secondary students. The same tendency can be seen in other western countries, including the USA (Keeton, 1985). After completion of the upper-secondary examination, boys and girls choose further education/training which reflects the division of labour according to sex on the labour market. Women are to be found mainly within the social, humanistic, educational, health and language fields, whereas men are to be found within the fields of natural sciences mathematics, technical sciences and economics.

Traditionally, women have not chosen the fields of education from which managers at higher levels are today recruited (engineering, business, etc.). A change is taking place, however, in the sex-related choice of education/training as a result of cutbacks within the fields traditionally chosen by women, and intensive propaganda has begun to influence women to choose, for instance, various forms of engineering. The fact that subjects are now combined in an untraditional way (e.g. language and economics) has also had a certain effect. In addition studies in business administration attract far more women today than they did earlier, a development that is also being experienced in the USA.

Prior to this position, women constituted only a small percentage of MBAs in the USA where the possession of an MBA degree is often regarded as a good background for making a career within trade and industry. In 1960, women constituted only approximately 2% of all international management students, while 20 years later the percentage of women had increased to around 35% of international management students (Adler, 1986/87). Women received about one third of the MBA degrees awarded in the USA in 1987, whereas it was only 2% in 1967 (Powell, 1988).

The fact that girls choose mainly education or training that is traditional for women, and are rarely to be found within the fields that more easily lead to positions of power and influence, is not just a Danish phenomenon. For instance, it is well documented that less women than men choose (natural) sciences and technology (Kelly, 1984; Whyte, 1986). While science does not seem to strongly facilitate a managerial career, engineering often does.

So far, we have localized more circumstances which contribute to limiting the female potential for leading positions viz. the fact that women have until now generally chosen fields of education/training which do not lead in the long run to management positions. Below we will provide a picture of the number of female managers, some at the national level within the public and the private sector; some within a number of different organizations, and finally, some in a number of comparable countries.

2.5   Female managers

Out of the total number of managers in the private sector of the labour market in 1986 in Denmark, 8.2% were women (Carlsen, 1987). This represents an increase from 6.3% in 1983. The percentage is relatively high compared to other countries; however, it should be pointed out that this survey includes management functions in a broad sense at both higher and lower levels (e.g. senior shop assistants, senior book-keepers, forewomen, shop managers, shop foremen, junior shop foremen). Carlsen (1987) has selected the occupational groups which relatively clearly indicate functions at the lowest level upwards. The method is based on reporting from enterprises on the titles of leading salaried employees and not on descriptions of the content of the management function. The investigation shows that in 1986, 4.6% of female salaried employees were managers as compared to 35.2% of male salaried employees. This is an increase for women from 3.6% in 1983. The investigation is only partly representative, but it indicates that the number of female managers in the private sector of the labour market increases by approximately 12-15% annually; that the percentage of managers who are female is increasing slightly by between 0.5% and 0.8% annually.

As the statistics mentioned include top salaried employees even at a low level, it is only in part relevant for our purpose to find out why there are so few female managers. If executives at higher levels are extracted, the percentage of women in this higher level is clearly smaller than the percentage of women holding management positions in general and the increase for women from 1983 to 1985 is somewhat less, viz. 0.5% to 5.4%. The group of executives at the highest level shows stagnation in the percentage of women in leading positions varying from 3.3% in 1983, 4.0% in 1984, 3.0% in 1985 to 3.7% in 1986. As always when it comes to statistical data, one must be careful. It is difficult to imagine that the number of female executives could change so rapidly. A drop from 4.0% to 3.0% would mean that one out of four female executives would leave their positions over a period of just one year.

As is shown in the above, the result is somewhat imprecise as regards the representation of women in management positions when all kinds of job categories are included as in the statistics used by Carlsen. For instance, women constitute 100% within the categories of "forewomen" and "senior computer operators", however, these jobs do not rank on the same level as "executives" where the percentage of men is 97 and "heads of computer departments" where

the percentage of men is 100 (1985). It is important to remember that statistics
are produced and that the techniques used to produce and to process data are
social constructions (Kirkham & Loft, 1991). Statistics can not reflect complex
phenomena. How jobs are classified is a matter of expectations, judgment and
negotiation. Status, identity and pay are associated with the grading of a job. A
particular job may be classified differently depending on the job holder and it is
likely that gender is significant here. It may be more important for men to have
the title of manager and the cultural expectation that men have higher position
than women may lead to men more often being classified as managers. The
legislation and institutional pressure on organizations to show 'nice' figures in
terms of the representation of women and minorities among higher ranks may
lead to women being classified as managers. In both cases the title and the classification tell us more about the politics of classification than gender representation in 'true' managerial jobs.

It is probably common that jobs are ambiguous in terms of them being managerial or not, also if one accepts the criteria of having subordinates. Borgert
(1992:43) writes about a consultancy project where he was supposed to conduct
some seminars for group managers. According to the executive, the persons
concerned needed "support in their leadership role". But when the seminar
started the participants thought the seminar unnecessary because they did not
think of themselves as managers and the seminar series ended abruptly. Apparently they had some vague responsibility for a work group of 3 to 4 persons,
including themselves. It is perhaps not a coincident that most of the participants
in the seminar were women.

The ambiguity of many jobs and their openness in terms of classification in
combination with other errors in statistical material makes aggregated data much
less reliable than it may appear. In order to obtain a more precise picture of a
possible segregation one should look at the percentage of women within the
individual fields and look at the percentage of female executives within these
same fields. Salaried employees is a broad concept; in some fields there will
probably not be many female salaried employees (such as technical) and in others there will be a majority of women, yet still without their representation at
management level.

A rough criterion for the percentage of women and men holding management
positions is the use of statistics of wage earners in the highest income bracket. In
an English investigation, these were defined as 2.5-3% of all full time employees
with the highest income (Fogarty et al, 1981). These statistics showed a reduction in the number of women holding management positions between 1968 and
1979. In 1968 women constituted 2.1% of the group; 11 years later the number
had been reduced to 1.85%. Legislation and a general increased awareness of
women's liberation, and even policy declarations from enterprises and other employers concerning equality between the sexes, etc. have had a certain minor
effect in increasing the number of female managers at lower levels. Yet prob-

lems with the economy in Great Britain and subsequent reductions in the total number of management positions have probably had the opposite effect.

2.6   Specific organizations

The statistics referred to above concern various countries as a whole, or major sectors within these countries. The statistics give an overall view of the conditions and clearly point to the fact that the percentage of women in leading positions is very low. Yet this type of statistic provides only an aggregate picture, and widely different types of management jobs are conflated. Even though a specific category is singled out, for instance "directors" or "personnel managers", mass statistics are still likely to provide a very rough and imprecise picture. An additional and more concrete picture may be obtained by looking at the number of female managers in a number of typical organizations, which has been done, for instance, in the present investigation. In this section we will not go into depth about organization levels. Instead we will give some representative examples of circumstances at concrete levels.

Fogarty et al (1981) investigated women in top jobs within a number of specific British organizations in 1968 and 11 years later in 1979. Within an industrial enterprise, female managers constituted 2.7% in 1968, 11 years later the percentage was 3.3. One out of every 30 managers was a woman. Of managers at higher levels, women constituted 1.3% and of managers at somewhat lower levels 3.8%. The female managers were distributed unevenly within the group of companies. Thus in one department concerned with marketing surveys, 40% of the managers were women. But even in the case of manufacturing subsidiary companies, variations were large. In one or two of these companies women held 5-10% of the management positions while there were, by and large, no female managers in the remainder. In another industrial enterprise, the investigation centered on the research division, as in the other departments, the number of women in leading positions was low. At the three highest levels of managers in that division the percentage of woman was 3%, 10% and 10% in 1968 and 11 years later (1979) the percentage of women at these three levels was 4%, 10% and 15%, respectively. The two enterprises have thus increased the percentage of women in leading positions, at least at the lower levels, by approximately 25%.

A comparison of the number of women at management level within the British Civil Service proved difficult, among other things because of differences in classifications and statistics. A minor increase is discernible, however. Yet the number is small, below 10%, and female managers are to be found, first and foremost, at the lower levels.

An investigation of the BBC showed that out of 100 of the highest positions, only one was held by a woman. In 1969 there were 7 women (out of 224) at the three highest levels, while there were 6 (out of 396) in 1979, i.e. a reduction in the percentage of women at the highest levels from 3% to 1.5%. At the overall management level, i.e. including the lower middle level and up to senior posts, the frequency of women increased from 5% to 7% during the same period. After a correction for the effect of certain reclassifications of job levels this meant that the percentage of women in management positions increased, but only slightly. It may be mentioned that 36% of the total number of employees at the BBC were women.

In the central administration in Denmark women constitute 24% of all those who are university graduates and 8% of all "managers" ("Lige nu", 1988). Within ministerial departments approximately 9% of the women are "managers" as compared to 26% of the men (Maegaard, 1986). The number of female middle managers within the central administration has increased slightly (from 9.4% in 1983 to 10.1% in 1987) (The Equal Status Council, 1990).

It would be reasonable to speculate that the number of female managers would be related to the number of female employees within an enterprise, in other words, that more female managers would be found if, for instance, women constituted the majority of the employees in an organization. A German investigation shows that the total number of women employed by a firm is not a reliable indicator of the percentage of female managers and that it is not possible to make any general statements as to the type of sectors or firms in which women have achieved leading positions (Antal & Kresbach-Gnath, 1986/87). From this investigation it transpired, for instance, that very few female managers are to be found in the large retail chains although a large percentage of the employees are women. In a chain of department stores, Karstadt, only one out of every 3,550 female employees is in management. An opposite example is to be found in the German railways where women constitute 5.4% of the employees, and yet women hold 17% of the leading positions. To identify the basis for these differences it would be necessary to undertake a detailed empirical analysis of the two different organizations.

2.7   Summary and suggestions for explanations

On the previous pages we have found documentation that women are to a great extent to be found on the labour market even though one third of women are in part time employment (in Denmark). However, the fact that the female potential for management is somewhat lower than the male potential does not explain the *extremely* low number of female managers. We also found that a gender division of labour exists, both in the labour market and within the educational system and that in general (and internationally) women 'choose' education and training that do not count very much in relation to formal definitions of management. Furthermore women are to be found in jobs which do not offer the same career prospects or pay levels as those of men. Courses at technical schools and also education in the field of management at business schools which would both make it easier to obtain leading positions have attracted only few women, though this number is increasing, especially at business schools. Lack of technical and economic education, in turn, contributes to reducing the number of potential female managers.

It should be pointed out that many top jobs do not require prior formal education. The private sector of trade and industry, for instance, has not had the same tradition of higher education as has the public sector (in Denmark). Also investigations have shown that even though women have the same educational background as men they are not promoted as frequently (Halaby, 1979; Maegaard, 1986). According to the two investigations mentioned the unequal status of men versus that of women results from the unequal access to management positions, the unequal status taking the form of hierarchic segregation.

An American investigation of MBAs showed that the progress of women was simply slower than that of men even though there were no differences when they started either in salaries, work functions or other factors (Devanna, 1987). According to the investigation, women were required to prove their ability to take on the next task at a higher level whereas men were expected to be able to take on the task. The great problem with regard to the slower progress of women is (according to Devanna) that at some time or other they usually end up outside the so-called fast track. It seems that when women invest in the same education and qualifications as men, they may get equal access to 'male' jobs but they do not receive equal treatment on the internal labour market once they are hired.

Persson-Tanimura (1987) feels that it is not sufficient for a woman to make the same investments as a man. She must make larger investments even to achieve the same salary. Halaby's (1979) investigation of job-related differences between the sexes supports the thesis that, for example, differences in salaries between the sexes within an organization as well as differences in rank between the sexes is less a question of difference with regard to education/training and experience but rather a question of the different importance ascribed to the resources of men and women within the remuneration system. Obviously if the work done by women is from the start regarded as being of less value than the work done by men, women will progress more slowly or else they will have to show a better performance than men in order to be promoted.

Even in Scandinavian societies which have achieved a certain equality of status, the following factors appear to contribute to a system where there are fewer female than male managers:

– there is a smaller percentage of women than men on the labour market;
– many women work part-time (this applies perhaps not so much to those with personal ambitions to achieve management positions);

– women choose the 'wrong' education/training in relationship to a managerial
  career;
– there is a division of labour according to sex, with women in occupations with
  fewer possibilites of career advancement
– there is a time effect (as a rule there is a time lag between entry onto the labour
  market and the possibility of becoming manager), which means that an increase in the percentage of women with the 'right' education/training does not
  immediately affect the percentage of female managers.

However, these factors cannot in our opinion more than partially explain the
extremely low number of female managers. Other explanatory models must be
found in order to explain why women continue to play a dominant role in the
lowest paid jobs of low status, often at the bottom of the career structure. This
still happens in spite of legislation on equal pay, equal status campaigns, etc..
But why do differences and inequalities between the sexes exist at all and how
do these find expression in relation to the labour market and in relation to power
and influence in society in general? We will treat these questions in greater
depth in the next chapter.

Notes

1   Executives are defined broadly here, including managers for very small enterprises,
    minimum 10 employees.

3 The social construction of gender

The purpose of this chapter is to examine a number of commonplace ways in which to understand social and psychological differences between the sexes.[1] Another objective is to suggest some of the potential reasons for these differences between women and men, both in relation to the choice of education/training and career, the position within organizations, and the labour market, and also with regard to power and influence in society generally.

A central issue in this book is the difference between the management positions achieved by men and women. However, in this chapter we deal more generally with the theories which attempt to explain various forms of inequality between the sexes (gender construction). This chapter therefore concerns the production of gender differences in a broad sense. Later we deal more specifically with sexual similarities and differences in relation to management positions. The approaches here, which are discussed briefly and generally, deal with various levels, and are very disparate in their background and focus. They pose questions which differ in some respects and therefore they are not as such comparable or alternate.

Various theories have been developed and used to explain the differences in position of women and men on the labour market, the division of labour according to sex, and the domination of men over women. Many writers have pointed out the multitude of theories which exist in the field of research on the situation of women. Micro-sociological theories are concerned with differences between women and men, differential treatment of the sexes and the effect of structural factors on the self-perception of the individuals. Culture theory is an all-embracing category which deals with many aspects relevant for our purpose. Here we introduce the concept in order to show our main inspiration for the interpretation of the case-studies. Role theories are concerned with differences between the sexes as expressed through different expectation and behavioural patterns and possibly psychological characteristics. Socialization theories go more in depth than role theory as they are capable of dealing with matters relating to the formation of the child's identity which is thought to be relatively important for the later choices in life, including those of education, job and career.

3.1   Macro-sociological explanatory models

Within the field of macro-sociology we find Marxist feminist analyses of the relations between the sexes, patriarchy theories and a synthesis of Marxist and patriarchal explanatory models.

The traditional Marxist analyses of capitalism have concentrated on exploitation and appropriation and are based on concepts which are not directly related to the sex of the parties involved. Marxist feminism is both based on and is critical of Marxist theory. Whereas the Marxist analysis of capitalism concentrates on a primary conflict between work and capital and operates with categories that are gender blind, feminism emphasizes the importance of relations between the sexes. The aim of Marxist feminism is to investigate the specific nature of the oppression of women under capitalism in the light of the gender relations that preceded the capitalistic production conditions.

The concept of patriarchy has also been of central importance for the discussion of the gender relations. Various theories exist regarding patriarchy; some are based on a universal model, others emphasize material relations and analyse from an historical point of view the various manifestations of patriarchy in various social systems. In other words, there exist major controversies about the precise meaning of the concept, but most feminists will agree that the concept of patriarchy deals with a structure of oppression and domination in which men are capable of dominating women.

Attempts have been made to synthesize the two above mentioned theories; the Marxist theory in order to explain class relations and the patriarchal theory in order to define society as a system of social relations between men. Even though a hierarchy exists among men, they are seen as being dependent upon each other. They create a kind of solidarity which makes it possible to control the labour of women and maintain the original division of labour between the sexes which, within the framework of this concept, is seen as the root of the present situation of women.

3.1.1 Marxist approach

In using the word "Marxist" we refer to analyses claiming authority from Marx' theory in particular as developed in *Das Kapital* (1947) even though we are well aware that many different Marxist explanations exist. Some are based on the early writings of Marx and others on his later work (*Das Kapital*). However, a common factor of these major Marxist works has been that they have been gender blind. Gender has generally not been a central concept, instead the relationship between wage labour and capital has been emphasized and is the central concept in the analysis of capitalism.

It seems rather strange that gender has been omitted in later interpretations, when both Marx and Engels were actually concerned with the oppression of women. One of the first attempts at analysing gender in relation to capitalistic production conditions was made by Engels (1972) in "The Origin of the Family, Private Property and the State" in 1884. In this he defines the contrast between woman and man as a class contrast which arises as a result of the division of labour between woman and man. Engels and Marx describe this as early as in 1846 (in "The German Ideology") as follows: "The first division of labour is the procreation of children by man and woman". This division was the basis for the division of labour according to sex between production and reproduction. Engels imagines that the equality of status for men and women is not possible as long as women are excluded from the productive work of society and are obliged to take care of domestic work. Therefore, in his opinion, the possibility of emancipation is to be found in women taking part on a large social scale in production and this, in turn, presupposes the abolition of the monogamous family as an economic unit in society.

Engels proved a great inspiration for later Marxist feminist interpretations, and analyses of the relationship between man and woman and the family within the capitalist system. His analysis has constituted a basis for materialistic analyses of the relations between the sexes. One of the arguments that developed surrounds the functional relationship between the nuclear family and capitalism. It is said to be functional in the way that the continued existence of the capitalist-worker relationship is, so to speak, dependent on and conditioned by, daily and lifelong reproduction of labour, which takes place predominantly within a family. The concept of reproduction became a central concept for an understanding of both how the social conditions were reproduced and how the labour force was reproduced daily and through the generations.

The division of labour between the sexes meant that women assumed a special role in relation to the reproduction of the family and in relation to attention to reproduction in terms of generations. Reproduction in this context means all that is necessary to cover the physical, psychic and social needs of the family (or the individual). Historically, these needs are changeable and an average reproduction level is the level which throughout time has developed within the social group in question. The unpaid labour of women in the home serves to reproduce the labour force and thus the production relations. Barrett (1980) points to the fact that often the housewife is also a wage earner and that there may be a conflict between these two fields of work.

Owing to the structure of the family and to an ideology in which the wage labour of women is regarded as being secondary when compared to the work within the family, it is possible to pay the female wage earner a lower wage or salary than the male who is regarded as the primary breadwinner. In addition to this, women are regarded as being less stable in labour than men owing to childbirth and their dominant role in the home, therefore it is possible to value their labour at a lower price than the labour of men. Feminist materialists have in general argued that the position of women is structurally different from that of men, and that the experience of women in life is basically different from the experience of men. Most people have regarded wage labour as a necessity for equality between men and women, yet on the other hand it has been felt that the capacity for reproduction was the major obstacle for equality between the sexes (Firestone, 1971).

The early Marxist feminism (e.g. Dalla Costa, 1973) sees capitalism as the root of all social inequalities (and dissociates itself from Engels' assertion that the entry of women onto the labour market would end male domination). The oppression of women and the gendered division of labour are regarded as 'firmly established' in capitalist production relations and therefore should be analysed in the light of these relations.

Other Marxist feminists from a later period have argued that the oppression of women exists in countries that are not capitalist (e.g. Eisenstein, 1979). Therefore, it would seem reasonable to introduce a new concept that could explain universal male domination.

3.1.2 The concept of patriarchy

Patriarchy was used by Weber to describe a special kind of organization of the household in which the father dominated the other members in an extended family network and controlled the economic production of the household (Barrett, 1980:21-22).

Millet (1970) was one of the first to use the concept of patriarchy as a universal concept independent of the form of production and therefore independent of capitalism. In addition to this, she believed that class divisions were relevant only for men and that women transcended the ordinary class divisions. Women and men are described as being in a relationship of subordination and domination and patriarchy is defined as the structure of subordination and domination (Bilton et al, 1982:374). However, major controversies exist as regards the precise meaning of the concept. Basically the above-mentioned definition implies a hierarchy of social relations and institutions in which men are capable of dominating women. This understanding of power can be seen as rather crude in the light of the progress of power theory during recent decades (e.g. Clegg, 1989; Foucault, 1980) but we refrain from going into this issue here. Hemming (1987) defines patriarchy as the law of the father and the operation of this law on other individuals. This definition does not limit the concept to the family but includes all male authority as an expression of symbolic 'fathers'.

Most writers regard patriarchy as being precapitalist (e.g. Engels; Hartmann; Firestone). This early institutionalization of men's domination over women was not abolished under capitalism. The concept of patriarchy implies that the domination applies also at a social level by men holding the formal positions of power in politics and working life and women not having access to these positions. It does not imply, however, that women are totally powerless or are totally deprived of rights, influence and resources (Lerner, 1986). As a consequence of this, Lerner uses the concept of "subordination" which includes the possibility of voluntary acceptance in exchange for protection and privileges. Several writers have criticized the concept of patriarchy as being ahistorical (e.g. Barrett, 1980:10) and as being a concept that is not particularly useful for an investigation of oppression of women in capitalistic societies. Some writers have analysed the historical changes in patriarchy as a result of changed relations to capitalism and/or other forms of production. Among others Burris (1989) argues that patriarchy also changes in relation to different types of organizational control.

All supporters of patriarchal theories emphasize the relations between the sexes and presuppose that these are characterized by men's oppression and domination of women. Gender is more important for the analysis than the form of production. However, some patriarchal theories do not employ universal models, but use instead the different forms of patriarchy in different types of societies and within different organizations. This we regard as an advantage.

Opinions differ as to whether male oppression of women has been a characteristic of all human societies or whether in more primitive societies equality between the sexes had existed and the work of each sex was regarded as being of equal value. Shorter (1976:513) and Illich (1982) express two different opinions. Shorter believes that women today, in capitalistic countries, have reached at least "shouting distance of social equality with men". Illich believes that under capitalism we are witnessing a discrimination and oppression of women which has never been seen before. French (1986) takes a middle stand. She does not 'romantisize' the situation of women in pre-capitalist times, on the other hand she is very pessimistic with regards to women's future and refers to women (globally) as "the new poor". The only women who have benefited, French writes, are the well-educated, white middle-class women.

3.1.3 The dual systems theory

Hartmann (1979) has attempted to make a synthesis of the two theories described above, the Marxist theory to explain class relations and the patriarchal theory to explain society as a system of hierarchic relations between men and a solidarity among men which maintains the male domination.

In her paper entitled "The Unhappy Marriage of Marxism and Feminism" (1979), Hartmann has advocated an understanding of capitalism and patriarchy as two distinct, but equally comprehensive systems of social relations which meet and interact (thus the dual systems theory). In her opinion, the systematic subordination of women in advanced capitalistic societies involves the two sets of interrelated structures; patriarchy, understood as a system of male oppression of women; and the capitalist relations of production, which in her opinion intensified the hierarchical nature of the gendered division of labour and encouraged sexual antagonisms at the cost of class solidarity.

She describes historically men's struggle for "the family wage" as a means of keeping the competitive, lower-paid female labour within the home and thus securing the care/reproduction within the family which was necessary, among other things, to reproduce male labour. Competition intensified in the working classes in that women (and children) were offered work at lower wages and in that male workers used trade unions not only to protect their own situation in relation to the capitalist but also to secure an advantage over female workers by segregating women within the labour market in order to preserve the patriarchal privileges in the home. Hartmann believes that patriarchy had been established before the break-through of capitalism and that it was transferred to the industrialized society by means of the control system mentioned earlier. Thus the sexually determined division of labour came to apply also to wage labour. Hartmann concludes that the present status of women on the labour market and the actual arrangement of sex segregated jobs are a result of a long process of interaction between patriarchy and capitalism. "Capitalism grew on top of patriarchy; patriarchal capitalism is stratified society par excellence" (Hartmann, 1976:168).

The question is how functional the relation/alliance between capitalism and patriarchy actually is at the present time. Hartmann's understanding of society as being composed of independent levels or systems is also questionable (Crompton & Mann, 1986; Carlsson, 1987). Many no longer use the concept of patriarchy, but use instead male domination, the more specific notion of patriarchy having been transformed into an idea of a more general male domination which indicates a general oppression of women. Others refer to societal patriarchy. The problem with the concept of patriarchy and the idea of an alliance of patriarchy and capitalism is, among other things, that history shows that capitalism has in some instances contributed in removing some of the existing patriarchal privileges. Capitalism, with the state as intermediary, has made way for measures to achieve equality of status between the sexes which would be inconceivable if an alliance really existed between patriarchy and capitalism. It can equally be maintained that capitalistic societies contain forces which undermine patriarchy, and that a field of tension perhaps exists between the two systems. The problem with the concept of male domination is that it does not incorporate the hierarchic relations among men themselves, nor does it incorporate class relations and it tends to globalize male power. Furthermore, there has been a tendency to objectify women in the analyses and to accord them the passive role of those who reproduce a number of existing structures while men are given an active role in production (Esseveld, 1987). This is in part a consequence of the use of the concept of reproduction which subsumes 'typical' female activities under the working model (production). Therefore, it can be difficult to understand women not just as an oppressed group but also as actors on the historical scene (Benhabib, 1987). On the basis of this approach it can be difficult to understand women who are to be found in positions of both power and influence. The approach undermines the agency of women. The theories are to be found at a level of abstractions where it is not possible to perceive departures from the classical pattern, nor is it at all possible to explain why some women succeed in transgressing the vertical (and horizontal) division of labour according to sex.

3.2 Middle range and micro-sociological explanatory models

In the previous pages we have outlined various theories which at an abstract and general level provide explanations of the different positions of women and men in the division of labour. We shall now deal with tendencies at a more concrete social level and consider the social constitution of the differentiation and inequality between the sexes. Instead of focusing on society as a whole, middle range level and micro-sociology, we deal with various 'local' institutional conditions. First, a number of structural explanations of the different positions of women and men in the organizational hierarchy will be dealt with. Next, understandings emphasizing the significance of local, i.e. organizational, culture will be treated. Finally, role theories will be discussed as a part of the micro-sociological explanatory models. Role theory emphasizes the different expectations of the sexes that show up in different behaviour.

3.2.1 Structural explanations

Middle range level or 'meso' structural explanations are characterized by an emphasis on differences or inequality between the sexes, for instance with regard to their interest in work, career, etc. and location in the social structure which are explained as being conditioned by the opportunity structures and concrete circumstances of women and men respectively. Production of gender differentiations is thus perceived as a direct reflection of the actual situation of men and women on the labour market rather than the result of an abstract and general social influence at the macro level. Nor are the earlier individual life stories of the individuals particularly decisive as to their fate according to this view. The concrete, actual life situation and the possibilities and limitations that it implies are more important. Thus it is the local level that is central. The opportunity structure is closely related to the division of labour according to sex. The most prominent researcher using this approach is Kanter (1977).

She describes how the opportunity structure is of decisive importance for the expectations of women and of men, for instance with regard to promotion. She also refers to an investigation which shows that the motivation and expectation of men with regard to promotion were significantly higher than those of women, but so were the real prospects of men of being promoted. The opportunity structure within an organization contributes to shaping behaviour such that it becomes a self-fulfilling prophecy.

People who are on a career track tend, in Kanter's opinion, to develop attitudes and values which urge them on further, while those who are not on such a track "tend to become indifferent, to give up, and thus to 'prove' that their initial placement was correct" (Kanter, 1977:158). She does not make any distinction between the sexes here.

She believes that the findings as regards sexual differences in work behaviour i.e. that men are more ambitious, goal oriented and engaged in their work and that women are more concerned with the work relations, should be reevaluated. If it seems that women are less motivated or engaged, it is, in her opinion, most likely to be because their jobs give rise to fewer possibilities in the future. She refers to an investigation which shows that in general, the jobs of most women entail fewer possibilities of promotion than those of men; as the possibilities for advancement increased the percentage of women in such jobs decreased markedly. A Canadian investigation (Marchak, referred to in Kanter, 1977) of 307 white-collar workers in 20 firms of whom half were women showed that the women mainly held jobs in which they had the least control over their own work, in which there was the most machine work, in which there was the lowest pay, the least job security and the least chance of being promoted.

A Danish investigation of banks (Mygind & Humeniuk, 1987) showed that the differences in self confidence of female and male employees in banks could be ascribed to the different positions of the two sexes in the possibility of promotion structure of the enterprise. Women were more often placed in positions with less possibility of development and promotion.

As has been shown, the jobs of women often hold less possibilities than to those of men, both with regard to influencing the job content and with regard to possibility of promotion (the so called dead end jobs). It is therefore reasonable to assume that women will take a more instrumental attitude to wage labour.

Two sociological investigations by Dubin and Orzach, referred to in Kanter (1977) show, however, that the popular view of women as being less work-oriented than men must be questioned. In a sample of men (factory workers) it appeared that work was not the central element in their lives and in a sample of women (nurses) it appeared that work was the central element in theirs. In an investigation of teachers and nurses, the women employees took a greater interest in their organizations than did the men and those who had 'sponsors' took the greatest interest. Men with few possibilities (e.g. of advancement) resemble more the stereotype of women in their attitude to work, they limit their expectations, seek satisfaction outside the job, discontinue their career early and create social contexts in which more importance is attached to personal relations than is attached to their jobs.

In addition to this an investigation carried out by Rose and Fielder (1987) has shown that women can be just as engaged in their work and just as interested in meaningful work as are men. Like Kanter, Fagenson (1986) found that women's orientation towards career varied in relation to their level in the hierarchy. Thus the investigation supports Kanter's theory that the opportunity structure is of central importance for career aspirations. Reverse causality cannot be excluded, however, career aspirations being the basis for placement within the hierarchy and opportunity structure.

Also important in the behaviour of employees within the organization (including their career prospects) is the question of whether they belong to a majority or a minority within a group, or within the department or the organization as a whole. The composition of the sexes (which is of interest in this context) of individuals in groups, in organizations, in schools, and at universities has become a subject that has attracted more and more attention in sociology (e.g. Kanter, 1977; South et al, 1982; Izraeli, 1986/87). It is believed that a number of structurally conditioned mechanisms start working in relation to a minority, irrespective of sex. According to Martin (1985), 'well' mixed rather than single-sex groups are advantageous to both men and women within an organization. According to Martin, men benefit more from mixed groups than do women. Martin believes that mixed groups are a precondition for women having success in hierarchical or male-dominated organizations.[2] Many investigations show that awareness of the number of various categories of human beings (in addition to race, sex, etc.) and a conscious intervention affecting the numbers of these categories can minimize the alleged negative effects of a majority of one sex over another.

A Dutch investigation has shown, however, that it is not irrelevant (which is claimed, for example by Kanter) as to which sex is in the minority (Ott, 1987). An empirical investigation in which female police officers and male nurses were compared, both of whom are in the minority in their field, has shown that while female police officers actually experience a number of the problems described by Kanter, male nurses experience mostly advantages from being a minority among female colleagues. At the same time the investigation has shown that while the male majority within the police groups rejected women when they reached a critical mass, the same was not true in the group of nurses. The conclusion to the Dutch investigation must be that it raises doubts about Kanter's theory which optimistically points to number (i.e. percentage) rather than sex as the main problem which keeps women back.

The structural approach does not explain why women find themselves in jobs with few possibilities of promotion more often than men do, for instance, it does not at all touch on socialization based on sex, but maintains that structural and situational conditions are decisive for the behaviour of a person. The consequences of structural conditions (opportunity structure, composition of the sexes) and the reproduction of these conditions, are explained in part, but the structural conditions as such are not explained.

3.2.2 Organizational culture

While the structural approach draws attention to patterns 'out there', i.e. regularities in behaviours, social practices or relations between different people, culture pays attention to ideational phenomena, i.e. the level of meaning.

A culture is defined and understood in various ways. Commonly, culture is seen as pointing to collectively shared patterns of meanings, values, assumptions and expectations that guide perceptions, cognitions and emotions. It creates and guides a collective, subjective logic which forms the unspoken, often unconscious subtext of social life.

There are many different schools and orientations within anthropology, ethnology, sociology and organization studies which express different views on culture (Alvesson & Berg, 1992; Keesing, 1974; Smircich, 1983). It goes far beyond the purpose of the present chapter to provide an account for those and we will only indicate the idea of cultural interpretations of organizations from a gender perspective. By talking of organizational culture it is cultural ideas and values on a meso-level that are seen as significant for understanding how gender is created and recreated at work. Normally, the organizational level can not be treated as isolated in relationship to other kinds of cultural configurations, but must be seen as interacting with societal, occupational, class and organizational subcultural (for example divisional or departmental) configurations (Alvesson, 1993).

Recently, a number of studies have been inspired by a cultural framework in studying gender and organization (Alvesson & Köping, 1993; Calás & Smircich, 1991; Mills, 1988; Mumby & Stohl, 1991; Symons, 1986). It is assumed that cultural values associated with maleness are favoured characteristics of many organizations (Morgan, 1986). It is thus assumed that overt practices clearly discriminating against women are a less significant factor than the embeddedness of cultural ideas and values that permeate organizational life on a depth level, and which are only partially possible to detect in observable structures, practices and behaviour. According to Mills (1988:356) discrimination and sexism can normally be assumed to be part of an organization's culture: "gender discrimination, far from being obvious, and overt, is embedded more or less unconsciously, in the processes that make up an organization's culture".

Different studies have pointed at different aspects of the gendered and gendering elements of organizational cultures. Language is for example seen as typically pro-male. Riley (1983) argues that the way organizations explain, motivate and legitimize their operations can reproduce and reinforce male dominance. The language of political symbols for example often draws upon sporting and military images to engender team spirit. Knights & Morgan (1991) discuss corporate strategy and claim that this discourse, rooted in the military, has a strong macho element and thus reinforces the masculine gender identity of managers and consequently in a subtle way discriminates against women in management.

Many studies recently have focused on sexuality and organizations, including sexual harrassment, efforts of management to control (restrict) sexuality at work-places or to use sexual attractiveness of primarly female employees either to enhance the power and prestige of superior male managers and as a symbol of organizational success or as a vital element in customer-producer interaction in service work (Burrell, 1984; Hearn et al, 1989; Hearn & Parkin, 1983; Mills, 1988, etc.).

Most, if not all, aspects of organizational culture can be seen as being gen-dered or at least relevant for understanding how organization constitute the gen-der identities of men and women. Not only personnel policies and practices and informal social interaction but all spheres of organizational life, from formal structures, communication patterns and styles of decision-making, indeed the very concept of bureaucratic organization itself, in direct and indirect ways, may express and reinforce asymmetrical assumptions, ideas and expectations about gender.

Needless to say, a cultural approach to gender and management points at com-plexities in terms of facilitating social change. No simple suggestions for social interventions emerge as planned cultural changes must be seen as a very difficult enterprise. Cultural analysis nevertheless provides important insights into our object of study and we will draw upon its insights, partly in the empirical investi-gations, but even more so in the final chapter, where we try to develop some new theoretical ideas on gender and organization.

3.2.3 Role theories

Role theories have some similarities with culture theory as both draw attention to expectations and norms. A particular role is contingent upon a cultural con-text. Roles are, however, a very specific and relatively superficial part of a cul-ture and can be treated without any ambitious consideration of its larger cultural context. The behaviour we expect of a person in a specific position as a male or female is called a role. Roles are normative. It is a question of expectations regarding an 'ideal' behavioural pattern. These social expectations can be passed on through textbooks, mass media and also by family, friends and colleagues. These expectations may differ and give rise to role conflicts.

Most jobs/positions in a working life are characterized by roles which are associated with either a female or a male role. Also because sexual roles de-scribe the sexes as opposites to each other there is the result that a woman in a traditionally male occupation may be regarded as unwomanly by her co-workers and possibly by herself and that she may therefore experience both an outer and an inner conflict when she breaks the pattern. The different gender roles are learnt through socialization. If there is a departure from the common roles there arises a kind of 'error' in the socialization. Therefore the so-called socialization bodies (family, school, mass media, etc.) become of considerable importance and we now focus on how these bodies treat girls and boys, women and men differently. Several investigations have shown, for instance, that attitudes to the two sexes differ and that as a consequence girls and boys are treated differently (see for instance Lensink, 1983; Spear, 1983).

Several investigations have shown that examiners who thought that a specific exam paper was written by a woman rather than a man regarded its content and professional quality as being inferior (Dipboye, 1975). Likewise, a number of investigations have shown that textbooks (in for instance physics and biology) tend to stick to a number of stereotyped roles for girls/women; they are shown in inferior functions, generally a little helpless but possibly good at domestic work, although without knowledge of major technical aspects, etc.. The picture that is communicated is that these scientific subjects are not for women (see e.g. Hilmo, 1983; Lensink, 1983). Other common stereotypes, based on the different roles expected of the sexes, are, for instance that men are presumed to be intellectually superior to women, to be more emotionally stable and to want meaningful work to a greater extent than women, etc.. These stereotypes have been repudiated by several systematic investigations within the field (Dipboye, 1975; Reif et al, 1975).

The fact that women and men are believed to have different psychological characteristics because they are expected to be different can have very limiting effects on both women and men. For instance, the stereotyped view of the leadership role is that it is dominating, competitive, aggressive, rational, etc., while the stereotyped view of women is that they are non-competitive, non-aggressive, irrational, emotional and unambitious. Roles are normative, however, and therefore historically changeable, thus the expectations of women and the role of women today differ from those of 30 years ago. What was not earlier questioned in life is now being debated. An example is sexual discrimination.

What is positive about the role theory and the concept of expectations is that it offers possible solutions to the problem. If the problem is that of different attitudes to girls and boys, and women and men, an attempt can be made to influence these attitudes. Curricula may be changed, sex equality campaigns may be initiated, etc.. The role theory appeals to common sense and from the perspective of reform it is easy to work with. Having said that, we should add that this way of thinking presupposes reflective agency on the part of the actors. The role theory is underpinned by simplistic conceptions of power.

According to Connell (1987:50-54) the problem with the role theory is that its view of sexual differences and the situation of women versus men is abstract and it does not provide a concrete explanation of the relations between the sexes. Literature on the role theory focuses on attitudes and disregards the realities behind the attitudes. As an example Connell mentions that we do not talk of class roles or racial roles, because the exercise of power within these areas is more apparent to sociologists. But when it comes to sexual roles it seems that the biological dichotomy conceals the fact that there is a power relation in this area at all. The role theory is seen by many social psychologists as a kind of social

determinism. It emphasizes the way in which individuals are caught in stereotype positions and these are made even more effective by other people rewarding
conformity and sanctioning departures from conformity. But why, asks Connell
(1987:50-54), do other people resort to sanctions? It cannot be explained by their
role expectations; people resort to sanctions as a question of individual will and
choice. The social dimension of the role theory is ironically dissolved into volun-
tarism, in a general assumption that people choose to maintain the existing customs, what happens in the sexual role theory is that the element lacking in the
structure is supplemented in a concealed manner by the biological sex category
(Connell, 1987). The sex role theory simplifies sexual complexity and tends to
reduce all masculinities and femininities to one dualism. Tolson (1977:22-46)
has, among other things, pointed out that there is no universal category of masculinity, and that we must acknowledge that masculinity is not simply the opposite of femininity but that there are many different kinds of masculinity within
different cultures. Also masculinity varies in different social classes.

Connell (1987) states four major reasons for abandoning the sex role theory as
a framework for analysing sex from a social point of view. First, it is arbitrary
and cannot theorize about power and social interests. Second, it is dependent
upon biological dichotomy and lacks understanding of structure. Third, it is dependent on a normative standard case and systematically misunderstands resistance; and fourth, it lacks a method to theorize gender historically. Sex role
theory does not have a method of understanding changes as a dialectic arising
within sexual roles. Even though Connell's points of criticism are important, we
believe that it is possible to use the sex role concept in various ways if it can be
supplemented with analyses of other major aspects. For instance, an analysis of
power relations is an important aspect.

3.3 Power

Other writers have also pointed out that the concept of role is inadequate to
analyse social sex, unless it incorporates aspects of power, control and interest
(e.g. Holter, 1984).

A distinction can be made between the macro-oriented power where women
are subordinated at a social level and the micro-oriented power, i.e. at the organizational level, in the home, etc.. Obviously these social and organizational levels
cannot altogether be distinguished from each other; if it is assumed that society
is characterized by certain general features as regards sex (division of labour
between the sexes, different social influence, etc.) these features will also exist
within organizations and vice versa.

Galbraith (1983) describes various kinds of power and how this power is exercised. He speaks of three kinds of power: compelling, compensatory and conditional power and says that to some extent male authority must historically be

ascribed to compelling power (the greater physical strength of the husband). Compensatory power (rewards by way of clothes, jewellery, etc.) has also been a possibility when it came to ensuring that women submitted to the will of men. However, the subordination of women, which was felt to be the natural order of things, was achieved only in part through explicit conditioning, upbringing, training, education, etc.. The greatest effect has been through women's acceptance of what has for a long time been regarded as the right thing by society and culture i.e. implicit conditioning (Lukes, 1978). The conditioned submission was based on a belief that the masculine will was preferable to women's own will. There was a corresponding belief held by men that owing to their sex or the related physical and mental characteristics of their sex they were entitled to dominate. These views have in particular been questioned by the women's liberation movement which has attempted to remove the belief that submission and compliance by women is normal and desirable.

An important aspect of the power conditions is that non-conscious (or taken-for-granted) ideas about relations between the sexes and their resultant power over one another are passed on. The historical superiority of men with regard to physical power and the later and less pronounced compensatory power has created deep-seated notions that men are naturally the more powerful. These ideas are passed on from generation to generation and continue to affect our expectations.

A way for men to preserve their power has been described by Lipman-Blumen (1976) who has developed a theory regarding sex segregation, a so-called homosocial theory of sex roles. It is men who control the resources, money, education, positions within trade and industry, political contacts, etc. and can satisfy most of their needs through other men. They are also more interested in other men, gaining their acknowledgement, etc.. Often a selection will take place among men, for instance in top positions (homosocial reproduction). Because men have the resources, other men and women will turn to them. This means that the behaviour of women (and men) within organizations can be explained by way of the power structure.

Many aspects relating to sex can probably be understood by means of structure and power, but if one is to understand the relation between structure and practice, and what maintains the structure, it is important to find out what is behind the conditioned power or "the gendered substructure" (Smith, 1987). According to Acker (1992:255),

The gendered substructure lies in the spatial and temporal arrangements of work, in the rules prescribing workplace behaviour, and in the relations linking workplaces to living places. These practices and relations, encoded in arrangements and rules, are supported by assumptions that work is separate from the rest of life and that it has first claim on the worker. Many people, particularly women, have difficulty making their daily lives fit these expectations and assumptions. As a consequence, today, there are two types of workers, those, mostly men, who, it is assumed, can adhere to organizational rules, arrangements, and assumptions, and those, mostly women, who, it is assumed, cannot, because of other obligations to family and reproduction.

Neither those exercising power or those that are subject to it are necessarily conscious of it. Haug (1984) has, for instance, asked the relevant question of why and how women themselves take part in their own oppression. She has argued that self-sacrifice is an action.

Ethelberg (1985) describes how male domination is maintained and how the conditioned power is communicated, for instance through change in conviction. She describes how the social oppression of women is transmitted to women's personality and how this expresses itself in three different personality strategies in relation to male domination: adaptation, overadaptation or protest. According to Ethelberg, personality strategy is the way in which the personality acquires knowledge of the fact that it belongs to a second-rate and relatively powerless category. Adaptation is a characteristic of the majority of women. The implicit conditioning is not questioned. The resulting personality style is that of the 'good girl'. Overadaptation results in the girl feeling inferior and developing a depression and passivity. Protest results in her being in opposition to male domi- nation and in that instance she will be regarded as unwomanly and as one who causes problems. Male dominance is therefore to be regarded as being derived from the social oppression of women and not as originating from a particular characteristic of men.

The oppression of women is seen as an integral part of the organization of society, it is also seen as important for the maintenance of this type of organiza- tion. Therefore, the oppression must be transmitted in such a way that women 'accept' it on the one hand, assuming the unpaid reproduction work, on the other hand accepting the lowest position in the labour market. Furthermore, Ethelberg notes that this complex process is to develop in such a way that they themselves regard it as an expression of their female characteristics.

Athough this last argument may seem rather functionalist and does not leave much room for women to 'break' the rules and influence the power structures we believe it is important to bear in mind that organizations do benefit from the fact that husbands in general are more 'free' to work hard and advance than their wives usually are because of other obligations. As long as these practices in domestic life are reproduced gendered organizations prevail.

3.4   Explanatory models in the field of socialization theory

While the micro-sociological explanations concentrate on the actual external social conditions and also on patterns of ideas that characterize the 'immediate surroundings' of individuals, perspectives in the field of socialization theory concern instead the constitution of the sexes as a psychological and socio-psy- chological process. The main emphasis is thus shifted from sexual differences as an outcome of external forces, to inequality as embedded to varying degrees in the different mentalities of men and women constituted in social contexts, which the individual has encountered in his or her life history.

Socialization theories put great emphasis on the importance of the background, childhood and later development of the individuals. Men's and women's way of functioning thus becomes an expression of their life history. The approach is therefore radically different from the micro-sociological, structural perspective which heavily emphasizes both conditions specific for various situations and also the importance of external advancement possibilities and restrictions. The perspective of role theory is clearly closer to a number of socialization theories but it puts more emphasis on the external restrictions and sanctions inherent in the idea of the importance of roles. It does not go into detail about the psychological level.

We make a distinction between two kinds of socialization theories: psychoanalytical and sociological. The former emphasizes, first and foremost, the importance of primary socialization, in particular the interaction between the young child and his/her parents, primarily the mother. The early separation and individuation process is regarded as being of importance for the establishment of certain psychic structures in a person. When we consider the theory of sociological socialization it is more about continuous development and the learning of cultural patterns which children, adolescents go through, for instance from mass media, school and their perception of the division of labour of adults, etc..

3.4.1 Psychoanalytical socialization theory

Theorists such as Chodorow (1978), Gilligan (1982) and Keller (1978), amongst others, have developed ideas based on a psychoanalytical theory about the psychological background for the differences in the emotional development of children and their identity. Chodorow finds that as the personality develops in early childhood there are sexual differences resulting from the mother-child relationship. Here the *division of labour* between father and mother in relation to rearing ('mothering') the child is the focal point for the relationship between man, woman and child. This is a dimension Freud did not attach any importance to.

The child lives, in early life, in a symbiotic union with the person who takes care of him/her (generally the mother). No limits are as yet drawn to allow him/her to distinguish between him/herself and the outside world. The outside world (the mother) is experienced in the early period as an extension of the child him/herself. Through his/her experiences with regard to satisfaction and frustration, joy and pain, the child learns to distinguish between 'I' and 'the other', between subject and object. Gradually, the child can distinguish between him/herself and the outside world and he/she acknowledges the outside world as a world consisting of objects external to him/herself.

The acknowledgement that the child is an independent individual and not a part of a symbiosis with the mother who has satisfied all his/her wishes and needs comes as a painful experience for both sexes. The child discovers his/her needs and his/her dependence and a longing arises for the re-establishment of the original unit. At the same time, there is a growing satisfaction with the autonomy he/she experiences. This development process will be of importance in later life as to whether the child strives for autonomy or symbiosis.

Theorists using a psychoanalytical basis believe that the most important influence on the perception of male/female by the individual is found through the early experience with the parents. From this influence, the self-perception of the individual is created, and his/her perception of sex and reality. Much can go wrong during this process. Here we will focus on the differences for girls and boys in this important development process, according to Chodorow and others.

This development process is believed to bring about different sexual identities in the two sexes. Boys base their sexual identity on opposition to what is feminine and thereby create an independent identity and consolidate their male sexual identity. In other words, an identification is established with the male (with the father or a father figure). The continued identification of girls with their mother means that the separation process of the daughter is inhibited and the separation from the mother becomes incomplete. It is easier for the mother to differentiate herself from the boy than from the girl and it is difficult for the girl to differentiate between herself and her mother. Therefore, the girl will not experience the same separation as does the boy, but will feel more closely connected to her surroundings, to the mother and to other people.

Owing to her different pattern of attachment to the mother, the girl grows up with a less well-defined ego and a greater need for emotional closeness in her relations, while the boy develops more clearly defined limits to his ego and a greater need for separation in his relationships.

As masculinity is defined through separation and femininity is defined through closeness, male sexual identity will be threatened by intimacy while female sexual identity will be threatened by individuation. Sexual differences in the formation of personality, as described by Chodorow in her analysis of early childhood relations, reappear in the middle of childhood. This appears from studies of children's games (Gilligan, 1987). We can see that Chodorow and Gilligan attach greater importance to the pre-Oedipal phase than does Freud. In this connection they emphasize that the division of labour between the sexes will be of decisive importance for the development of the children. The boy is 'pushed into' the Oedipus complex while the girl usually gets more unclear limits in relation to her self because of the continued identification with the mother. Her Oedipus conflict is not completed.

The different socialization of the sexes could, if we accept this theory, to some extent explain the greater interest of women in social relations. Their choice of education, training and career makes allowance for this need, whereas men endeavour to obtain autonomy, and their orientation is perhaps towards management positions.

The socialization theory can be criticized for not making sufficient allowance for the complexity of the person and, in addition to this, for overemphasizing the importance of sex in early socialization.

The development of the child in a specific way under given circumstances is not a mechanical process. The child participates in a social interaction under certain conditions, but the child is also party to the interaction and can presumably follow his/her own path; for instance, mix male and female elements as well as elements not easily categorized in gender terms. Subordination (closeness) and independence (separation) can exist alongside each other in the life of the child. As also pointed out by Connell (1987) there is no universal development pattern, nor does such a pattern exist in the special social context.

In particular, it may be mentioned that the interaction between the mother and the young child is not determined totally by the sex of the latter, but by the conceptions regarding the child, for instance sex role ideologies, etc. and a number of other circumstances including the similarities of the child to the parents in ways other than the purely genital. Girls may resemble their mothers as regards temperament, hair colour, and looks to a lesser degree than do their brothers, etc.. In general, the separation/individuation process, which according to psychoanalysis is complex and renders the child vulnerable, is determined not only by the child's sex. Other influences are: the social situation, background, personality, age of the parent, the child's position in the family order; important separations (e.g. as a consequence of illness), the constitution of the child, his/her biological instincts, the division of labour between the parents, whether the mother works outside the home, whether she has received further education or training, etc.. A large number of influences play a role and they are well documented by many writers with approaches that differ in some respects, see for instance Erikson (1955), Miller (1981), Berner (1984).

The importance of the sex of the child in his/her early development must be elucidated in more detail before the importance of the aspects presented by Chodorow, Gilligan and others can be assessed. More careful considerations are needed as regards the significance of the long term consequences of the importance of the sex (of the person who undertakes the mothering) in the early socialization. Later (Chapter 4) we will see that sexual identification is of great importance to women as to whether they become interested in/motivated for a career outside the home or a more traditional female career in the home.

3.4.2 Sociological socialization theory

In addition to the psychoanalytically inspired socialization theory, a sociological variant exists that provides a more social explanation of sexual differences. It attaches greater importance to the outside world in the establishment of differences, i.e. the attitudes which the child meets, the expectations made on the child, and so on. For example, at an early stage, children have different demands made on them depending on whether they are male or female. They are formed for instance by statements such as 'small boys don't cry' and 'nice girls don't do that'.

Sex role expectations are regarded as having a significant influence on who we become, how we behave, how other people see us, and how other people behave in relation to us. By accepting and incorporating the socially accepted rules, the child incorporates the cultural norms and rules of society. Thus the child learns to live up to the expectations of how he/she should behave. As the child grows older he/she encounters various socialization agencies such as school, friendships, media influences, sports associations, etc. and through these agencies he/she is provided with models for the behaviour suitable to his/her sex. The expression 'secondary socialization' is understood here to mean the socialization taking place outside and as an extension to the socialization within the family. The secondary socialization can modify or confirm the primary socialization.

A number of investigations are concerned with differences in the experience of girls and boys as regards sports and competition (Hennig & Jardim, 1977; Harragan, 1977). The investigators believe that boys/men have more experience in winning/losing, and in risking a stake, whereas girls/women see risk as entirely negative with the chance of losing, or being hurt and injured and therefore something which should be avoided. Most men regard taking a risk as something which can affect their future, something which may involve a future gain rather than a loss (Hennig & Jardim, 1977:27).

According to Lever (in Gilligan, 1982), girls prefer to discontinue a game when questions of doubt or disagreement arise, while boys apparently enjoy the discussion about the game just as much as the game itself. This game experience is a kind of secondary socialization. However, the preconditions for handling the game in a specific way, and possibly the choice of game, originate from the primary socialization. Mills & Murgatroyd (1991) argue that game playing versus play prepares boys and girls differently for their understanding of organizational life.

In addition to this, the perceptions of social stereotypes of the sexes, of masculinity and femininity, will in various ways reinforce the early sexual identities. Stereotypes can be found, for instance, in textbooks. Several textbook analyses have shown that the sexes are presented in a very stereotypical fashion in many of them (Hilmo, 1983; Lensink, 1983). One example Hennig & Jardim (1977:55) discuss is an investigation (from 1973) of primary and lower-secondary school books. This showed that,

when good things happened to a male character in a story they were presented as resulting from his own actions. Good things happening to a female character (of which there were considerably fewer) were at the initiative of others, or simply grew out of the situation in which the girl character found herself.

3.5   Discussion

The approaches discussed differ considerably both in their focus and in their level of abstraction. They concentrate on various aspects of the problem discussed here – differences between women and men. From the general societal inequality with regard to power and influence to gender differences with regard to priorities, ambitions, etc..

The macro-sociological explanatory models describe the oppression of women at an overall level and are interested in very general patterns. Early Marxist feminist approaches emphasize the capitalist conditions as almost decisive for the situation of women. Sexual differentiation is built into the capitalist production relations. On the other hand the patriarchal approach has focused on relations between the sexes rather than the 'nature of capitalism' and many theories of patriarchy have seen the oppression of women as universal persistent through different historical periods and across different cultures.

A synthesis of the two theories, Marxist feminist and patriarchal, is an important contribution in attempting to surpass the limitations inherent in both approaches. But as in the original theories, the synthesis also tends to make the situation of all women in contemporary society uniform, which is a consequence of the abstraction inherent in the analysis. It is difficult to record change on the basis of patriarchal theories. It seems that historical and cultural variations in inequalities between the sexes cannot be dealt with by the concept of patriarchy. A number of overall explanations of social inequalities between men and women can be provided by focusing on society as a whole, but gives us no idea as to how, and to what extent the inequality is constituted institutionally. The analysis does not end by ascertaining that male dominance is still prevalent. The question is when, how and for what reason do we have male dominance? The analyses are rarely concerned with variations in the class and the race of the women studied, nor in other concrete historical aspects which might provide a more varied understanding of the oppression and lack of equality of women.

Middle range and micro-sociological models are concerned with the importance of social structures, organizational cultures or gender roles. Structural theories draw attention to external, 'objective' circumstances in the production of inequality between the sexes, e.g. how the opportunity structure and the relative composition of the sexes may influence motivation, career orientation, etc.. A number of general explanations of the different treatment of the sexes are provided by the role theories and they are attractive because they provide a number of 'model' solutions.

These models cannot capture the complexity inherent in the behaviour of individuals, however. They are not concerned with the life of an individual prior to his/her life within an organization or with the aspirations held by individuals upon entry into an organization. In this context the external conditions are regarded as causal for the behaviour of individuals. However, role theories must be regarded as insufficient for an analysis of gender differences, since themes of power and the interest in preserving the status quo are not included. The power concept was incorporated in our critique as an essential element for an understanding of these aspects.

It is important also to be concerned with the constitution and preservation of the interests related to power. To ask the question: which practices are maintaining power? Unless this is acknowledged one can easily get into the situation which faces some of those in the women's liberation movement for some time, viz. of regarding the category of men as the 'main enemy'.

Theories of organizational culture to some extent share the focus of cultural assumptions, expectations and norms with role theories, but have a broader theoretical orientation. They make it possible to consider the dynamic aspect of gender production as well as the asymmetrical power relations inherent in cultural ideas and social practices. Like the other middle-range theories, organizational culture hardly takes into account the life history of organizational participants. Gender is seen as being constituted first when men and women enter the workplace.

On the other hand, socialization theories, both the psychoanalytical and the sociological, can capture the background and life history of an individual. Psychoanalytical theory goes into the subject in more 'depth' than does the sociological, and almost by definition tends to over-emphasize the primary socialization at the cost of the secondary socialization that takes place through affiliation to a place of work or through university training etc.. Obviously, this is inherent in the focus of the psychoanalytical approach. On the other hand, sociological socialization theories seem to overemphasize the effect of the socialization agencies on the fate of the individual. The point is that within the present framework of socialization theory it is difficult to distinguish between possible contradictions between primary and the secondary (and tertiary) socialization, which could be of special relevance for an understanding of processes of change in the life of human beings.

Finally, we will say a few words about biology, although, we like most other social scientists in the field of gender, neglect this dimension in the book. Biological factors could, for instance, be of importance for the attitudes and philosophies of the life of human beings. These are rarely touched upon, perhaps because biological factors have indeed been misused in the name of science. They have been used ideologically when needed by specific political or other dominating interests. We cannot exclude the relevance of genetic differences between the sexes. The problem is, however, that it is difficult to decide what differences are the result of the experience gained in life (through socialization) and what, if anything, are the result of the biological factors. We do think that social scientists should emphasize the social and cultural construction of gender but maintain some self-critique regarding the risk of 'social reductionism' and be open to the idea that biological factors and deeply rooted psychological differences may be of some relevance for illuminating gender phenomena.

Having pointed at a rather wide set of primarily sociological dimensions and foci of significance for understanding gender production in general, and gender at work in particular, we have established a repertoire for considering and theorizing various aspects of gender, managers and organizations. We will not concentrate on any particular theoretical approach in the book, but connect to various sources as they appear relevant when we overview and critically discuss research on female managers (Chapters 4-6) and then account for our three empirical studies (Chapters 7-9). In the final part of the book we draw upon a cultural understanding of gender and organization.

Notes

1   When we use the concept "gender", there is an implicit understanding that gender is socially and culturally 'produced'. It has been common among some feminists to make an analytical distinction between sex and gender, a distinction which was difficult to translate into Scandinavian (Swedish, Danish or Norwegian), because there is no such distinction in any of these languages – it is all gender (KØN). In order to make the Anglo-saxon distinction many used the expression "biological (KØN)" and "social (KØN)". This distinction is not maintained to-day, it depends on the context if KØN means sex or gender. We believe (like e.g. Calás & Smircich, 1991; Flax, 1990) that the distinction is superficial, a way of making a dichotomy beween body and spirit.

2   The statistics referred to in Chapter 2 about the number of female managers in the German railroad (Antal & Kresbach-Gnath, 1986/87) seem to contradict this.

4 Similarities and differences between female and male managers

This chapter deals with similarities and differences between women and men in relation to management positions. Often when the subject of female managers is discussed, the question is raised as to whether women are different from men. It is a question which arises from the assumption that differences of sex (inborn or more significantly acquired) may influence the behaviour of managers. These assumptions of sexual influences must be seen in the context of the various cultural conceptions and expectations of the sexes, of which we gave an account in the previous chapter. It is important to consider the situated nature of research results and ideas on the topic. The characteristics of female (and male) managers probably change with changing societal conditions. In the first part of this chapter we deal with the question at the individual level, role theories and socialization theories are relevant here; in the second part we deal with the question at the organizational level, where a structural explanatory model is used.

4.1 Leadership style

There has been a tendency in literature to transfer in a mechanical manner the ideas and theories regarding differences in the values, priorities, interests, of women and men in general to female and male managers. We shall endeavour to avoid this tendency in what follows and deal only with investigations that have been carried out on actual managers. Therefore laboratory investigations – which seldom include practising managers in the sample – will not be dealt with here. (For a survey of such studies and a number of other investigations, see e.g. Dobbins & Platz, 1986.)

There are a number of writers who are of the opinion that women do not function as managers in the same way as men do. Bayes (1987) has investigated whether women in high ranking positions behave differently from men. She carried out in-depth interviews of American women and men who were at the highest income level of the Federal Government, the Health and Human Services Department and the Treasury Department, and also collected data through interviews and questionnaires from both women and men at the same income level in the Department of Social Services and the Treasury Department in the State of California.

The investigations showed that the expectation that women and men might have different attitudes to leadership style and have different behaviour in similar situations were not supported by the data collected. While some women exhibited a management style which was open and 'participatory' or democratic, other women favoured control in their management style. Men, too, varied in their management style in degree of openness and participation. The only area where some male and female respondents agreed that women were different from men was in the area of their dedication to work. Women were perceived to work harder, to take their work more seriously, or even too seriously, and to be less concerned with monetary rewards than with recognition when a good job was done.

Bayes' conclusion from the investigation was that women in public bureaucracies do not manage by using a different leadership style, nor is any different leadership style reflected in the attitudes they express regarding organizational structure.

Kovalainen (1990) raises the question whether there would be differences between female and male managers with regard to work role descriptions and attitudes towards subordinates in a country with quite another cultural background (Finland) and another business tradition than for instance, the USĂ. Her study of 100 male and 100 female bank managers showed no major differences. A slight difference in managerial attitudes towards subordinates was noted, however.

Comprehensive research by others has come to the same conclusion. Bartol (1978:806) summarizes her examination of different investigations as follows: "In most cases, there are either no differences or relatively minor differences between male and female leaders on leadership style, whether the leaders are describing themselves or being described by their subordinates".

Powell (1988:165) reaches the following conclusion as to whether female and male managers differ or not, "they differ in some ways and at some times, but, for the most part, they do not differ".

When any differences between male and female managers cannot be found to be demonstrated in investigations of the actual behaviour of managers this may be due to various circumstances. The first and most obvious is that the real (deeper) differences are not very great. A related reason is that female managers have adapted their style to the male model, and they have had nothing unique to contribute. A third reason is that behaviour and attitudes are questioned in ways which do not capture the specifically female outlook.

As opposed to the above mentioned studies, a number of other writers maintain that there are clear differences between women and men in their management style. As a rule, this assumption is based on theoretical considerations and has been derived from assumptions about the character and the importance of the gender socialization (see e.g. Grant, 1988).

Loden (1986) is one writer who, as opposed to those mentioned earlier, emphasizes differences between female and male managers. Loden presents certain empirical examples in support of her own ideas. However, there are a number of objections which can be made to this work. Firstly, many of the differences mentioned have been based on interviews with individual managers who often refer to experiences which concern differences between women and men, and not women and men as managers. Secondly, she overgeneralizes from her findings and the results are expressed in terms of wishful thinking rather than in critical and reflective terms.

An example of differences between female and male managers that Loden mentions is their differing ability to deal with conflicts. Loden's data, based on 171 male and 145 female managers shows that male managers mainly use a win-lose approach to resolve a conflict, i.e. they would compete in order to win over forces of opposition to secure their own positions. The assumption is that to resolve a conflict, a trial of strength is required in which one person must win and another lose. The objective is to become the winner. The female managers have a tendency to use a win-win approach to resolve a conflict which is a more communicative approach. In solving the conflict they make allowance for the feelings of the other party. Only if male managers were unsuccessful would they then avoid the conflict, which may be seen as the reverse of their original competitive approach. When it is impossible to win, men avoid the conflict. Their objective is to avoid losing. Compromise was employed by men only when competition and a show of strength could not be employed effectively.

Loden found that the female managers favoured co-operation and adaptation which is a strategy of consensus rather than a strategy of competition. The strategy of consensus takes longer but has the advantage of preserving relations. However it can result in female managers not getting their own way. At this point compromise was also used as a strategy. Loden is of the opinion that in general female managers focus less on action and more on consideration.

Loden (1986) writes that while men feel best using the strategies of competition or avoidance in situations of conflict, these are two strategies which women rarely employ. Conversely, the two approaches employed by women, co-operation and adaptation, are those which are the least attractive to men.

Loden also attributes a more intuitive management style to female managers and refers to the book "Intuitive Management" by Agor (1984). Agor found a significant difference between female and male managers whereby women showed a stronger preference for an intuitive management style than men. However, the use of intuitive thinking by men increased as their position within the organizational hierarchy was improved. She is therefore of the opinion that female managers and male managers at the highest level have much in common in their approach to problem solving.

It is tempting to see Loden's work as part of a 'propaganda campaign' for female managers. She is worried about the crisis within the American business world and feels that feminine leadership could play an important role in a revitalization of American enterprises. She feels that the traditional male management style is less effective seen in the light of the present productivity and moral crisis. In its place she puts the female qualities and talents which, she feels, are desperately needed if the present crisis is to be solved.

Marshall (1984:13) has another point, namely to refute the thesis that "women are different from men, therefore they will not become good managers". On the basis of various investigations she concludes that women are very similar to men in their style of management. Marshall points out that the most frequently reported difference is that female managers score higher than men in the supportive side of management. Marshall concludes that the differences between women and men are very slight and that the female qualities may be those that will be in more demand in the future in management positions. Women might perhaps become better managers than men.

There is a striking contrast between Loden's and Marshall's two interpretations of the differences demonstrated between male and female managers. Loden inflates the differences to dimensions which give, in her book, a distorted impression of the actual conditions. Marshall, who has, as already mentioned, a different point of departure, attempts to show that female managers are not inferior to male managers. However at the end she undermines her conclusion by maintaining that in general women could perhaps become better managers. Strictly speaking it is difficult to see a basis for an opinion on this since as mentioned above her investigations have shown that there are no demonstrable differences in management style now so why should they be expected in the future? Better arguments must be found if this claim is to be made. For instance one could imagine that a larger number of women in leadership positions would have an effect since there is then a possibility that a larger number of 'typical' women would be recruited (i.e. atypical as compared to present female managers) and because the larger number in itself would render it possible for a closer approximation to be made to the characteristics of the 'typical women' and thereby bringing about changes in their management style.

A brief summing up of the research must be that most empirical investigations show very few and only slight differences between the sexes in their management roles. When it comes to behaviour, attitudes, etc. the similarities between men and women in management positions are more striking than the dissimilarities. In a summary of the empirical research, Butterfield & Powell (1981:130) conclude, that "It is now commonly believed that actual (leader sex) differences in the behaviour of real leaders are virtually non-existent".

4.2   Different job reactions

Even though there are apparently no major differences in the behaviour of managers, there can be differences in the way in which they experience their job. Reactions to their job may differ and these reactions may find expression in psychological effects such as stress. A number of investigations question whether female and male managers differ when it comes to stress factors. The general impression is that there are significant differences.

A British questionnaire (Davidson & Cooper, 1984) in which the respondents included 696 female and 185 male managers showed that women experienced higher pressure levels from stress factors both at work, at home and within the individual herself. They also experienced greater manifestations of stress than did male managers. Women in junior and middle management experienced the highest occupational stress levels.

Potential stress factors were noted on the basis of earlier investigations. Respondents had to score (according to the Likert scale) the degree of stress they felt in relation to each statement. Potential stress factors had been divided into three areas, namely those encountered at work, at home and within the individual. The female managers scored significantly higher in stress at work. They lacked female role models, and felt exposed to sex role stereotyping. They felt pressure to achieve and felt their treatment was unfair vis-a-vis men when it came to prospects of promotion and career. They experienced discrimination and prejudice and felt that their job-related training was inadequate as compared to that of colleagues of the opposite sex. Finally, they felt that colleagues of the opposite sex received more favourable treatment by the management.

In the home there were also a number of factors which gave rise to stress. The fact that the female manager earned more than the husband/partner, lacked support for domestic chores, experienced conflicting feelings of responsibility in coping with both family and career all gave rise to stress. Also having to decide whether to establish a family and have children created stress.

When considering the areas wherein female managers have the highest amount of stress score and diverge most from the score of male managers, one finds that most of these are within the area of work. Also, in one way or another, they are associated with prejudices and sex discrimination and are therefore factors which are outside the control of female managers themselves. As for the male managers they experience the greatest amount of stress arising from the authority/leadership role as well as from the (unsatisfactory) magnitude of their salaries. The female and male managers who are most exposed to stress are those, who suffer bad health, smoke too much, consume too much alcohol, are dissatisfied with their job and perform poorly. It is of course difficult to say what is the cause and what is the effect or to point at underlying significant factors.

The stress symptoms of the female managers are most often psychosomatic and find expression in inferior results in work performance. They lack enough self-confidence to voice their opinions. They feel incapable of being a success, and of coping with conflicts. They react emotionally to problems at work and lack self-confidence in the performance of their job. On the other hand the greatest stress symptoms of the male managers show themselves as a nervous stomach and a larger consumption of alcohol. In only one area did they score higher than the female managers, namely in stress resulting from not being able to produce work at a satisfactory rate.

In an earlier investigation carried out by Cooper & Davidson (1982) of 135 female and 500 male executives in the UK they found correspondingly that the psychosomatic symptoms were more common among female managers than among their male counterparts. Headaches, migraine, irritability and anxiety were reported more frequently by women than by men.

Weinstein & Zappert (1980) using 123 female and male MBAs in employment also found that women reported having depression and nightmares, and possibly breakdowns more often than men. Also they found that women had more non-specific physical complaints.

From Davidson & Cooper's investigation (1984) mentioned above, it appears that the female managers showed more stress symptoms related to family/domestic issues. It also appears from the investigation, however, that there were demographic differences between female and male managers. On average, female managers were older than the male managers and they were more often single. If they had children, their children were older. Also twice as many of the female managers were divorced. This pattern seems to be consistent. The marital status of female and male managers differs, male managers are likely to be married whereas half of the female managers are likely to be single (see Powell, 1988), also male managers tend to have children whereas less than half of the female managers in a recent Danish study had children (Billing, 1991). In addition to this, the female managers Davidson & Cooper (1984) studied, were concentrated at the lower management levels and they were often the first of their sex to have the jobs in question. They had fewer subordinates and earned less as compared to men at the same level. All these factors limit the value of comparisons as factors such as age, family conditions and job level may affect the observed results. A more general problem concerns possible differences between males and females in terms of reporting stress symptoms. It is likely that men and women differ in terms of self-perception and reporting of bodily symptoms. Nevertheless, certain tendences concerning gender differences may be treated as 'true'.

What implications arise from the fact that male and female managers differ in their ability to combine family and work? Obviously, it causes mental pressure for female managers, a fact which has also been demonstrated in an investigation carried out by Etzion (1987) this time on female and male engineers, i.e. professionals whose situations may be regarded as similar to those of managers. Etzion found that there were no differences shown in the importance that women and men (51 of either sex) ascribed to success at work and in the private sphere – but that there was a significant difference as to what they believed caused burn-out. The burn-out of men was mostly related to lack of success at work but not related to difficulties in the private sphere. The burn-out of women engineers, on the other hand, was primarily related to difficulties in the private sphere and only thereafter was it related to lack of success at work.

It must be noted that there is no obvious harmony between the organizational demands made on female managers and their functioning in relation to these. Many of the stress factors are related to internal organizational matters which include discrimination, a point which will be taken up later. Other stress factors are related to the tension which exists for most women and in particular female managers between their work/career and family. Jick & Mitz (1985) refer to a number of studies which show that parenthood is a more important stress factor for women than for men. That it is not (yet) a problem for men is due to what we described in the previous chapter (3) as regards the historical organization of the parents' role in the familiy and the sex role expectations that are incorporated in these.

Many people will claim that as long as more flexible working conditions, reasonable maternity leave arrangements, sufficent child-minding possibilities, and a more equitable division of the housework and responsibility for children, do not exist, it will be impossible for many women to become, or even wish to become, a manager. The traditional socialization of women has always told them that it is their responsibility to take care of home and children and possibly other family. Therefore becoming a female manager will appear to most women to be a tenuous utopia, unless there is an untraditional division of labour in their home or unless the children have grown up.

Some writers have in fact emphasized that, if anything, traditional female socialization is an antithesis to leadership (Healy & Havens, 1987) while the qualities which are associated with male socialization are regarded as essential for the successful manager. At the same time the fact that women are associated as a category with the home front has meant that they are not regarded as being qualified to assume masculine roles and high-status positions (Hennig & Jardim, 1977; Kanter, 1977). Still, female managers exist. What differentiates them from women in general? We will look at this in the next section.

4.3 The managerial woman

In the previous chapter we described how the socialization process and the normative sex role expectations contributed to putting girls and boys on their different tracks, the girls most often not going on to a career in the traditional sense.

We pointed out that the theories mentioned often were not capable of showing the complexity of the individual and thus incapable of finding out why he/she deviates from the ordinary pattern. We will go on to examine whether female managers have some characteristics in common. It should be pointed out that only very few of the investigations are detailed enough to give a full impression of the life stories of female managers. An exception is Hennig & Jardim's *The Managerial Woman* (1977) and therefore it is this which we will examine here.

Their investigation concerns 25 female managers who have all achieved top positions in the USA. All of them were born in the USA between 1910 and 1915. Their social background was upwardly aspiring middle-class. The fathers of 22 of the 25 had management positions within the private sector of trade and industry, and the other 3 were college administrators. Their mothers were full-time housewives apart from one who was a teacher. The 25 women had several characteristics in common, either they were only or first-born children or had an upbringing on a par with first-born children, all of them had had a very close contact with their father who had encouraged them to be independent, believe in themselves and not be afraid of taking risks. He had more or less given them the impression that they would have to be (like) a man in order to be a success. From childhood they had engaged in traditional masculine activities and they developed a preference for men rather than women early in their lives. The mothers were described as "typical", which meant that she had done "the right mother-type things" (Hennig & Jardim, 1977:82). One of them describes her parents as follows, "My mother was a warm, fluffy pillow, not terribly exciting, while my father was always dynamic, a really charismatic personality" (1977:8).

This typical view of the parents and their roles led to their seeing these roles as divided. This led to an unsolved conflict which was not faced until much later in their lives. Half of these women had married divorced men or widowers who were at least 10 years older than themselves, and who had a considerably higher income than they themselves. None of them had children.

All these women had had a good relationship to a male superior who had supported and encouraged them. For this reason alone it is difficult to say what has been the greatest influence in their progress, was it the presence of a mentor or a particular socialization that was 'not typical of women'? The last factor is probably the more significant. In addition, they would perhaps not have had a good relationship to a male superior if their own father had been emotionally or physically more absent during the socialization process.

Hennig & Jardim (1977:107) imply, however, that these women were all very conscious of their future at an early age, and that they rejected their mothers' traditional view of things and followed their own ideas.

It is as if they were setting the stage for the future. Their choice of their father as a role model, their dislike of 'traditional' women, their preference for co-educational activities were predictors of what they would do: attend a co-ed university; major predominantly in a professionally oriented area rather than in the liberal arts; establish much closer relationships with their male peers than with other women (men would confirm them, women would consider them odd); choose a career related to their fathers' and work almost exclusively in the company of men. All of these choices would be made during college and in the first years of their careers.

It must be borne in mind that these women grew up during the 1930's and their family pattern has been quite traditional. However it can be assumed that this would be atypical today (or at least tomorrow) for female managers. Now the mother will often have had a job or received an education during their children's adolescence, at least if the female manager belongs to the younger, under 40, generation of managers. Is the social background the decisive factor for career aspirations, or is it the identification figure, in this case the father? Often they are obviously closely allied. A Danish questionnaire investigation of men and women managers (Carlsen & Toft, 1986) concluded that social background is of greater importance for the career of women than of men and more women than men (18% and 4%, respectively) reported a strong attachment to their father.

4.4   Discussion

The large majority of the previous investigations shows that male and female leaders/managers are by and large similar. However, one can have certain doubts as to the reliability of the existing research into leadership in general. The research seems unable to produce unambiguous and concurrent results and there are therefore those who wonder whether traditional concepts can actually capture the phenomenon of management. Andriessen & Drenth (1984:514), for instance, conclude in a survey of research into leadership, that "The only point of agreement is that existing approaches have largely lost their usefulness for the further development of the field".

Many writers believe that research into management employs narrow, deterministic, rigid models which appear abstract to the practitioner and incapable of capturing the potentially most interesting and important aspects (see e.g. Calás & Smircich, 1988).

In recent years research into organizations has to some extent changed its view of management from being a question of planning, co-ordination, support, supervision and control into being something which is to be seen as defining reality, and exerting mental influences. It is emphasized that leadership is concerned with the handling of symbols and control of meaning. Concepts such as "symbolic leadership" and "management of meaning" have become popular (Peters, 1978; Smircich & Morgan, 1982, etc.). It is possible that this theoretical shift reflects changes in management practices and organizational conditions. Such a new avenue of research has, however, not yet been taken up in the study of sexual differences in leadership. Thus, it is still an open question whether this way of looking at things would modify the present day view of male and female managers as being by and large homogeneous in their leadership.

Until further research is carried out, one must therefore assume that as regards important behavioural categories there are only very few differences between women and men in management positions. This may have several causes: it is

possible that women and men are alike when it comes to the aspects most relevant to the tasks. Another option is that personal characteristics are of less importance than external structural circumstances for managerial work. The job and its
organizational context is perhaps more significant than the person having the
job.[1] A third possibility is that rigorous selection of people for management
positions is made with the effect that those either interested or selected are alike
but differ markedly from other men generally, and – perhaps in particular –
other women generally.

These are open questions. Whether it is the job which shapes the woman or
the woman who shapes the job cannot be answered with certainty. There must be
great variation depending on the type of job as well as the person holding it. One
could imagine that a certain selection takes place in particular for women at the
middle management level and upwards where the number is small such that
those considered for jobs are rather atypical and possibly similar to many men in
values or work behaviour. If this is the case it is not beyond belief that a large
increase in the number of women recruited to management positions could reduce the present selectivity and perhaps increase the difference in managerial
styles between these women and their male colleagues. An increased number of
women in important positions in working life could perhaps also change wom-
en's roles in these positions. The increase could influence the socialization of
those in the process of becoming female managers but also others at the work
place so that the element of male dominance could be reduced and thus lead to
greater 'gender variation' in managerial jobs.

This is mere speculation. However, it is important to point out that studies of
female and male managers that are available for one thing are rather problematic, for another they also concern a small number of women and prove difficult
to generalize over larger groups of women, which would include the 'recruitment reserve' for management positions. As has been mentioned earlier, quite
extensive material is available dealing with the emotional reactions to working
life of both men and women. The stress reactions are in general more clear for
female than for male managers. This applies generally for women and men in
employment, i.e. also for those who are not managers or professionals (Jick &
Mitz, 1985:408-418). The relation to the job of the different sexes shows the
contrast between identical behaviour on the one hand and different emotional
reactions on the other. It can perhaps, be explained by factors outside the job or
perhaps by factors in the interaction between work and the private sphere. Obviously, sexual differences exist here. One cannot rule out the possibility that biological factors also may matter. Another possible interpretation is that differences are a reflection of different inclinations of men and women to respond to
issues of stress and health in conversations or questionnaires rather than any
'objective' differences in terms of stress and causes of stress.

The reported discrepancy can, however, also be interpreted as showing that
women in management positions are not as similar to men, as is indicated by the

studies of the behaviour of managers. Perhaps the research into stress shows subtleties which other studies cannot capture regarding how a person functions or does not function in her/his job?

At least we can assume that a given situation which results in different reaction patterns from the different sexes should also have definite, even if minor behavioural implications. It is to be expected that a situation in which people react differently and there is some discretion, should have the effect of these same people acting differently in some respects. Alternatively management jobs may often be so narrowly structured and limited by external factors that a manager does not have very many options. His or her behaviour is thus not determined by values, preferences or psychology, but by the constrictions of the material and sociocultural context.

Finally, it is appropriate to remind the reader as well as ourselves that management and managerial jobs are social constructions (cultural artefacts) which can take many forms. It is very likely that research efforts to measure managerial behaviour, values and reactions are insensitive to such variations when using questionnaires and other means which aim at facilitating comparability through the use of abstract, standardized scales. It is even more likely that international (cross-cultural) and historical variations are neglected in large parts of the thinking and research within the field. Management as a specific function and a specialized profession is a rather recent historical invention and it is not impossible that the end of this century will be reevaluated by forthcoming generations as peculiarly management-focused (Smircich, 1985).

Like gender, management must be seen as a social phenomenon which over history is constructed and reconstructed. It is important to bear in mind that we are interested in the combination of two 'moving targets' – women (gender) and managerial jobs. This motivates a) some suspicion to the research within the field for being parochial, and b) a preparedness to **not** look for law-like, eternally valid patterns, but for results and viewpoints that may be relevant primarily for a particular time period, in a specific cultural context. This insight is easy to cope with in our case studies, where changes are salient, but is somewhat more difficult to keep in mind when considering a-historical and static questionnaire investigations. Given the fact that most research in the area is not that old and we concentrate on a certain cultural context (highly industrialized societies which have reached a comparatively high degree of gender equality during the 1980's), we do not want to overstress these problems either.

In this chapter we have dealt with similarites and differences between female and male managers. In the next chapter we shall deal with possible differences in the treatment of women and men in assessments on their way to a managerial job. We shall explore further which factors facilitate or prevent women from attaining leading positions.

Notes

1   This would be in harmony with Kanter's (1977) point of the significance of the structural position for a person.

5 The way to – and from a management position

In Chapter 3 we referred briefly to investigations which showed that sex role expectations of girls and of boys differed and that these different expectations had the effect that their performances were judged differently, as a rule to the advantage of the boys. Below, in a research review, we examine whether the sexes are also treated differently in the context of organizations. We look at whether women and men are treated differently in assessments and at some indications on discrimination against women in management positions. In addition to this, we examine whether sexual stereotypes make themselves felt in management positions. Finally, we concern ourselves with the question as to whether the composition of the sexes within an organization is of any importance to the possibilities of women becoming managers. Does a larger number of women within an organization mean that women will hold more management positions? After having looked at these questions at the organizational level, we go on to look at some explanatory models at the level of the individual which explain the small number of female managers using these factors relating to the individual.

5.1 Discrimination in connection with assessments

Extensive literature is available which takes as its focus sex discrimination in various organizational contexts. Most of this literature is American, and it may not be possible to strictly generalize all the results to other countries. Many studies are also now rather dated, and there may be great variations over a couple of decades within the field of gender studies. However, it cannot be denied that these results, when carefully considered, are relevant for the understanding also of, for example, contemporary Scandinavian conditions.

Discrimination may take place in all kinds of situations in which the working life of women and men is assessed, influenced and decided upon. Schooling, vocational training, first employment, type of tasks in the job, development at a specific place of work, employment changes, promotion, career prospects when a young manager, constitute the central fields in which women and men can be influenced in different ways. All these factors may give rise to different results as far as careers are concerned. It is important to note that this discrimination not only affects the career opportunities of those who are treated unfairly, they are also affected psychologically. Discrimination involves a socialization aspect and affects self-esteem and identity, making it difficult to separate outcomes of 'discrimination' from other dimensions of subjectivity.

Here we are concerned only with discrimination, that is, differential treatment which is not motivated by 'relevant' criteria. Differential treatment may occur for other reasons. For instance, workers may have different interests or biological preconditions (e.g. in connection with pregnancy or in relation to heavy physical work) but this is a difficult issue. Further discussion falls outside the scope of this chapter.

Discrimination may be harsh and drastic or subtle, indirect and perhaps even unconscious, not only for those who discriminate, but also for those discriminated against. Subtle and non-conscious processes weigh more heavily. Implicit conditioning and the construction of certain forms of experiences, beliefs and self-understandings constitute the central expression of the exercise of power in modern society (Galbraith, 1983; Lukes, 1978). In this context, crude, conscious discrimination, motivated with ill-will, aiming at the repression of women, is of less interest than the unconscious and unintentional results from prejudice, stereotypes and a lack of knowledge. We do not believe that the wish of directly working against women, analogous with (gross) racism is the great problem.

Gender discrimination, like discrimination of other groups which does not however attract the same intensive attention in mass media or in research, is shown by many different groups such as personnel administrators, managers, colleagues, subordinates, customers or clients and others. Women are not necessarily discriminated against only by men. Other women may contribute heavily to discrimination.

A major problem when investigating discrimination concerns the possibility of finding standards or criteria by which to compare the differences in others' assessments of women and men. Discrimination means that a person is not assessed fairly or given opportunities based on the person's characteristics and performance, etc.. One perceived characteristic (gender, age, race, religion), irrelevant of context, creates a biased perception of this person's other characteristics, abilities and behaviour. We are here talking about non-conscious, nonintended discrimination. As assessments of the characteristics and performance of human beings are very often difficult and subjective, researchers find it hard to demonstrate with certainty that a specific outcome is based simply on discrimination. It is possible to obtain indications, but hardly firm evidence on discrimination, if a group or category is strongly underrepresented in higher posts, e.g. less women (blacks, working class, immigrants). In order for the outcome mentioned to 'explain' (to be perceived as) discrimination, it must be assumed that the population from which recruitment takes place includes women and men with similar qualifications, and abilities for the job in question.

There are different views of the similarities between women and men in the context of working life and in the context of relevant background, mental, intellectual and motivational characteristics for management positions. If it is assumed that women and men are, by and large, alike and offer the same performance, have the same motivations and interest in their careers, it is therefore natural to regard the underrepresentation of women in high posts as compared to their higher representation in lower posts, as being conditioned by discrimination. If it is assumed that women and men are different, owing to socialization, etc., it is more difficult to put forward the thesis of discrimination, at least in a stringent form. This is not to object to the idea that discrimination may take place. The problem for the case against discrimination is that if two groups differ then comparisons are problematic and it is harder to prove that one group is discriminated against. The fact that women and men with the same formal qualifications are assessed differently could, in fact, be due to them being different and not to the prejudices and biased evaluations of the person assessing them. Usually, research into discrimination does not have access to a 'true' picture of how people actually are with regard to their personal characteristics.

In spite of this note of cautiousness, there are extensive indications that cultural expectations and perceptions exist which affect the way in which the two sexes are perceived, assessed and treated. These pervade society at all levels, not least in the context of work where major parts are traditionally perceived as 'male spheres'. Several writers have discussed the different expectations of men and women within organizations and these writers have basically concluded that it is not necessarily what women do or are capable of that results in their slower progress in the enterprises, it is rather what the people who engage and promote them expect of the women which determines their career progress (e.g Halaby, 1979; Devanna, 1987). These expectations are usually based on sex-linked behaviour.

These differences in cultural expectations may change into more subtle discrimination. When women are expected to be different from men, they may also be assessed differently with regard to professional qualifications. Forisha (1981:21) refers, for instance, to an investigation (Cecil et al), which demonstrates that men are regarded as potential leaders/managers whereas women with equal qualifications are regarded as clerical workers. In addition to assessments being made differently on appointment, it has been demonstrated that more routine tasks were assigned to women (Terborg & Ilgin, 1975). They also received lower pay and were promoted more slowly (Day & Stogdill, 1972).

Dubeck (referred to by Mills, 1988:362) studied the recruitment of college graduates for management positions in an industrial enterprise in the USA (the Midwest). She observed that the male recruiters were interested in knowing the person's qualifications for the job when the candidate was male, but were more concerned with the person's interest in the job when the candidate was female. In the case of female candidates, the questions and comments centered on whether the applicant was career-minded and whether she would leave the job when or if she got married. In considering qualifications women were assessed on the basis of much narrower criteria than men. The question of whether a man had a relevant educational background was disregarded if, for instance, it was felt that he would fit in. The same recruiting personnel were much more uncertain about this ability to fit in when the candidates were women. Dubeck further observed that this kind of recruitment process prevented the promotion of qualified female candidates. For men, great importance was attached to 'managerial experience' whereas this qualification was not investigated for women. This quality was regarded as an advantage in connection with promotion, therefore the expectation that women do not have it contributed to limiting their promotion in the organizational hierarchy.

It is generally experienced, and well-documented in research, that male applicants tend to be selected more often than their female competitors for management, scientific and semi-skilled jobs (see Nieva & Gutek, 1980). In assessment procedures men tend to be assessed more positively.

To understand sex discrimination one should distinguish between what concerns the perception as such of different people and how these are generally received and treated. It is one thing to allow the sex of a person to influence one's perception of the qualifications and qualities of the person in question which obviously have nothing to do with gender per se (such as intelligence, emotional stability, interest in the job, etc.). It is quite another matter to treat persons of different sexes differently even though they are not perceived as being different. A person can be recruited on the basis of sex because of a wish to adjust a 'sexual imbalance'. Preconceived opinions may exist about women giving the job a lower priority because of actual or future children. Possibly, employers often exaggerate the importance of women having children while no significance is attached at all to male employees with children (Billing, 1991:117-119). In addition, the way career ladders function often disfavours women. It cannot be overlooked, however, that 'realistic' evaluations on the part of employers in this respect can to a certain extent contribute to explaining the following type of phenomenon. Rosen & Jerdee (1973) mention an investigation undertaken by Harvard Business Review. 1,500 of the subscribers to the magazine who held management positions were sent two questionnaires. The replies to these led to three conclusions:

– Managers expect male employees to give the highest priority to their job when career and family obligations collide whereas they expect women to do the opposite;
– when a person's behaviour threatens his or her ability to do the job, managers make a greater effort to accommodate a male employee than they do for a female employee;
– unless the guidelines are unambiguous managers are biased to the advantage of men as regards selection, promotion and career development decisions.

Perhaps prejudices, and stereotypes have also strongly influenced this investigation. On the other hand, working life has by and large adapted to the general social constructions and conditions of the sexes that characterize early socialization, family patterns (gender expectations in relationships), etc., and which have the effect that women do not as often as men give work and career the highest priority. This does not motivate the use of stereotypes, however. Perhaps conditions have changed somewhat since this investigation in 1973 and as regards the stereotypes of managers regarding female employees.

The studies referred to above illustrate conditions which are probably shaped by cultural conditions that discriminate against women. But they may also contain elements and considerations concerning culturally determined but actual differences between women and men – which put pressure to bear on men to have paid work and on women to be in charge, to a greater extent, of the reproduction sphere. It is difficult to separate stereotypical beliefs from realistic expectations. Quite a number of studies are available which more specifically illustrate how a person's sex in itself affects the perception of that person. Female and male performances of exactly the same kind have appeared in several studies to be evaluated more positively if the person undertaking the evaluation thought that a man was behind the performance (Nieva & Gutek, 1980). This has been the case both when the performance concerned writing scientific articles, painting pictures, constructing mechanical objects, dealing with emergencies and doing housework. Thus, there is a clear tendency that performances rendered by men are judged more positively than performances rendered by women. Often good results achieved by women are ascribed to 'coincidence' or some other external factor while good results achieved by men are regarded as a result of his will or ability.

The picture is not unambiguous, however. Although there is usually a pro-male bias in evaluation, a small number of studies have also found a bias in favour of females. Nieva & Gutek (1980) refer to studies that have considered managers, lawyers and manual workers. These studies have found a bias toward women. A number of investigations have also concluded that there was no unfair treatment because of sex when it came to assessment of performance.

On account of this, we must qualify our understanding. One cannot simply say that women are persistently misjudged because cultural expectations distort the ability of perception even though it may freqently be the case. Nieva & Gutek (1980) note the following factors as being relevant:

– Distorted perceptions arise from insufficient information. Notions about the importance of sex will play a role first and foremost if there are few other clues. Many laboratory studies simplify and isolate the situation and emphasize sex strongly. At the same time background information and anything else that complicates the situation is missed out. Therefore a greater degree of sex discrimination is often noted. In this connection we find that in his field investigation Powell (1988) noted that there was no sex discrimination in the assessment of students being admitted to university. However several experimental studies found there was discrimination. Powell suggests that access of richer information in real life reduces the discrimination salient in experimental studies.

– Sex-related bias also has to do with 'sex role incongruity'. Thus in areas which are regarded as being 'female' or 'male', cultural attitudes will have a greater influence. As relatively many jobs are traditionally 'masculine', especially management positions, one may assume that male applicants and candidates for these jobs will benefit.

– Discrimination in assessments is also influenced by the level of qualifications or the level of performance involved.

According to Nieva & Gutek (1980), women are assessed less favourably than men, when they are well qualified and manage well, while women are assessed more favourably than men when both are not well qualified or render a performance which is not good. This implies a system of rewards that differs for men and women. In brief, a sex-related evaluation bias (discrimination) is a greater problem for successful or competent women in situations which are not unambiguous and where proper knowledge about the person is lacking and in situations where a behaviour is expected which is not congruous with sex roles.

The tendency to give a specific group preferential evaluation and to treat another group unfairly does not apply only to the sexes. In an investigation of stratification within organizations, Pfeffer (1977b) used a sample of American BA and MBA students a number of years after their finals. He found that socio-economic background was of importance for their progress and income level even when competence (operationalized into academic qualifications) was kept constant. Pfeffer suggested that this is related to the fact that the progress made within the enterprise is determined by the social equality between senior executives and the group investigated (which is in part illustrated by socio-economic background). It also appeared, however, that the importance of socio-economic background was greater in small enterprises than in large; greater in staff positions than in line positions; and also greater in the fields of economics, insurance, etc. than in manufacturing functions such as production. According to Pfeffer (1977b), background and social equality play a greater role within fields of work and organizations where the employment of objective criteria is difficult. In technical jobs it is, presumably, easier to determine 'pure' competence. In large enterprises more systematic and qualified evaluation instruments are employed, according to Pfeffer. This is in accordance with the importance of social equality/inequality of the sexes. As well as concluding that the degree of coincidence and assessments based on objectively irrelevant circumstances are greater in situations which are diffuse and difficult to evaluate, we can also point to the importance of the social background of women in organizations and management positions. It is probable that women with a working class background are even more likely to be unfavourably evaluated than women with an upper middle class background. This aspect has not been sufficiently investigated, however.

5.2 Discrimination against women in leading positions

As already mentioned, it may be difficult for women to be promoted within the organizations. Symons (1986) had compared the world of management to a territory which was reserved for a few insiders. She describes the problems of becoming a member of the world of management which she calls the tribe. Using a sample of 67 female managers she investigated the rites of initiation that were necessary in order to become a member. The problem of getting access to the territory turned out to be in part a structural problem which has been created by the segregation of the sexes on the labour market. Getting out of the female job ghetto at all constituted a great problem. It is less surprising that it is difficult to be promoted if one has been in a secretarial post, than to understand that there is also a serious recruitment problem for those who had an MBA. It was more difficult for women than for men to use their education to enter a career job according to Symons. Becoming a member of the tribe at all constituted a problem. Creating credibility and being included in the promotion potential was contrary to the normative expectations of women. The women felt that they must be able to prove that they were not only the equal but better than men.

I believe that women still have to be exceptional to get ahead, which is unfortunate. I look at the women in this company, and they're all exceptional. Some of the men here are average but there are no average women (manager in Toronto, quoted by Symons, 1986:385).

An investigation by Harlan & Weiss (1980) revealed two subtle forms of unforeseen discrimination. The first concerned the promotion pattern. Middle management supervisors gave the highest points to older and less aggressive women who, Harlan believes, constituted a lesser threat and were less dynamic. The other concerned evaluation. When a male manager did something wrong, he was corrected, but if a female manager did the same it was ignored, according to an interview with Harlan (in Collins, 1982). Collins thinks that the supervisors were not interested in confronting female managers because they thought that they would break down if they were criticized whereas they could criticize male managers and afterwards go out and drink a beer with them.

Another form of discrimination is mentioned in an investigation undertaken by Bayes (1987:18) from which it appears that a number of the female interview respondents noted, that if a woman makes a mistake, "it is because she is a woman, whereas if a man makes a mistake, it is because he was a poor manager, not because he was a male". The respondents were in positions which Kanter (1977) refers to as token positions.[1] According to Kanter, tokens will symbolize the sex category to which they belong. As is often the case within the field (and in social science in general), this finding is not as clearcut as it may appear. Reported incidents can not always be taken at face value and the meaning (i.e. threats, coaching, discouragement, misunderstanding) of the reported messages may be more ambiguous than respondents and researchers claim. Therefore messages, also from people who perceive themselves as victims of discrimination, must be carefully considered and critically evaluated. Nevertheless it indicates the presence of sex discrimination in the sample.

The problem is that the management role has traditionally been related to the category of the white, male, middle class and a part of this is managerial practices that have contributed to keeping women in a traditional position on the basis of sex roles, for instance secretary. This is an experience that may be encountered in connection with meetings with outsiders where the woman is assumed to be a secretary and not a manager. Other ways in which sex is made into a conspicuous point in the interaction is where, for instance, during a business conversation the woman's looks are commented on or questions are asked as regards her marital status. It appears from Symons' article (1986) that women handled such problems with humorous comments or by ignoring the remarks and reverting to the business talk, which was the most effective method. Nevertheless (as pointed out by Symons), such comments on the sex of women are often experienced as irritating features because they are a reminder that the sex of women constitutes a problem in the work situation. Therefore it will remain a challenge for women to handle their sexual identity as long as they are a minority in the world of management.

5.3   Sex stereotypes and management positions

The problems mentioned above are related to the nature of management. As men have traditionally held the management positions, management can in advance be assumed to imply some idea about 'masculinity'. Among others Schein (1973, 1975) refers to investigations which show that management is primarily seen as being related to masculine characteristics. Therefore successful behaviour at work is also understood to be masculine which has the effect that women are expected to fit the role badly. Masculinity is normally assumed to include management potential which women by definition lack to a greater extent than men and this is something which they are probably to an even greater extent, *expected* to lack.

Hearn & Parkin (1986/87) refer to Weber's three ideal types of forms of authority and, by implication, leadership. Firstly, leadership can be seen as coming from traditional authority which originates from a socially accepted status, for instance the father's. Secondly, leadership may be understood as the product of the qualifications and charisma of 'great men'. Thirdly, leadership may be taken for granted as the normal role play relating to rational, legal authority within bureaucracies. Even though the above-mentioned interpretations are distinct in Weber's understanding of the theory, elements of all three of these seem to be present in many mainstream studies of leadership. In many management models, the necessary and desirable qualifications are assumed to be masculine whatever that more precisely means. When women demonstrate such qualifications and become managers, the language is, according to Hearn & Parkin (1986/87:38), often distorted because women are assessed differently from men. "Aggressive becomes 'over-domineering', and assertive is viewed as bossy and strident." Women are thus expected to act within the framework of their sex role. They should preferably act as 'real women' and this picture is difficult to maintain when they have become managers and show qualifications that women are not expected to have.

As regards the stereotypical perception of the management role to the effect that it requires male qualities, Dipboye (1975) mentions that an attempt was made to determine characteristics which distinguished between the efficient manager and the inefficient manager and that neither personality traits, characteristics or the like could be found which consistently could distinguish between good and bad managers. The characteristics of a good manager depend on the situation, says Dipboye. There may be much truth in this. At the same time, researchers into management have not been successful at explaining the phenomenon properly (Andriessen & Drenth, 1984) and this leads to certain difficulties of relating sex to (successful) management in that one does not have much knowledge about what characterizes a good manager. When considering how perceptions of the sexes affect the functioning of women in many kinds of managerial positions, the effect of conceptions of the sexes both historically and in a specific situation should not be disregarded. Forisha (1981:23) summarizes it as follows:

In summary, then, there is evidence that men and women can both be highly competent in similar professional and managerial positions. It would also appear that women sometimes fare best when they incorporate both interpersonal skills and high levels of competence in their leadership styles. However, there is also evidence that women are sometimes less effective than men and there are suggestions that this may be due to the negative impact of their peripheral position in the work sphere. If women are denied challenging assignments, if women are underestimated and hence rewarded for underperformance, and if they begin to think less of themselves both because of stereotypical attributions and the accomplishment of less difficult, routine tasks, then women may indeed differ from men, and not in a positive direction.

In order to be able to understand the consequences of sex stereotypes it is thus necessary to take into account their 'substantial' effects (via socialization and development of the personality). People may become what, at first, other people expected them to be. Sex stereotypes may, in other words, have the effect that many women actually have worse preconditions for functioning in managerial positions – and that it takes time before these are overcome.

5.4   The importance of the composition of the sexes for discrimination

Many feel that sexism and discrimination will drop markedly when more women are employed within an enterprise. Therefore many believe that the critical factor is not gender per se, but the ratio, the number of women. A theory on critical mass has been proposed (see e.g. Loden, 1986) which implies that an actual effect on the enterprise and a balance between the sexes will not arise until women constitute more than 30% of the total number of employees. When this share has been reached, working with women will be taken as a matter of course and female managers will have been in the enterprise long enough to be able to reach positions of influence (see also Chapter 3). The claim is that a mixed composition of the sexes is required if women are to have success in hierarchic male-oriented organizations (Martin, 1985). Also Kanter (1977) has described how very few women in the context of male dominance will be treated unfairly and have difficulties of making a career, indicating that an increase of women will automatically make things easier for them. As we pointed out in Chapter 2 it is too simple a statement to expect that numbers of women increasing in an organization will 'automatically' result in more women in leadership positions.

Izraeli (1986/87) has investigated whether there was a connection between the share of women within an economic trade and the share of women among managers of this trade and whether the contribution of the number of female managers to net growth would be greater in industries where the share of female managers was larger. Izraeli found that there was a connection between the share of women within the industry and the number of female managers. The greater the share of women, the greater was the share of female managers within the industry. In addition to this, she found a connection between the proportion of female managers within a specific industry in 1975 and the rate of increase in female managers measured as the share of women in net growth of managers between 1975 and 1982. On the other hand, she found that the level of segregation in management did not change during the period in question. Segregation is to be understood as correlation between the number of female managers and women's share of the entire labour force. The latter increased in Israel from 32.6% to 36.9% and the former from 12.4% to 15.9%. That is, where the number of women in the labour force increased by 4.3%, the share of women among managers increased by 3.5% in absolute terms. On the basis of this, she concluded that management has become an occupation that is even more segregated on the basis of sex. On the other hand, one can perhaps claim that the rate of increase in relative terms in the number of female managers was higher than the increase in women in the labour force. The increase of the latter by 4.3% from 32.6% is considerably less drastic than the increase in female managers from 12.4% to 15.9%. In the first instance there is an increase of 13% and in the latter an increase of 28%. The Izraeli (1986/87) investigation includes in addition to general managers also lower and middle level managers. This is presumably why the number of female managers is relatively high as compared with conditions in many other countries.

If we make a comparison with an area within the private labour market in Denmark (approximately 25% of the total salaried staff is included) we do not find an increase in segregation during the period 1983-86. Women's share of the number of managers increased from 6.3% in 1983 to 8.2% in 1986 while the female share in total salaried staff increased from 39.2% to 40.9% (Carlsen, 1987). The percentage increase in the number of female managers was thus larger than the increase in the total number of female salaried employees. We must, however, once again point to the criticism expressed earlier of the above-mentioned investigation in which Carlsen tends to lump together a large number of different groups under the category 'management'. So the question is whether it really tells us anything as to whether segregation exists when the different categories of management are not taken into account.

Many have claimed that once women have gained access to an organization it becomes easier for more women to gain access and there will be a greater recruitment potential for the leading posts. However, some investigations have shown a somewhat different pattern. An example is an investigation carried out by Harlan & Weiss (1980). They investigated 100 female and 100 male managers in two large enterprises. They found that the resistance to the first women was very great and that it became gradually less as more women were employed in the firm. But when the share of women reached approximately 15% of the middle management group, it seemed that the men felt threatened. They feared that the women would take the next job that they wanted for themselves. Numbers tend to constitute a threat to men as it makes the increased competition with which men are faced more conspicuous. Resistance then becomes more open. Harlan & Weiss suggest that the resistance is unconscious; that men are simply afraid and respond at a somewhat primitive level. Therefore, it is impossible to talk of a linear progression in the promotion of women, let alone reduced discrimination when, for instance, they constitute 15% of all managers. As mentioned previously, new obstacles may arise. Thus, what they are touching upon is that interest and power conditions play a role and oppose equal treatment of the sexes in a situation of tough competition about high posts (cf. power perspectives, Chapter 3).

Many have tended to believe that a certain number of one sex would lead to some kind of deterministic behaviour from the other sex (cf. the whole discussion about tokens). This has been problematized by Skvoretz (1983). Skvoretz, like Ott (1987), suggests that a few men in female groups have a less negative experience than a few women in male groups, and this is because the sexual status of males is an advantage to them rather than a disadvantage. This means that the higher sexual status of men will in part compensate for the disadvantage of belonging to a numerical minority. But seen from the point of view of the female token person, a larger share of women in a predominantly male context will be an advantage to women because a larger heterogeneity will partially counteract the negative effects of the sexual inequality. For women token status can in general be said to be negative (Kanter, 1977). Whereas for men it can really be said to be positive (Skvoretz, 1983; Ott, 1987).

Mixed uneven groups may also be appreciated differently by male and female members. The fact that for instance men join a female group may increase the status of the group while women joining a male group may lower the status. Therefore one can see that because they also wish to advance, in their own interest male members feel compelled to resist more women joining their ranks because they regard this as a handicap for their own difficult attempt at advancing or reaching the top. Apparently, if too many women join a group it will have an effect. Harlan & Weiss (1980) found, for instance, that when the share of women was increased, i.e. when a group of women were placed together within the same category of managers or the same department of an enterprise, it was very easily made into and regarded as a female job and subsequently one could no longer recruit men for the department or the job. Therefore it must be pointed out that often it is no good generalizing on the basis of one investigation of a specific enterprise, stating that the same applies to all other enterprises, let alone from one national investigation stating that it is an international phenomenon.

As already mentioned many have been concerned with the phenomenon of the critical mass but here various examples have been emphasized which show that the number in itself does not release an automatic effect. Other factors which may be equally important may play a role. Is there, for instance, great unemployment within the area in question? Is there perhaps keen competition within the occupational group? This must be seen as a major reason why the resistance will in certain cases increase when more women join the group. Finally, there is the fact, as already briefly described, that enterprises with a high share of women, possibly with female dominance, tend to decrease in status, which in turn seems to affect wages and salaries. There are many historical examples of this, for instance it is the case in Denmark within the whole of the social sector, and in part the public sector and across the education sector.

5.5   The level of the individual

In this section we will look at some explanatory models which claim to be able to explain the small number of female managers at the level of the individual. The most frequent explanation comes from the socialization theory. Here it is proposed that as a result of specific socialization women develop other interests than pursuing a managerial career.

In Chapter 3 we have given a detailed account of theoretical explanations for sex differences on the basis of roles and socialization. Therefore, we will only briefly describe, how these theories are employed in relation to the problem mentioned. Often sex role theories and socialization theories overlap. Many studies are not sufficiently thorough to be called socialization studies, but this aspect we cannot deal with here. A person-oriented explanation says that lack of women in management is due to the socialization of women, that it contributes to furthering personality traits (forms of subjectivity) which are opposed to the demands forming part of the management role. Among these female traits are the fear of success and an unwillingness to take risks (see e.g. Horner, 1980). According to these theories, being a woman and making a career are incompatible and this should be the reason for women's fear of success. In Bayes' investigation (1987) many female and male managers mention a difference which constitutes a problem, viz. the mental condition of women which they describe, for instance, as being raised to become secretaries and not being able to let go of this mentality. They lack self-confidence, are unwilling to take risks, lack ambitions, neglect personal development potential and lack the ability to plan their careers.

Several objections have been raised to seeing female behaviour as merely a result of socialization specific to women. Riger & Galligan (1980) think, for instance, that this behaviour will be explained differently, if it is instead regarded as being determined by the situation. When, for instance, women are not promoted within organizations, this can be the reason why they take so much trouble about the actual work they have, which gives satisfaction and self-confidence. The person-oriented explanation will claim, on the other hand, that women devote themselves highly to the actual work because they have not learnt to plan or set long-term objectives. They do not regard this as a step on the way to further promotion. Women regard personal relations as an important part of their job satisfaction. On the basis of a person-oriented explanation, one would think that this reflects the deep-seated traits of women, but on the basis of a situation-oriented explanation one would think that women's need to be popular is related to their job situation and as they stick to jobs in which there are no possibilities of promotion, their satisfaction does not come from the job, but from the quality of their relations with colleagues. Riger & Galligan (1980) suggest that studies of women in management must make allowance for both person-oriented and situation-oriented variables as otherwise there is a risk that factors will be ignored which can explain important discrepancies in the findings. Nor do they think that fear of success is necessarily an internal motivation factor, but that it can instead also be a response to situational factors and that it is therefore not at all limited to women. This is in accordance with, for example, Kanter's (1977) view. The fear of success is in their opinion determined by the situation and is not found, for instance, within traditional female areas.

Also other characteristics of women and men have been claimed to come from socialization, however, on a closer examination these turned out to be sex role stereotypes which also greatly contribute to limiting the sexes to a number of roles accepted in advance and are thus, in a sense, 'real'. Dipboye (1975) has investigated five of these stereotypes regarding women and men. Men are said to be intellectually superior, emotionally more stable, they appreciate promotion and meaningful work more and are more self-assertive, self-confident than women. The successful manager thus has male characteristics. In his opinion, none of the above-mentioned stereotypes hold, but he points to a paradox in referring to investigations which show that women who are intellectually superior to men gain less self-confidence as their average marks increase at institutes of learning (among others Hollander, 1972).

Reif et al (1975) refer to a comprehensive examination of investigations concerning biological and socialization factors which concludes that the only difference between women and men that biologists, psychologists, socio-psychologists and sociologists all seemed to agree on was the greater interest of women in relations to others: "About the only testable difference between men and women seems to be women's greater ability in interpersonal relationships" (1975:13). Another earlier investigation (Ellmann, 1963 referred to in Reif et al, 1975) concluded that it appears that the differences between women and men are far less important than the similarities between them. It seemed, however, that the claim to the effect that women are more concerned with their colleagues and friends could be supported and that they were more concerned with the quality of supervision and job surroundings while men were more interested in the advantages of their jobs, possibilities of training, promotion and pay. The only major difference between women and men is thus, according to these investigations, the relation orientation of women – and what some call 'rationality of care' (greater interest in others). This stems from the primary socialization according to many writers (Chodorow, 1974; Gilligan, 1982), but one should bear in mind the role of structural conditions, as indicated above.

In Chapter 3 we examined the psychoanalytic socialization theory and how this interest in being connected with others comes from the early contact with the 'mother figure'. But is it this interest that has the consequences which for most women results in other priorities and choices than career, for instance giving priority to the family, when a choice is to be made? At any rate, the investigation mentioned below is remarkable. Dipboye (1975) mentions a survey of 1,528 highly intelligent children (average IQ 152). A follow-up survey of these at the age of 35 showed that more than 70% of the men were employed in academic or semi-academic jobs (professions). 48% of the women had wage labour – and those having jobs were school teachers, secretaries and the like, very few had received academic education. It was believed in these surveys that the most significant 'performance' of these talented women was their choice of highly intelligent husbands.

That women give priority to the family to a greater extent than do men appears also in an investigation of 300 male and female managers in a single company, referred to by Loden (1986). This study showed, among other things, that even though in relation to their jobs one third of the women had been asked to move, only 21% accepted this as compared to 81% of the men. It is claimed here that female managers with children do not give priority to their career to the same extent as do men, but consider all aspects, in particular the family.

When exploring why women do not have the same success as men on the labour market, the focus must shift from the biology/nature of women, to the cultural limitations emanating from sex role expectations. Obviously real differences between the sexes on account of socialization are important factors, but as mentioned earlier only one real difference has been found in most investigations, a difference, that is, between women and men and not between female and male managers. This difference is the rationality relating to care mentioned above. That women are often more oriented towards the family and ready to give their career lower priority is in accordance with this.

5.6   Discussion

By now extensive documentation is available to show that women and men do not differ with regard to personal characteristics, abilities, talents, etc. and at the same time it seems that there is a clear difference as to how their talents are utilized in their working life. Where women are concerned, as far as can be judged, it is not unusual for them not to exploit their possibilities. Often those responsible for this are heads of department, employers and other people within organizations who often unconsciously form estimations and decisions that treat women unfairly. But it is also to a great extent a question of internalized, learned barriers and obstacles in women. Thus, the problem is to be found in women themselves, at least from a superficial point of view. Alternatively, one could say that culture, via its agents of socialization, has placed the problem 'within' the subjectivities of women.

It is difficult to decide to what extent this internalized complex of problems which finds expression in lack of self-confidence, a tendency to sacrifice their own possibilities for the sake of the family, lacking ability to take a long-term, strategic perspective, etc. is conditioned by an early or a current long-term socialization or whether it is more a question of what is communicated socially in different situations and contexts. In the instances where women's behaviour is an expression of an early and/or lifelong socialization, it is, if anything, a question of characteristics that are integrated in the personality and which determine the work behaviour and contribute to the sexual structuring of the organization rather than an effect of work and organizational conditions. The latter may, however, influence, reinforce/reduce the personality traits. And these traits may be more or less sensitive to various work and organizational conditions. Career may, indeed, be more or less in agreement with 'femininity'[2] depending on whether it is a career within the army or within the fashion industry.

The above-mentioned ways in which women may behave in relation to their working life may, as pointed out by Kanter (1977), Riger & Galligan (1980), etc., also be regarded as reflections of more direct social conditions. In that case social communication will be of greater importance than a personality determined by socialization. It would probably be wrong to try to reduce the discrepancy noted earlier between the potential of women as far as talents are concerned, and the difficulty that is deeply rooted in subjectivity in taking the best possible advantage of this, to be solely a question of individual psychology or external social factors. The whole spectrum of social influence exists; from a repertoire of actions deeply rooted in the personality via socialization to a sensitivity to actual external conditions. The very interaction between internalized factors (life history) and those conditioned by specific situations (social contingency) is important. This aspect has not been sufficiently investigated in the literature.

There is sometimes a tendency to maintain a dualism between the characteristics/abilities (first and foremost talents) of women and various external or superficial internal limitations and obstacles. Sex roles and stereotypes are examples of the latter. It is then claimed that women are just as qualified as men for the work, but that 'only' prejudices, stereotypes, habitual thinking, attitudes, etc. prevent them from seeking and getting, for instance, management positions.[3] This viewpoint involves a trivialization of the consequences of socialization. It also involves a risk that the competence and qualities that are assumed to be important for functioning in positions at a high level, for instance management positions in contemporary bureaucracies, are not 'captured' correctly. Among these qualities are self-confidence, an interest in one's career, and a high level of ambitions. Differences between the sexes with regard to the distribution of these characteristics are socially and culturally shaped, however, in major respects these differences exert an influence even at a psychological level.

Finally, we would like to emphasize that many women (and men) may have good reasons not to be interested in becoming managers. In research and literature on women and management there is a tendency to defend a moral to the effect that women *should* become managers. The factors that explain the lack of female managers are regarded as an external obstacle which should be surmounted. This applies to both external and internal barriers. It is also implied that if the obstacle is successfully surmounted, women on a great scale will seek and get leadership positions. Such implicit thinking is probably also to some extent characteristic of this book. It should be emphasized, however, that it is very likely that many women and some men (traditionally and also at present) have values and priorities in life other than career jobs and management positions (Billing & Alvesson, 1989:74-76). It cannot be excluded that this situation will continue to exist even though prejudices and various barriers are removed and the possibility of women getting a freer choice is improved. The possible 'free choice' of women, which is different from that of men, can probably to a great extent be traced back to differences in early socialization of the sexes – which perhaps reduce the 'freedom' of the free choice. What remains is that one should not postulate career and management ambitions as the norm and something which women have for various reasons been denied.

Notes

1   This indicates that there are only a few women in these managerial positions. See further discussion in section 5.4.
2   Femininity is a cultural construction, ascribed to characteristics – orientations, values, traits – which are perceived to be typical for women.
3   In addition to this, there are various external obstacles within organizations, child-minding, etc.; however, we only deal with the socio-cultural level.

6   Ideas about women as managers

In this chapter we will discuss some of the popular ideas and arguments about women entering in management. We will consider Marshall's book *Women Managers. Travellers in a Male World* (1984) in which she systematically examines several studies. Departing from these studies she rejects various ideas and prejudices against the presence of women in management positions. Other studies are also included in our discussion.

By studying Marshall's book critically, we will try to examine the ideas and methods of argument used in this field. Her book illustrates the difficulties that must be handled in research in this area, if we wish to proceed any further in the discussion concerning women managers. It is easier to concentrate and discuss the topic more deeply if only one text is used at a time – especially Marshall's text which provides an overall exposition of major questions that are typical of thinking within this field. Hearn & Parkin (1986/87:40-41) see the book as "the most sophisticated analysis yet of women in management" and think that it "effectively demystifies and counters ... misapprehensions". We now turn to consider these misapprehensions, in detail.

According to Marshall, the following are the six most common reasons given by authors, researchers and laymen for the scarcity of women managers, particularly at the upper levels. The literature in this field focuses mainly upon various versions of these.

(1) Women are different from men, so they do not make good managers.
(2) Women do not have the same motivations towards work as do men.
(3) Stereotypes of women mean companies are reluctant to employ them as managers.
(4) Women believe the stereotypes too, and behave accordingly.
(5) Other people will not work for or with women, or make life difficult for them if they have to.
(6) When women go out to work, their children and husbands and homes suffer, and society suffers as a result (Marshall, 1984:13).

This last view has become somewhat outmoded and no longer seems to be an obstacle to women's work today. Marshall does not examine this last reason, but deals with each of the other five reasons which we will also discuss in the following. We are, however, aware of ideas about tensions between career and family and have examined this issue elsewhere (Billing, 1991).

6.1   Are women different from men and thereby less qualified than men for management?

The question involves two aspects: that of similarity/difference and that of competence. They are not necessarily interdependent. From this perspective, one can say that women are, on average, different from men but just as competent. Dissimilarities do not necessarily involve different grades of competence. The same job could be carried out equally well by two persons with different types of qualifications. Also different abilities might be useful in different types of managerial positions.

Quite a number of studies have dealt with differences between women and men as to their leadership styles. These have shown that style and behaviour are not directly linked to gender, and that women and men are very similar in their approach to leadership. As reported in Chapter 4, review articles typically conclude that "no research has shown sex differences in leadership aptitudes or styles" (Ferber et al, 1979:467) and that "women are no less qualified psychologically for positions in management than men" (Tkach, 1980).

Some studies have proved that there are some small differences, e.g. that women are more supporting and people-orientated. Many people think that this tendency speaks well for women's competence as managers.

Another study (Bachtold, referred to by Marshall, 1984) of 863 successful women within 4 different occupations concluded by testing that competence varied according to occupation. Yet another study indicated that successful managers of both sexes simply differed from the population in general in their similar characteristics regarding working values, personality, motivation, and background. The only exception was that the women were less often married.

Marshall's (1984:17) conclusion from her reading the literature was that "women are much the same as men, or very similar. Their difference are qualities you say we need more of in the future. Perhaps women will make better managers than do men".

The conclusion is not extraordinary. However, it involves an inadmissible generalization, at least if it is to be interpreted as saying that women in general are similar to men. Studies of female and male managers do not seem to give us much information on this issue, but what can be said is that the existing research indicates that, at the present time, women and men currently in managerial positions show considerable similarity.

Considering the small number of female managers and the extremely small number actually in top positions, it is possible that women in these positions are not representative of their sex in general (cf. Hennig & Jardim, 1977). One could say also that even male managers are not representative of their sex and therefore there is a similar selectivity in this group. This should permit drawing conclusions of studies of female and male managers, and see them as being 'biased' or 'selectively' representative of women and men in general. Considering that many more of all managers are male, they are probably more like (or less unlike) men in general than female managers are like women in general. This may change as the number of female managers increases. However, the very small number of female managers makes it very difficult to generalize from them to women in general which of course includes the 'reserve army' of potential female managers.

As a very small number of women attain managerial positions, we assume that they are a pretty 'atypical' group especially of the era that the studies Marshall (1984) is referring to were done (the beginning of the seventies and earlier). We cannot exclude the possibility that we are considering women whose personality, values, motivations, and lifestyles in many cases are closer to those of men in upper managerial positions and not to those of women in general, see also Grant (1988).

Some parts of Marshall's study support this idea of women managers' 'atypicality'. One example from the research she reviews indicates that successful managers do differ from the rest of the population, and that individuals from different occupations show clear differences in their personalities. The last point indicates that women and men in general are different, because they are – as mentioned in Chapter 2 – found placed in different occupations.

In spite of the research examining similarity/dissimilarity, amongst female and male managers, it is still an open question as to what extent women and men, outside the narrow and atypical circle that have become managers (especially female managers) show similarities/dissimilarities regarding their competences to become the future managers.

Questions also arise about similarities/dissimilarities between women and men who are managers as well as between women and men in general in terms of a static compared to a dynamic (developmental) perspective. The static perspective is that individuals are characterized by stable, deeply rooted traits and dispositions of the personality. The dynamic perspective is to what extent ways of acting, behaving, values and even certain personality traits are a result of socialization at the work place.[1] Attitudes and outlooks might also be an expression of the (managerial) position, one occupies, etc.. Thus we say, 'the job makes the man or woman', the social context of a position and the work content constructs the person in a specific way. This important dynamic dimension receives no serious treatment in most of the studies because they do not consider life development, socialization and its effect on personality development and the importance of specific conditions which effect behaviour etc.. One possible interpretation could be that female and male managers are not just similar in a fixed sense, but that similar conditions of socialization and of structure in time cause them to become similar. When male and female managers respond in a similar manner when questioned in surveys, for example, it might be as a result of their job structures and experiences which bring about a homogenization of attitudes, behaviours, etc.. Another possibility is of course that only a certain type of female is recruited to managerial jobs. This would make it difficult to generalize from this managerial group to women in general.

This question of whether women are different from men and therefore whether they are less capable than men to be managers is far too unmanagable and – as in much of the research on this question – it is very easy to answer simplistically. Obviously, many women, as well as men, have qualifications to act as managers. One problem with this research is that it assumes that we know what a 'manager' is.[2] As mentioned earlier it assumes a male-associated model of management. However, we can still suppose that there might be general gender differences as well as similarities between the small number of women managers and their male colleagues. We must add that the question of possible differences between women and men regarding their behaviour, personality etc. does not imply possible differences regarding their degree of competence. Whether men and women are similar or not will not tell us very much about their similarity or difference in terms of competence in carrying out various kinds of managerial work. It must be added here that 'competence' is not a simple 'objective' fact, but a social construct based on values which are not necessarily gender-neutral.

In the literature on gender and organization, the treatment of women often concentrates on their typicality. Of course texts in this area recognize that neither women nor men are entirely homogenous, but having devoted marginal space to acknowledging this, most texts focus on what is common for women. A statement such as the following captures how gender differences are perceived:

Women tend to judge themselves by standards of responsibility and care towards others, with whom affiliation is recognized and treasured. Women's moral judgments are closely tied to feelings of empathy and compassion for others, and more directed toward the resolution of particular 'real life' problems than toward abstract or hypothetical dilemmas. Arising out of their experience of connection, women's conception of moral problems is concerned with the inclusion of diverse needs rather than with the balancing of opposing claims.

In contrast, male self-identity is largely formed through the denial of relation and connection with others. In a culture that defines manhood in terms of separation and self-sufficiency, boys become men by breaking affilitative bonds, pursuing individual attachment, and avoiding attachment to others (Ferguson, 1984:159).

This perception of women and men is common also in the feminist literaure, very much (as Ferguson) inspired by Gilligan (1982) and Chodorow (1978). Many believe that women because of a different socialization have unique skills, and writers on women in management regard these as valuable for organizations (e.g. Grant, 1988; Loden, 1986) (see Chapter 4).

There is a tendency in the above mentioned texts – as in large parts of the gender/organization literature – to make rather general statements and downplay the possibility that women should not be treated as a single and homogenous group in relationship to these issues. It is, for example, possible that female managers and male managers might share common traits and behave in a similar way while the majority of those women who are not managers might differ from both female managers and from men.

At the same time we will admit that it is very difficult to avoid general expressions, notions about typicality and such like and the reader will have noticed that we are not able to avoid such statements either. The problem is not, however, references to general tendencies – there are often empirical as well as practical reasons for pointing at these – but an inclination to overgeneralize and fail to carefully consider when more or less general points are motivated and when these obscure variation and heterogeneity. Our critique of authors jumping between the two categories of female managers and women in general (the latter category almost exclusively made up of women who are not managers) concerns less the problem of general expressions than a failure to distinguish between two possibly quite different social categories.

6.2 Do women have the same motivation as men with respect to work?

As with the previous question, Marshall (1984) tries to answer it far too generally. Here too, she is not atypical. Various studies are examined which, in general, deal with women's wishes for a job, also their motives and various problems and difficulties in relation to their husbands and children. Studies of all kinds of women show their increasing interest (and economic necessity) in having wage work. They also show that women are less interested in, or at least less totally absorbed by the idea of a career in the traditional hierarchical sense than men are.

Women's motivation to work in general is, in this connection, of less interest. More interesting is the motivation of women who may form a potential recruiting base to manager positions, a motivation overrunning '9-5', and a motivation to work as managers. There are different kinds of motivation, varying from the need for a certain kind of wage work to the wish for a more demanding managerial position. In order to answer the question of whether women's lower motivation to (paid) work more than a normal week can explain the low number of women in managerial positions, it would be helpful to have a rundown of the career interests of these women who might have the qualifications to become managers. We have not encountered such material. Of course it is very difficult to determine and measure such qualifications, but it seems credible to assume that a large number of people do not possess those symbolic skills which are necessary to operate as a middle or top manager in a modern bureaucracy. This is not only a matter of individual traits, but also of class background.

Marshall's (1984) material consists first and foremost of studies about women, who are not directly compared to men, which makes it difficult to answer the question of relative motivation to work. Finding no reasons why women should not become managers, she writes that although a number of women appear to have certain ideas about careers which differ from men's ideas, it does not make women's potential as managers any less likely. She concludes: "Many women have motivations towards work similar to men's. Practical difficulties explain why some do not translate these into action" (Marshall, 1984:24)

There is an alternative interpretation better supported by the material which Marshall refers to. That is, that women often have a different and a 'less active' motivation to work than men, as well as a different attitude and consciousness about their career. However, it is very important not to see these factors as being 'certain' or static, or as being female factors in general, or as isolated factors. Variations in motivation whether towards or within the job are considerable both for women and for men. Any differences are not a manifestation of in built or 'natural' differences, but are a result of, amongst other things, socialization, family conditions, child-minding, economics, job characteristics, and so on. A considerable part of lower 'motivation' is the result of restrictions, caused by the family. Demands from husband and children confer a different kind of 'motivation' towards the careers of women. We cannot exclude the possibility that many women have other ideas (because of different socialization and gender ideologies) about a 'good' life than many men. Also, it is true that a great interest in 'getting on' does not necessarily result in success as a manager. Even if there should be more men than women willing to give priority to career it does not mean that men are more suitable for the job.

Nevertheless, the low number of women in higher managerial positions can possibly be partly explained by the fact that motivation for 'getting on' is often slightly lower in women than it is in men. Career and promotion are, both in the past and although to a lower degree at present, less prominent as driving forces for many women than they are for most men.

6.3   What is the importance of stereotyped ideas about women?

A much cited explanation as to why employers do not employ women in manager positions is that stereotyped ideas about women are not in harmony with the demands which managerial jobs are assumed to impose. Quite a number of studies have concluded that management in general is thought of as a male occupation (e.g. Schein, 1975).[3]

We shall comment on these studies and especially their interpretations which emphasize the importance of stereotypes. By stereotype, we mean a fixed and overgeneralized formula which may have a touch of truth, but which does not allow any possibility of complexity, or variation. Stereotypes indicate the presence of preconceived ideas which can distort interpretations.

The problem is that the possibilities of research subjects having complex or nuanced opinions are not taken into account in the design of the studies. The way the research is set up often prevents these qualities from being expressed and instead constructs stereotypes itself through 'forcing' subjects to responding in simplified ways. To what extent people really have the stereotypes put before them in the research situation is hard to say. If a questionnaire is used to make persons respond as to how women and men differ in general and they are asked to put x in check-lists the stereotypes are to some extent built into the research design. Hardly any space is left for non-stereotypical answers. Questionnaires used in the field do often not make it possible to register any complex aspects. The possible existence of stereotypes is not classified although it should be quite obvious that gender-stereotypical thinking exists and especially with regards to management/managerial roles.

The second problem with interpretations is the relationship between stereotype and 'reality'. A stereotype is fixed and unsubtle and can be false or debatable. Thus the statement that Scandinavians are tall and blonde is a stereotype if it means that all Scandinavians are supposed to be so. But if it is understood as a statement of a *tendency* that Scandinavians are more often tall and blonde than other nationalities – and it actually is so – it can hardly be considered a stereotype.

If there is a tendency that managers more often than people in general, have capabilities for managing, and are competition oriented, self-confident, objective, aggressive, and so on, and if men more often than women are associated with these tendencies then the researchers might be making a correct assumption. We cannot exclude this possibility.

Marshall (1984:26) thinks that Schein's and other similar studies have a certain validity because they enlighten existing stereotypes, but also emphasizes that these studies themselves are just stereotypes and nothing else:

They capture stereotypes by demonstrating the close correspondence of male and manager in both women's and men's eyes, and the relative incompatibility of female and male manager. They are not sufficient justification for excluding women from management jobs because, as previous sections have demonstrated, the stereotypes do not adequately represent women's characteristics and capabilities. Rationally, then, I can argue that employers should accept the research proof, change their negative opinions of women's suitability, and recruit them to management jobs.

Marshall rejects the studies by saying that they are just stereotypes (that means they are fixed in an unchangeable form). She refers to comparative studies of female and male managers. They include a very small and possibly atypical group of women and this presents a problem. We do not know if they have been influenced by their jobs and socialization in their working life differently from the influences that the majority of women (who have not got manager positions) have experienced. It is hardly possible to reject the ideas about women and men in general by referring to these studies.

6.3.1 The influence of stereotypes on women's ideas and behaviour

Sex roles are social constructions and influence and suppress women and men in certain expectations and behaviour. They are taught during childhood and socialization continues throughout life. Marshall states that this process has

a profound impact on core aspects of individual personality. As gender is a more central foundation of identity than most (if not all) other characteristics, sex roles have a commensurately significant influence on who we are, how we behave, how others see us, and how others behave towards us. Our sex role permeates all aspects of life, and takes precedence over other, more situation-specific work or social roles if they are compatible (Marshall, 1984:27; quoting Bayes & Newton).

In her overview of the sex role research, Marshall states amongst other things that the sex role prevents women from expressing themselves and limits individual growth. The sex role is considered to be a trap or a cage created by women themselves and by others through socialization, expectations and restricting mechanisms. Marshall (1984:36) reaches the following conclusion, which is in opposition to the view saying that it is women's acquired sex-role thinking which causes them to seldom achieve managerial positions.

Stereotypes trap women and men. But we create them so we can also change them. If attitudes to women changed, their views of themselves and their behaviour, would change too.

Stereotypes are socially created and sustained, and are not, therefore, indestructible. Women appear particularly sensitive to other people's expectations of them – if these changed, their sex role would be less constraining. They would also be able to develop the independent perspectives and values they express, enriching the work environment as well as their own lives.

We find this closing remark rather superficial. If sex roles strongly contribute to the identity of women and men, then it cannot be maintained that through changes of attitudes etc. they can be liberated from these roles. As we stated earlier, it might be that sex role thinking refers to a somewhat superficial picture of the conditions of social processes and the processes by which gender is constructed (Connell, 1987:47-54). The sex role concept refers, however, at least partially to these circumstances which are extensive, complex and have profound consequences, especially through the life histories of the individuals – and even a partial understanding of these circumstances sets limits to fast and simple changes of attitude and behaviour, at least with respect to women's recruitment and functioning in managerial positions.

If however, sex stereotypes are not as salient as the questionnaire research suggests, and we see this as an open issue, then of course the stereotype obstacle becomes less significant for understanding the relative absence of women in managerial jobs.

6.4   Subordinates' resistance to female managers

The small number of female managers is sometimes explained as a consequence of their unpopularity with subordinates or colleagues. The following studies are referred to by Marshall (1984:37).

A study from 1965 of 2,000 subscribers concluded that more than two thirds of the male and almost one fifth of the female *Harvard Business Review* subscribers were uncertain as to whether they would work for a female manager. In a later American study, in 1979, a large number of university graduates were asked about their preferences regarding the sex of the professional worker or manager in various professional occupations (medicine, accountancy, law, estate-agency, dentistry and veterinary science). The following conclusion was reached, about two thirds of the men preferred men in at least one occupation, and half of the women also preferred men in at least one occupation. About one sixth of the men, and less than one third of the women preferred women in at least one occupation. Finally about one fourth of the men, and less than one third of the women were indifferent towards the sex of the manager or professional worker.

Several studies have indicated that employers often express scepticism about women in managerial positions as they view them as being far too emotional, too likely to get pregnant and too apt to have difficulties in combining work and family life all of which reduce their ability.

Marshall's (1984) response to the widespread resistance against employing female managers is to claim that giving women more chances to show their skills would change the stereotypes and would better the relations between employees and female managers.

Once again, one could ask if changing stereotypes and removing prejudice is that simple, although it is probably much easier to reduce prejudice against female managers than it is to change those sex roles that women consider as part of their identity. Attitudes are by definition, more superficial than identity. Could there be anything else apart from sexual stereotypes which might affect people's attitudes to the different sexes in their roles as managers or colleagues in various occupations? Half of the women preferred men in at least one of the six occupations, while only about one third preferred women. It is interesting that these results were obtained from well-educated university graduates. A possible interpretation, although not very attractive, is that the women had 'substantial' background experiences of interaction with representatives of the different sexes within these occupations, in other words that they had some 'good reasons' for their evaluations. For example it could be a question of others' stereotypes or other circumstances which make it more difficult for women in managerial positions and other special occupations which lower performance (as perceived by the women and men in the sample). Alternatively the results show that the sex role stereotypes – if they affect the answers – must be very profound and must influence even persons who we would expect to know better because of their higher education and special occupations.

We are sceptical of the value of these studies. The data is vague and superficial, to say the least, and it is therefore impossible to draw conclusions from it. Our point is to show how difficult it is to produce 'objective knowledge' and inspire more scepticism within the area.

6.5   Closing remarks

The purpose of the previous review was not to specifically criticize Marshall's book or to correct it. On the contrary we believe this book makes several positive contributions which are also noted by several other authors (Grant, 1988; Hearn & Parkin, 1986/87). However, the study does reveal some important problems regarding analyses in the study of women as managers. The most significant problem is the difficulty in reaching well-founded unequivocal conclusions regarding the basic assumptions and statements about women's qualities, aspirations and problems compared to men's in relation to managerial positions. Despite extensive research, one cannot maintain that women and men are basically alike or differ regarding qualities, motivation, ideas about themselves etc. pertaining to this field. Furthermore, questions such as the following ones still remain unanswered:

– How do women who, with regard to age, experience, education, gifts, etc. are potential managers (i.e. 'the middle group') differ from or resemble female managers?
– What do any differences mean? Is any female deviation from the male standards as regards qualities, career orientation, etc. of any relevance to their overall capability as managers? These female differences might be negative, neutral or positive – with regard to manager positions in general.
– How does women's motivation toward work compare with men's motivation? As mentioned earlier, it might be fruitful to distinguish between various groups – such as women and men in general, women and men with some sort of interest in their career, women and men who are parents, women and men who are already managers, etc.. The problems and obstacles which affect women in relation to managerial positions requires us to study these various groups. The specific motivation toward managerial jobs must be studied too,

separately. A person can have a high working motivation and/or a career interest without wishing to be a manager.
- What sexual stereotypes do we deal with? How important are they? At one extreme stereotypes can be so influential that they blind people to 'reality' and distort their perceptions. 'Proof' of something else is not accepted. At the other extreme stereotypes can be vague and thus easy to reject. We must differentiate between the reality and the prejudice that goes into the creation of a stereotype. To what extent do they reflect something real, and to what extent are they a matter of distortion?
- How influencial are stereotypes and sex roles to women? To what extent do sexual differences depend on these stereotypes and what is the importance of a profound (socially and psychologically, perhaps to some degree biologically conditional) gender identity? How we deal with these questions will be influental on which socio-cultural changes that are rendered possible.

The problems discussed in this chapter must therefore, in our opinion, be considered to be open and unanswerable until further and more differential studies take place. What we have in mind is firstly, that social science can only reach temporary and uncertain answers to complex questions. Secondly that the roles of women and men as a result of changes in society, are not static categories but are changing concurrently with cultural and historical factors. 'Truths' based on gender are therefore changing throughout history, as the construction of gender changes.

Therefore the problems seem impossible to solve once and for all. They are notoriously open and ambiguous. In more controversial and political respects certain points of view may be perceived as necessary, but with regard to the present analysis, critical problems, uncertainties and ambiguities pose more interesting, indeed more varied questions. We are very much in agreement with Flax (1987:638), when she writes,

Confronted with complex and changing relations, we try to reduce these to simple, unified, and undifferentiated wholes. We search for closure, or the right answer, or the 'motor' of the history of male domination. The complexity of our questions and the variety of the approaches to them are taken by some feminists as well as nonfeminists as signs of weakness or failure to meet the structures of preexisting theories rather than as symptoms of the permeability and pervasiveness of gender relations and the need for new sorts of theorizing.

Our book aims at illuminating uncertainties and complexities, rather than providing clearcut answers, although we depart from Flax's poststructuralist approach, in the sense that we want to show different contemporary empirical patterns and tendencies and are not interested in, for example, deconstructions of any empirically supported answer to questions regarding women, organization and management.

Notes

1 There are, of course, other and even more 'dynamic' perspectives than the socialization perspective, such as some versions of identity theory and poststructuralism, in
   which the situated and discourse-dependent nature of subjects are emphasized. Here
   the idea of viewing the individual as a coherent whole is rejected in favour of an
   opinion which views the individual as discoursively (linguistically) constituted (e.g.
   Shotter & Gergen, 1989). We have not seriously considered this idea in the present
   study, because it tends to neglect the life history of individuals and it does not correspond with our experiences and observations of individuals' orientations often showing considerable consistence over space and time.
2 Female secretaries told us that they performed managerial duties, but they were not
   formally recognized as managers, neither were they paid accordingly.
3 This was mentioned in Chapter 5, and we will come back to this in Chapter 11.

Part Two: Three case-studies

Introduction to the case-studies

In this and the following two chapters we shall analyse three empirical studies. These are in-depth case studies of three organizations, each with different qualities and characteristics pertinent to our topic. The three organizations are; the National Board of Social Welfare; the Scandinavian Airlines Systems; and the Ministry of Foreign Affairs. These organizations are described and interpreted with regards to the following:

- the number of female managers compared to the number of male managers, also compared to women in the organization as a whole, or in relation to women in other relevant categories (e.g. in the two public organizations, the number of graduates);
- the numerical proportion of women and men in other areas in the organizations;
- the field of activity and major tasks within the organizations;
- common personnel and organizational conditions, e.g. recruiting policy, organizational structure and cultural characteristics (e.g. collectively shared values, understandings and norms);
- career patterns. Methods of recruitment and selection of managers. Common principles and average and deviating patterns;
- prospects, external objections and internal barriers for women as regards managerial positions;
- gender differences with respect to leadership style;
- general gender perspectives on the organization in question, including its neutrality or 'bias' from a gender perspective.

In particular, we study the organizational conditions which impede women moving up the career ladder, and also in a few cases, conditions which encourage them to achieve higher positions and function in these.

All the above aspects are dealt with in the following three chapters. However, there is considerable variation in the extent to which the various themes or aspects are examined in the chapters contingent upon the specific circumstances of the various organizations. Therefore it follows that the three chapters are not homogeneous as regards their topics. Since the organizations in question differ to a considerable extent, therefore different aspects have been found worthwhile and interesting to study. For example in an organization with few female managers, it becomes harder to study how they function compared with their male colleagues, whereas in an organization with many female managers there is no point in studying specific impediments to women moving up the career ladder.

The three organizations were selected based on the assumption that they could give a broad illumination of the issue of gender, management, and organizations. Thus the National Board of Social Welfare (BSW) was selected because the number of female employees is quite high, as well as females in managerial positions. Also one could hypothesise that the nature of the organization, the area and its activities, ought to imply relatively few obstacles to women advancing into management. SAS was chosen because the number of females is high, its major areas of work are both typically male (engineering, flying) and female (service) and because, unlike the two other organizations in question, SAS is a private company. The Ministry of Foreign Affairs (MFA) was chosen because it is a high status organization and because the number of female employees among graduates is relatively low and very low on the level of managers. It can thus be regarded as a 'pro-male' organization in which structural conditions or cultural beliefs and meanings preventing women from climbing upward were expected to be relatively salient. Additional considerations and reasons for choosing these particular companies for case-studies will be explained in the introduction of each of the organization studies.

We emphasize that our study is not a stringent comparative one. We have chosen a free presentation in which the case-studies are not very tightly connected to each other. We think that the research field is far too new and unexplored to make a more rigorous effort in that direction. We believe also that rigorous approaches seldom produce interesting results. This study is explorative and aims at generating ideas and empirically supported discussions and theoretical ideas. In other words we pursue the interesting topics we meet in the study rather than adhering to a definite plan. A more open-minded approach and varied picture of the cases is thereby possible.

We are interested in studying why there are so few female managers, how female (and male) managers function in their positions and how they experience being managers. These questions can be answered partly by looking at organizations where there are relatively few female managers and partly by studying organizations where they are more predominant. There are different themes of interest in the various organizations due to their different character, the possibility of making strict comparisons in a narrow meaning thus becomes reduced. Also, the character of the field requires a flexible study. The field of gender and organization is very complex and not very accessible. Results depend amongst other things, upon the willingness and ability of the interviewees to generate interesting material. This is, besides being dependent on the researcher's skills and the personal characteristics of the interview subjects, also contingent upon the organization. Different organizations can reflect different gender issues. They might encourage or discourage the disclosure of interesting information to various degrees. For these reasons, the depth and the possibilities in different case studies will vary.

Because the study is loosely structured, we shall present the results for each organization in self-contained chapters. References to literature and conclusions are available in these chapters and it is possible to read each of the organization studies separately. However, we discuss and sum up a number of topics in Chapter 10, and also draw some further conclusions in Chapter 11. We feel that taken together, the three following chapters give a broad empirically based picture of our research field.

7 The National Board of Social Welfare

In this chapter we concentrate on an organization (BSW), selected according to the following criteria: it is public, it has a rather low prestige (according to the employees) compared with other organizations in central administration and it has a relatively high number of females (at staff as well as at managerial level). The organization is within the Danish central administration consisting of a social welfare department plus an administrative (and planning) department comprising in all, 264 persons, 141 women, and 123 men at the time of the study.

The study has mainly been concentrated on the social welfare department. The gendered division of labour is also seen in the university graduate labour market which results in the fact that the recruitment potential for managerial positions in the administrative department is less among women. Here there was one female manager when the interviews took place. In the social welfare department there was the same number of female and male heads of department, three of each sex. There is also a female supreme manager for the social welfare department and a male director as manager for the entire organization. In the social welfare department, there are 78 women and 50 men, 128 in all. Graduates consist of the same number of women and men – 31 of each (in the department of administration there are 28 graduates, 11 women and 17 men).

For the purposes of collecting data we have used the partly structured interview method, that is qualitative single interviews with selected persons (mainly in managing positions). In all, 11 persons were interviewed, 9 managers (7 in the social welfare department, the male director for the organization, and 1 female personnel manager in the department of administration) and 2 of the university graduated. There are five female and eight male managers in the organization. Before further analysis of the different ways of presenting the problems we shall first give a short introduction to the organization.

7.1 The history of the organization

The organization was established in 1970 through a merger of three different directorates. Physically the new organization at first was spread out, being located at 7 different addresses. Not until 1976 in connection with the operation of the Social Security Act and the decentralization of a number of tasks to the municipalities, did the organization get its present address.

From 1976 management changed from control through directives and rules to control by agreements, guidance, and consulting, or 'soft' control. This control is now practiced by contributing and influencing ideas and action. The working tasks were changed, from being specific to being more general, i.e. apart from traditional discussions and written counselling, experience and guidance is now made available through pamphlets. Lectures are delivered, and consultant activities offer guidance and advice. One might say that the organization has changed from a traditional bureaucracy to outwardly-facing service-oriented organization.

The formal tasks can be summed up as follows:

– in cooperation with the Ministry of Social Affairs, to follow the development and contribute to the updating and revision of rules, guide-lines, and so on;
– to contribute to the decision basis of the Ministry, the counties, and the municipalities (accounts, budget estimates, consequence analyses, amongst other things, on the basis of the social and health and experimental programmes of the municipalities);
– to contribute to the development and arrangement of social professional knowledge and experimental activity;
– to take care of the supervision of the Social Security Act by discussing complaints and carrying out investigations
– to administer some state institutions;
– to take care of the education of 'home helpers' and others.

Since 1970, several rationalizations have been carried out in BSW as the tasks were delegated to the municipalities after the municipal reform. Here they obtained more self-government and more (municipal) self-financing. The rationalization caused many staff reductions. Furthermore, BSW was subjected to a number of large cuts, first and foremost because of the delegation of the functions to the municipalities, but also afterwards as a result of further demands for cuts associated with efforts to reduce the costs for public expenditures contingent upon problems in the Danish economy.

It was necessary for the organization to adapt to changing situations on several occasions such as amalgamations, the decentralization of tasks, the changing of controls and steering circumstances, retrenchments, cuts in the number of employees. But the number of staff was in part cut-back in such a way that no one became unemployed, despite the fact that the end result was a halving of the original staff. Those who were 'set free' got some help to find another job. Other reduction was achieved through retirement, and also BSW devised new ways to survive, amongst other things by selling activities on a consultancy-basis.

Its historical development and these constant changes contributed to the fact that the organization is felt to be very dynamic by the staff. However, there is a division between those colleagues who are more traditionally oriented and thus considered to be unfavourably disposed towards change, preferring a more static organization, and those colleagues who are campaigning for decentralization, which mainly means a decentralization of tasks and decision-making from the department to the municipalities.

The fact that the organization has been faced with heavy cuts, first and foremost because of the restructuring, has meant in practice that there has been a more effective solidarity amongst the staff than usual, across trade union organizations and professional groups. The staff has agreed on the basis that whatever one's position or rank, it is necessary to stand together, as opposed to other places of work where staff members some times are played off one against the other. Thus a common threat has given rise to a degree of solidarity. Gradually, the staff and management are starting to question how long they can make these cuts and still function as a viable organization. History also reveals that the organization still lags behind in the sense that it still handles things in the 'old-fashioned' way, the so-called centralized, and regulation-oriented way. Those who believed in the old customs and practices did not disappear with the onset of decentralization, since people were fired according to the rule 'last in first out', although the word 'out', in practice, meant getting help in obtaining a new job. For some of the staff it has been a difficult change-over. To play it safe they have chosen to take the jobs that are called the B-tasks. A- and B-tasks and A-and B-teams were discovered – or if one takes a less objectivistic stance, proposed as labels for the internal social differentiation – in another study of BSW (DIOS, 1985). These labels seem now to be deeply rooted in the consciousness of the staff (see section 7.5). Other members of staff take the opinion that it has been very exciting to experience all the changes and the rapid development. The possibilities for survival of the organization are compared to a cat's, "it has been attacked nine times and has survived nine times". They believe it says something about its capacity to survive, and also about the creativity within the organization. The collective experiences are viewed as a clear strength by the employees.

7.2   The prestige and career pattern of the organization

Although it seems to be a dynamic organization from the staff's point of view, the commonly held belief is that the organization has a low prestige today, because social work has a low status when compared to work in other sections of the central administration.

Social services is considered to be something we all understand, and moreover to be a typically female job. In total there are more women than men employed in the social department. In order to undertake social work in Denmark at least, you are not expected to have had a very long education. This has an influence on the prestige of the organization. On average, therefore there is a lower level of education than in other comparable administrations. A lot of people with middle-level training and even some unskilled people have at times been employed. Another important factor for how BSW is perceived by its staff concerns its relationship to the Ministry of Social Affairs. The latter which BSW to a considerable degree interacts with, and to some extent competes with, is generally seen as more powerful and prestigeous.

The fact that the organization is considered to have a relatively low status means that career-minded people do not enter or at least do not stay long in BSW.

If you are a really career-minded person you apply for a post in a more distinguished department, or in the private trade. For lawyers and economists this is clearly a side track. As regards career it is a low status department so to apply for a post here to a considerable extent shows an interest in social care and a kind of idealism too (male graduate).

Apart from the high number of females, the organization is characterized by the fact that the people who apply for a post in this organization are not specifically career oriented, according to interviewees. Those who work in BSW have applied for the post because of an interest in the matter and the challenges which they will face. They possess a great deal of idealism, interviewees said. The dress and style are also more relaxed in this organization compared with the other administrations and departments (e.g. the Ministry of Foreign Affairs, see Chapter 9).

That the organization is contained within the social sector might also explain the high number of females. Many women have an interest in welfare work and are educated for a job in the social sector. Among the employees there are many non-academics with typically female educations: social work, teaching, and other middle-range trainings. Previously, there were many law graduates, now it is more mixed. They come from other academic backgrounds instead of the more traditional (e.g. now a number of people with a social science background have been recruited). There are quite a number of applicants from people with academic backgrounds, especially because of the character of the work and the good reputation of the organization (and perhaps because of unemployment among graduates in this country). There is a widely held opinion that the applicants know about the good climate at this place, they know about work conditions and the work tasks, and that they find it is a good place to work.

Some of the young staff go on to apply for a job elsewhere, e.g. for a job in the Ministry of Social Affairs, especially those in the group of academics and especially those from untraditional academic backgrounds. There are also a number of more experienced elderly staff who leave, for early retirement for instance, but this is because the job has changed so much that they can no longer keep up with the times, informants told us.

But apart from those two groups, there is a tendency for the staff to have long service – and also that the people who apply for a job elsewhere often return from both the private and the public sector jobs. One of the reasons why people return is that they are disappointed with the climate they experience elsewhere, we have been told.

7.3   The organizational atmosphere

The National Board of Social Welfare is considered to be very different from other departments with more 'lee-way' for each staff worker. It is highly appreciated that the staff make proposals, and that they actively put various problems on the agenda and so on, but as financial resources are limited, these proposals are not supposed to cost anything.

Somehow people are very concerned about each other, and the atmosphere is good. It really is. There is safety in the system and much care and concern, considering it is a work place. More than I have seen at other places (female manager).

Each person has more freedom and has more margin. If you want to get on and you have an idea, then no one stops you (male graduate).

The atmosphere in the workplace is described as very caring, unambitious, and helpful. This supportive network was proved in connection with the first heavy reduction of staff when everything was done to help people find new jobs. It was considered to be a collective problem which should be solved by everyone as a joint effort.

There is little prestige or status associated with being 'busy'. The staff leaves at about 4.30/5 p.m.. They have normal working hours. This means that the workplace is not "family oppressing" (as one male manager put it) if you also have family commitments. People are not expected to be available day and night and there are not so many urgent tasks as in other departments.

Many of the men are described as very family oriented and some women and also men are employed on a part-time basis which is very uncommon for men in the central administration. Part-time commitment does not necessarily mean less interesting tasks, quite the contrary, as some of the interviewed persons, albeit on full-time, emphasized. They think that the part-timers often have more resources, spend the best time of their day on their work, and that they get the most interesting tasks.

The majority of the staff (men and women) believes that the men in the organization are more "sensitive" or empathetic than the average man: "I would not say that they all sit and cry in the corner but they are sensitive in the best sense. They are concerned with their families and children, and overtime is up to you" (male graduate).

Picnics and children at work are accepted by all:

We agree on the fact that on one specific day we bring all our children and then you cannot work, everything is chaos. The manager finds it okay. But they are also more 'soft' than others (managers at other places) (male graduate).

The men who apply for a job and remain in the BSW are presumably 'softer' than the average man, sensitivity may even increase through the internal social-ization in the administration. However, it is well-known, according to several of the interviewed persons, that the traditionally career-oriented persons do not remain in the administration.

7.4 '68 democracy spirit

There is a predominant collective norm in the organization saying that you do not "put on airs" (according to several managers and assistant secretaries) this being synonymous with breaking 'the social norm'. On the other hand it is neces-sary to 'break the social norm' if you are looking for a managerial position. (This is perhaps best expressed as switching to another norm system, i.e. the importance of doing something different.) However, it is acceptable for people to apply for managerial positions. Why are there then certain rules for not being too ambitious? A male graduate explains it in this way:

Ambitious people are not popular, this would mean they had become hard. Ambitious people don't fit into this environment. And if someone becomes a manager, it is better if they stay soft in order not to get too powerful.

The formal structure of the hierarchy is accepted, but not the fact that leaders of project groups can be appointed. No one is 'allowed' to achieve a higher status than others, outside the boundaries which the formal hierarchy marks out. There is a '68 spirit[1] in this organization which raises a barrier against anyone applying for a managerial position. One possible result of these organizational conditions is that the effectiveness and the achievement level of staff will not be very high. At least, it is hard to imagine that people who demand of themselves and others high individual achievement will be stimulated in this organization. Although the overall achievement level appears to be reasonably high, it is possible for an individual to 'free wheel'.

The system in this organization appears to involve a contradiction. On the one hand the major part of the staff is engaged and commited to the work, but on the other hand, too much commitment makes it difficult for them to adhere to the collective norm and not to break the 'social norm'. Both norms exist side by side, and will tend to push people over to the B-team (see section 7.5) where they are not 'blamed' for being too ambitious and also to encourage 'over-commited' career-minded staff to leave the organization.

A preliminary conclusion is that the organization in question has some con-trasting elements, not the classic ones between the sexes or between manage-ment and workers or other divisions, but for example between rule-oriented and decentralization oriented persons, between those with different expectations of involvement, and between those with expectations of breaking and not breaking the 'ambition norm', between those with the '68 spirit and those with individual interest in taking initiatives, and between A- and B-teams. The following para-grahps explore the team structure.

7.5 A- and B-teams

According to those who were interviewed, A- and B- teams exist to varying degrees and on various levels. The division into A- and B-teams is between those people who get the exciting tasks and those who do not. The allocation of people to either an A- or a B- team depends on who wants the exciting jobs, and on who defines them. Generally speaking, the traditional 'regulation-oriented' people belong to the B-team and the others to the A-team, however, it is not quite that simple. Interviewees suggest it is generally a question of 'personality' and not of gender. The educational background is not so important, the question is whether you get the 'outposts' or not (internal jargon).

The managers believe that they recognize which people from their office be-long to the A-team and which to the B-team. However, they know less about the staff from other offices. Project groups are established using staff from various offices and the managers in question select the staff according to how they per-ceive the capabilities of the staff members. However, the staff can also define their own interest in a specific task. Some of the interviewed managers believe that there are self-perpetuating processes, and that some members of staff may be able to do more demanding tasks but they 'are not allowed to', as they are kept in the B-team. This means that some of the people continue to get the repetitive, traditional work whilst others get the more interesting tasks. If and when a group has carried out a task satisfactorily they can then easily be given as their next task something more 'challenging'. Thus some of the principals feel that it would be appropriate if the management were to switch the A- and B-tasks, in order not to give the exciting tasks just to the one team. Given the likelihood that this would mean an equal distribution of tasks, at least by A-people perceived as less interesting, there may be resistance to this idea. To a large extent this division of labour between A- and B-teams, shows similarities to the traditional labour division between sexes. Perhaps this distinction between social groups fulfils a function comparable to the one which is often a result of the labour division between sexes, and is also a result of other forms of division of labour between contrasting groups (natives/immigrants, majorities/minorities, etc.) One group (A, or male/native/majority) takes care of the interesting work, while the other group (B, or female/immigrant/ethnic/minority etc.) undertakes the less stimulating work and is 'kept' in a secondary position.

7.6   Promotion

In earlier times the criterion for becoming a manager was to have been a good
administrative employee. A reward was given for having served well and for a
long time. It was possible for non-academically graduated individuals to be promoted to the rank of manager, whereas nowadays only those with an academic
background[2] obtain positions in the central administration. Today, candidates for
managerial jobs must be professionally qualified and also must have contributed
something of noticeable value before being regarded as suitable for a managerial
position. The managerial qualities required, according to the interviewees, are "a
willingness to work on a co-operative basis", and "a capacity to solve problems".

   The recruiting for managerial positions takes place mainly from within the
organization and from within the Ministry of Social Affairs. The promotion
board asks people to apply for any unoccupied managerial positions. Those who
are considered must have been perceived as outstanding in some way or another.
The promotion board is made up of two managers and three staff representatives. The board decides whom it is going to interview, and on consultation, the
board makes a recommendation. If they do not agree, they might decide to recommend more than one person. Then the head of BSW receives the recommendations and makes the final recommendation. The ministry receives this recommendation and makes the final decision on the appointment. In only 2 cases in
over 10-15 years has the ministry declined to follow the recommendation made
by the BSW.

   It is not detrimental for a candidate to have worked outside the organization.
There are even some people who think that it is a disadvantage to apply for a
managerial position in the same department in which the applicant has worked.
A male manager found it difficult to make the transition from being a co-worker
to being a manager in the same office. The employees in an office do not always
agree on who should be recommended. Obviously there may be a problem if
there is more than one applicant from the same office. The unsuccesful candidate might subsequently leave. It appears that it is usually amongst the academically qualified that specific mechanisms come into force, since they are the only
people who are formally qualified for the competition. The clerical staff are
mostly interested in obtaining a sympathetic and competent person as their manager.

7.7   Barriers for women?

In the Social Welfare Department we have not been able to identify mechanisms
which would make it more difficult for women than for men to advance to managerial positions. Professional capability and potential managerial skills are two

criteria which the department believes that men as well as women possess. Therefore, the result is that there are just as many female as male managers. However in the administrative department this is not quite the case. But here there are not as many female as male graduates. Women graduates are 40% and they have one out of four managerial positions. Furthermore, in the Social Welfare Department managers have been recruited from more untraditional academic backgrounds when compared with those in managerial positions in the central administration. In the Social Welfare Department women are not hindered by having the 'wrong' kinds of educational backgrounds and therefore they have the same opportunities as men to become managers.

Here we are only considering the conditions within the organization. We do not discuss the possibility that women might not have the opportunity to take a deeper interest in their work outside of the normal working week, as a result of their domestic circumstances.

In most cases women are treated similarly to men (according to the interviewees). 'Proof' of this statement is that a sex quota argument was used in only one case. This means that given a choice of two equally qualified people, a woman ought to be appointed (in the event a man was appointed but only after some trouble).

In contrast to this indication of gender equality, women's lunches were introduced. Someone had heard of a similar phenomenon in another administration office and had thought that it would be a good idea to try a similar scheme. It was initiated by the graduates. At the first lunch meeting the women discussed the presence of any problems specific for women at the workplace, and the conclusion was that they had none – but decided that it was nevertheless a good idea to continue these meetings. Some female interviewees note however that these meetings are not given high priority.

None of the interviewees think that there are barriers or any other kinds of difficulties which hinder women advancing in the system. Even the director of BSW has spoken out in favour of women as managers. He gives the following reasons: "I consider the female element in negotiations as very important, because it gives us the opportunity to be human beings rather than civil servants".

There exists a positive atmosphere toward female managers who are described favourably by the subordinates interviewed, e.g. "They are more strategic, have less hidden agendas, are better equipped to solve conflicts, are very professional" (male graduate).

On the whole, however, the differences between the sexes and their way of working are seldom noticeable. None of the interviewees had noticed any problems from subordinates in accepting female managers. Only a few of the interviewees mention any differences at all between the role of female and male managers. A slight difference mentioned is that where perhaps some of the men are more goal-directed, the women are more attentive. However, it is hard to know whether this statement mirrors real differences in orientation (or even shared

beliefs on this matter in the organization). The previously mentioned sex stereotypes (gender expectations) and other beliefs may influence the perceptions toward women and men in this particular way. It is hardly possible to rule out that
the same behaviour can be perceived and interpreted differently depending on
the gender of the person 'behind' the behaviour.

In the organization, people believe that the job influences the person much
more than vice versa. In other words, the demands of the job are more important
than the gender responses of the person, who carries out the job. It follows that
there is a tendency within the organization to differentiate between managers on
the basis of their competence rather than their gender. The gender is assumed not
to interfere with the evaluation of competence. Thus, it is more a question of the
'male' or 'female' methods and characteristics used in management, irrespective
of actual gender, which are important in the managerial job rather than the actual
gender of the manager, e.g. "you can find tendencies in men as well as in women
that lead them to run the business on a housekeeping basis, and to often pay too
much attention to detail", as one male manager put it.

Apparently, it is hard to see any strong sex differences within management in
this organization. The female managers can give examples of particular power
games (Ås, 1982), but they only met these in other situations which were outside
the organization (where women were in a minority). No one says that they have
been faced with discrimination because of their sex in this organization.

7.8   Discussion

With regard to this particular organization, the National Board of Social Welfare, it appears that there is no indication to support the view that men and
women are treated differently, or the view that women are likely to experience
specific barriers in their career and in their promotion to managerial positions.
On the contrary, the organization in question must be considered 'gender neutral'. By calling BSW gender neutral here we mean that neither sex is (formally)
discriminated against.

Between men and women any dissimilarities as regards their preconditions,
their opportunities and their desire to move up the career ladder and function
well in a managerial position do not seem to affect this organization in any
problematic way. At least this is not a problem with regard to the group within
which the recruitment to managerial positions takes place. Appreciable gender
differences as regards relevant previous qualifications and/or interest in becoming a manager do not exist in the organization in question.

This account of BSW is in direct contrast to most of the results of other studies of female managers, their situation, background, recruiting conditions and so
on. Many studies have been made (especially English and American) which
show that women have more difficulties in 'getting on' (Chapters 4 and 5). The

factors involved are many, according to Legge (1987), ranging from the under-mining effect of the sex role stereotype to the effect of careers taking place on men's terms, and from the effect of women's exclusion from the informal net-work of the organization to the problem of being visible. Many of these factors place women in double-binds which we discussed in Chapter 4. These can lead to the following, "unless women behave very similarly to men, they will not be considered suitable as managers ... if they stray too far from stereotypes of femininity, they will be sanctioned for deviance" (Marshall, 1984:37).

One of the major handicaps with regard to women's career advancement is their role in childbearing. It is often mentioned as an important impediment to advancement. For example, when a male biochemistry manager was asked if women had the same opportunities for promotion as men had, he responded:

No – yes and no. No instantly, because women have this terrible biological hazard of going off and having children, and the women I know, that have got to the top, have either been single or not had children ... and I keep trying to think of women who've got chil-dren – I don't know any (Homans, 1987:95).

Although different authors have different opinions about what causes the prob-lems that women encounter, they do agree on the fact that the difficulty in achiev-ing a career is greater for women than for men, and the difficulty lies especially in attaining top managerial positions. Walters (1987:21) for example in an analy-sis of the conditions and difficulties encountered by women in the British public administration states:

It is clear from all the available evidence, that women practitioners never make it to the top of the service in anything like the same proportions as the men with whom they enter the service. Proportionally, more women than men leave the service and of those who stay, less make the jump into the Under Secretary grade either at all or early enough to progress beyond it. Women stay back, drop out, and are 'cooled out' for many reasons.

The question is how to interpret this obvious contrast between the majority of the findings in literature and our empirical data? We could make the assumption that this other literature is overgeneralizing. Or, it could be said that the organiza-tion that we researched is highly 'untypical', and therefore its characteristics cannot be used to throw into doubt other general statements about barriers, inter-nalised gender thinking, etc.. If the majority of organizations operate in the way described within the main part of literature, then there are good reasons for mak-ing these general statements, and it would be misleading to give extremely marginal exceptions any greater importance.

In the first instance, our study of the National Board of Social Welfare must however be deemed to support the hypothesis that much of the available litera-ture does not consider sufficiently the variations within different fields and orga-nizations. Through the use of 'deviant cases' or examples established understand-ings can be modified and enriched (Silverman, 1985:21).

Our intention is not to make any quantitative statements about the relative existence of equality at work places with respect to career and management positions. Instead we shall try to explain the specific circumstances and conditions which contribute towards equality of the sexes in the organization in question which, in contrast to the general literature on this issue, seems to be almost utopian. By citing the conditions and mechanisms affecting the sexes in our organization, we can contribute towards an understanding of the various factors which encourage or discourage the creation of a socialization and career structure within the work situation which is not gender oppressive.

We believe that our study supports the fact that both discrimination and equality vary within one society at any given time (in history) and that it is important to expose the social conditions and mechanisms which generate this variation. Our study provides us with an opportunity to look at equality-generating dimensions in the organization, which is an opportunity to a large extent ignored in the literature as a whole, which almost exclusively takes an interest in inequality.

How can we explain the equality that exists in the organization? We believe that the following aspects are significant:

– the homogeneous background qualifications of both sexes
– the lack of division of labour between the sexes within the organization
– the division of labour between sexes within the generally similar working field outside the organization
– the specific characteristics of the field of work (social work and administration), which can be said to be 'gender-neutral'
– the recruitment and selection of people with certain personalities
– the public sector nature of work
– the 'minimalized' organizational hierarchy

These aspects overlap to a certain extent, but we deal with them all separately in order to achieve a deeper understanding of the organization and its equality in terms of promotion and managerial duties.

The academically trained male and female employees, in whom we have been interested in this organization, tend to share the same educational background. Education as well as experience varies only slightly between the sexes. This means not only that the 'objective' or 'formal' promotion potential is no different, but also that the sex stereotyping potential on the local level is not allowed to flourish as easily as if e.g. most men were law graduates and most women were social workers. We therefore assume that the values and ideas which support the similarities rather than the differences between men and women are stimulated at this place of work.

The absence of a gender-dependent division of labour in the organization also supports equality. As far as we can discern, gender is not a determining factor with regard to which positions people occupy or which tasks they attend to. The clerical staff, which includes many female employees, is to some degree an exception, but this group cannot be candidates for managerial positions because they do not have a university degree. One could perhaps say that in the Danish public administration it is more caste (or class) that matters. If you do not belong to the proper caste, you cannot be considered manager potential. Caste/class has to do with educational background – only people with a university degree are promoted. This is a result of a strong union-alliance between the academically trained and the employers (the state) in the public sector, which has led to the former group's monopoly of the 'managerial labour'.

The composition of the staff and the conditions under which they work are obviously to some degree a result of the gendered division of labour in the general field of similar work outside this organization. The number of academically educated females is considerably larger within the social welfare field than in other fields. Also, their number is greater in political administrations within the social care area, than within many other comparable fields within the Central Administration. Within the law profession, a higher percentage of women have applied for a job in the social care field than within most other work areas which employ law professionals. This general labour division affects the administration, however, in a way that neutralizes local gender labour division. The fact that a relatively large proportion of the total number of academically educated females and highly educated people apply for jobs in the social work field results, at least in this case, in a reinforcement of gender equality. A local gender division of labour hardly exists at all. This offsets the balance toward sex stereotyping, which otherwise exists at the majority of work places according to the literature in the field, and it might create a basis for equal opportunities for promotion for both male and female academically trained workers.

To a certain extent the gender related labour division is based on the overall gender composition (the ratio of men to women) within an organization. The number of men and women at a place of work is what is considered to be decisive in determining women's career and promotion opportunities by structurally oriented writers like Kanter (1977) (see Chapter 3). Our study is in harmony with this particular viewpoint. However, the sex ratio within the entire organization is not the main issue as regards career- and promotion opportunities.[3] What is more important is the horizontal and vertical gender related labour division. The literature we have mentioned in Chapter 3 does not deal with this question at all. An equal sex ratio within an organization would not promote women's career opportunities if all the women were employed as clerks and secretaries, and therefore with the present rules, could not advance to managerial positions, and if all the men were employed as graduates and therefore could have promotion opportunities. In other words the traditional division of labour between the sexes within the organizations would not promote the women's career opportunities at all, irrespective of the overall sex ratios.

The sex ratio could be said to be sufficient explanation for the favourable conditions at this place of work with regard to highly educated women's career prospects. However, there is some indication that these conditions are not always sufficient to create full equality. Some other studies have proved that even in organizations where a large number of women have the same qualifications as their male colleagues, the women are still promoted to a lesser extent than are the men (see e.g. Juristen & Økonomen, 1981; Magisterundersøgelsen, 1986; Walters, 1987).

It is our belief that the specific characteristics of the actual social field of work are of central importance to the gender equality that exists. In general in each basic activity area or field certain values, ideas, ideals, expectations, norms, rules and so on have been constituted and institutionalized. These cultural manifestations vary depending on the field, for example; primary school education, elite sport, free-lance journalism, nuclear power station work, librarianship, etc.. Thus we can talk about occupational, industrial and/or organizational cultural contexts. In the organization that we have studied the field can be defined as social work at a central administrative level. Obviously, the field affects the organization, but it is broader and not equivalent to it. The organization is also determined by its specific conditions, e.g. its history, management, resources etc. Within the framework of a specific activity field, organizations vary in terms of attributes which are common within the entire field and which are organizationally specific. In many respects, a more important social category than the organization are the social functions which in dominating or peripheral form, can be executed in various kinds of organizations and/or professions characteristic of the organizations in question. Van Maanen & Barley (1984) speak about "occupational communities" to describe those labour groups. Bourdieu (1979) takes a different attitude and talks about "social fields", by which he means the arena of activities, rules, abilities, rewards, prestige and so on within which a certain group acts. This arena represents the 'sounding board' in which everything – statements, behaviour, structures, etc. – are given symbolic meaning.

The organization that we deal with is characterized by its social work on a professional-administrative level. This influences the organization and constitutes a kind of profession that most of the employees belong to. For this social group and this activity field there are certain ideas about forms of subjectivity (personal beings) that are important. Masculine stereotypes are not very positively evaluated. On the contrary celebrated virtues are social consciousness, humanness, softness, empathy and solidarity.

On average women are said to possess these attributes to a greater extent than men. This may be interpreted as a result of genetic differences, socialization background and/or experience. Thus women are believed to be very suitable for this type of social work. At least, this has been claimed very often when discussing gender determined educational and professional choices.

In the National Board of Social Welfare the suitability of women to the social welfare work is, however, only of marginal significance, as the administration does not deal directly with this kind of work. Instead the daily tasks are mostly law interpretations, the preparation of recommendations, guide-lines, and so on. There is more paper work rather than interface with people. Indirectly, however, the social welfare work still affects the organization. This is because both the social field and working culture which characterizes the organization share the kind of ideology and values predominant for people in this kind of work. People not directly but also indirectly working with social welfare are for example often socially progressive toward, conscious of and positive to equality.

It can also be said that the combination of highly qualified/relatively prestigious administrative work (in relationship to 'average' work in the surrounding society) and social welfare matters together creates a work setting which cannot be considered to be either 'male-' or 'female-oriented', but 'gender neutral'. As we mentioned before, half of the academically graduated workers in the social department are women. This indicates that the organization combines work that otherwise tends toward being dominated by women (in social welfare), or by men (in the central state administration). The organization is therefore a synthesis of 'female' and 'male' cultural elements.

We can see from this analysis that there is a certain selectivity regarding who is recruited and who remains in the administration. Often it is sensitive, 'soft' men, described as family-orientated rather than career-oriented. Quite apart from the consequences resulting from the structure of the activity field and the characteristics of the professional culture or occupational community to which the majority of the staff belongs, we must say that career opportunities are rather limited in the administration. There are relatively few managerial positions compared to those in many other parts of the central administration – about 1 managerial post for every 10 academically trained workers. For non-academically trained staff promotion to the managerial level is impossible.

We can assume that the recruitment of less career orientated workers reduce the competition mentality. This makes life easier for those social groups, who historically speaking have not been associated with career advancement and promotion to managerial positions. Other social groups who traditionally still have certain career oriented ideals and are faced with expectations of being fighters, have an advantage in situations where these ideals are fostered and rewarded. But in BSW the competition mentality and abrasive characteristics are not rewarded. The atmosphere created by a non-competitive egalitarian organizational culture is more conducive to work done by women and presumably by many 'sensitive' men as well.

Moreover, the fact that the Welfare administration is in the public sector is of central importance in generating equality where competition is not so pronounced. Although the organization has been faced with abolition threats, this has been primarily a result of factors other than the achievements and the competition capability of the organization. The impression is that individual performance is not very strong in this organization. There is time for 'being social'. As for the managers they sometimes work more than a normal week, but most work a little less than that which is usual within, for example, the Ministry of Foreign Affairs (Chapter 9).

Although the managers in the BSW have problems in combining work and family commitments these problems are said (by the interviewees) not to be as great as they are within other state sectors, ie. some ministries, and within the private sector where the pressure can sometimes be even greater.

Finally, there is the weak hierarchy within the BSW which results from conditions within the organization. The difference between managers and subordinates is not very apparent. The staff have representatives who have an influence on the appointment of managers. The minimalized hierarchy is partly a result of the fact that it is a social welfare field, and also that people with certain ideals, values and political opinions have applied for jobs (many of whom have their roots in the '68-generation which makes them neither military, macho-oriented nor impersonal or bureaucratic in their managing style). It is important in this respect to note the large percentage of highly educated people within the organization.

All the factors mentioned can presumably make management either more difficult or easier. From the point of view of many women it can be easier, for two reasons. The majority of women may prefer a softer managerial style and would have difficulties in adopting a military style which is so far removed from the common expectations and ideals associated with women. Also the weak hierarchy makes it possible for a person to be promoted to manager without losing too many of their social contacts and their solidarity within the workplace. It is often said that women consider their social needs to be of central importance and are interested in having good and close relations with their colleagues (Billing & Bruvik-Hansen, 1984:175-179; Gunnarson & Ressner, 1983). In many other workplaces eventual promotion could mean that these good relations could not be fully maintained. However, in the BSW the minimalized hierarchy means that career advancement does not necessarily cause any loss in that respect.

Notes

1 "'68 spirit" refers to the ideology prevalent in the students' movement in many western countries in the late 60's. The student movements were (at that time) characterized by being leftists, activists, progressive, informal and non-hierarchical.
2 An "academic background" is interpreted narrowly in Denmark. For example social workers are not defined as academically qualified. A university graduate has at least 5 years of university studies.
3 Actually, if one looks at the entire BSW, and disregard the closure of the managerial labour market, women are clearly underrepresented as regards managerial jobs.

8   SAS

8.1   Introduction

One of the criteria for our selection of SAS was that it should be a contrast to a public company which had a relatively similar numerical distribution of the sexes. Another criterion for the choice of this organization was that it appeared to the public to be 'modern' and 'progressive' with regard to staff; an image that has predominated for the past 5-6 years. This image has been somewhat disturbed by the financial crisis experienced by SAS in 1991/92. It has resulted in SAS having to dismiss 10-15% of its employees and having to adopt a more stringent employee policy. The investigation was undertaken in the period 1987-89, and therefore any restructuring, reductions, etc. that have taken place since 1989 have not been taken into account. The management espoused an interest in 'female characteristics' in its management style during the 1980's and had to the public also introduced new ideas for organizational changes. These were communicated primarily through the personified picture of SAS that the public holds, and said by Jan Carlzon, the managing director. Thus from an ideological point of view the organization at the time of the study lives up to values that have been highly sought after by some writers on women and management, e.g. alternative organizational ideas, a 'flat' structure and a decentralization of power and influence.[1] Consequently there is reason to examine such a company with its claim to have toned down hierarchy, with a view to investigating whether this type of hierarchy is of any importance for female managers.

After a short introduction to the method used, a general introduction to the company is provided so that the reader may understand the basis for the specific problems dealt with here. Then the composition of the sexes within the organization and in the management posts is described. The recruitment of managers is studied and it is here that the various barriers to women's access to the management posts are discussed. One section deals with the special problems faced by female managers. Finally an account is given of Scanweb which is a network of female employees who have come together from different divisions and regions (countries).

8.2   Method

The investigation was concentrated on the divisions within SAS that had a reasonably large percentage of female employees, i.e. mainly managers and other employees within the Business Service Division and the personnel department in

SAS Denmark. The study also included a number of managers within other administrative divisions.

The managers were employed at various levels, such as head of division, heads of department, personnel managers etc., a total of 16 people were interviewed (5 male, 11 female) of which 13 were managers and 3 were otherwise employed. The reason why more women than men were interviewed is firstly that this project concerns in particular the situation of female managers and secondly that the experiences of female managers may be of particular relevance for understanding the gendered nature of management and organization. The male managers were selected for their comparability with the female managers, in similar fields of work and positions.

The interviews were, as in the other two case studies, semi-structured, qualitative individual interviews with great flexibility in which the individuals could touch upon areas which they felt were essential. Each interview was of a duration of one to three hours. In addition to this the participant observation method was employed in connection with major meetings in the Scanweb network of women.

8.3 Description of the organization

8.3.1 General and historical

SAS was founded in 1946 by three private companies in Denmark, Sweden and Norway with the objective of establishing a joint air service across the North and South Atlantic. In 1950, the company was extended to cover European and domestic air traffic. During the same period, the governments of the various countries joined the limited liability company as co-owners so that the state and private companies now owned 50% each of each of the three countries' shares in SAS. The Danish and the Norwegian shares are each two sevenths of the whole while the Swedish share is three sevenths. SAS obtained first refusal on domestic air traffic routes and an exclusive right to overseas air traffic.

Until the end of the 1960's the market grew steadily, but after that trouble set in. In 1973 the oil crisis arose and the world market stagnated. Technological developments were slower and SAS started to experience problems which in 1979-80 were reflected in an actual loss.

SAS continued to use the old solution models of cost control, reductions in costs, rationalization and attempts at increasing productivity. Decisions were reached on the basis of technical rationality (the belief that one best solution could be found and that the company's functioning could be optimized in a machine-like way), which did not work very well in a market with variations and uncertainty and changed conditions as regards competition (Edström et al, 1985, 1989, chapter 2).

The old philosophy had worked as long as the market grew steadily in a predictable way. However, in a situation of increased competition this philosophy provided no solutions to the problems now experienced by SAS of lost market shares, unsatisfactory profits, low efficiency and a low morale among employees.

From having been originally almost exclusively an airline both as regards concrete activities and also ways of thinking SAS has developed more and more into an company concerned with travel. When Jan Carlzon became the new Chief Executive of the organization in 1980, the transformation process of SAS accelerated and the primarily product-oriented company became more service and market-oriented. This means a reorientation from relatively standardized offerings to a more flexible and differentiated way of relation to the customer. This is still a characteristic of the company today. The foundation for change had been laid before Carlzon took up his position, but he became to a great extent the advocate of and symbol for the new philosophy.

SAS is one of the largest companies in Scandinavia and is often described as a colossus.

To be employed in SAS in general one must firstly realize that this is a colossus. It is a very large administrative system. We have approximately 20,000 employees and this is something that makes itself felt (male manager).

In addition to its airlines, SAS consists of SAS Hotels, SAS Service Partner, SAS Leisure and has a share in other companies. Altogether 30,000 people are affiliated to the activities of SAS on a world scale. Approximately 20,000 are affiliated to the airport activities in Scandinavia and of these approximately 7,800 work in Denmark (1989).

In 1984 the airline was divided into seven divisions of which five are marketing and technical divisions, while the other two are the administrative divisions, Business Services Division (BSD) and SAS Data. BSD sells services within areas such as personnel and wage administration and is responsible for major fields of management and personnel development within SAS. SAS Data is responsible for planning, programming, operating and maintaining the central data systems within the airline company.

The individual divisions have a status as independent units with an independent right to reach decisions and also responsibility for the economy of the unit. The division of the company into these units was an attempt at "flattening the pyramids" (Carlzon, 1987) and lessening the "colossus" image. Of course, the rhetorics of the CEO hardly mirrors the social practices and intraorganizational relations in a clearcut way. As will be seen below, interviewees repeat this rhetoric, which indicates that it at least to some extent corresponds to their experiences and perceptions.

This investigation is first and foremost concerned with the administrative sector of the company. When comments are made on the company based on our own empirical material, they therefore concern primarily the administrative sectors of SAS Denmark which will be referred to as SAS.

8.3.2 Description of the new strategy and organizational structure of the SAS company

In order to understand organizational and management conditions within SAS from the perspective of gender, it is important to show the major changes to the company that have taken place within SAS during the 1980's. These affect in various ways the dimension of gender within SAS. However, we will deal explicitly with the subject of gender and management later in this chapter.

The new strategy for SAS was launched with the following main characteristics. Importance was to be attached to the passenger paying full price "Businessman's Airline" (in that respect Carlzon did not even think of businesswomen). Marginal capacity was to be filled with tourist class passengers with a clear differentiation between the two segments of the market (Edström et al, 1985, 1989, chapter 2). Resources were to be concentrated and the organization was to be designed so as to make allowance for the 'adaptation to need' of the segments. This strategy reflected a new philosophy within the company in which primary importance was attached to the 'needs' of customers (especially the comforts of business class passengers) and no longer to the technical and operational possibilities/characteristics of the company. From the original strategy in which decisions in SAS were centralized and reached on the basis of technical rationality, SAS changed to a strategy in which decisions were to a greater extent reached on the basis of a market viewpoint and also on a decentralized basis within the more general guide-lines prescribed by the philosophy of the company as well as management textbooks. SAS now showed a balance between the logic of production and the logic of the market that differed from the earlier balance (Edström, 1988).

The new philosophy of the company and those values, norms and assumptions related to the philosophy were pointed out to the employees through course activities and in writing. The philosophy emphasized self-confidence, individual responsibility and satisfaction of employees and customers. As stated in the pamphlet, "SAS Culture", "Satisfied customers and satisfied employees are our best asset".

To most people, the changes were positive and these changes were not attributed to Jan Carlzon alone. His charisma might have been necessary to implement the changes, but the staff of SAS was accorded much of the honour; "if they had not been willing to do their part, nothing would have happened" (as one interviewed female employee said, who had been working in SAS for 20 years).

In the old days a 'team spirit' was to be found in SAS, staff were proud to be with SAS, then came a period when this spirit was less pronounced.

Then suddenly we became innovative again and invented new products, such as divisions into classes and new service components. We were able to do all this ourselves. Then suddenly once again people become proud to belong to SAS (female manager).

After that the team spirit in SAS became important again, according to interviewees.

The interaction between staff members was regarded as an important precondition for the successful change of the company. When a company is to compete in the field of service it is essential that the staff support their ideas (Normann, 1983). The climate within the organization is important not only for internal reasons (good atmosphere, cooperation, low staff turnover) but also for external reasons in relation to the customers and the market. The climate within the organization is evident to its customers and will affect their view of the quality of service and thus eventually their satisfaction (Schneider, 1980). One way of increasing the involvement of the staff was to employ new types of managers who were not only specialists within their fields but also capable of making other people function. As one female manager expressed it, "being a manager became much more of a social phenomenon".

The fact that the attitude had changed as regards the "management profile" appeared, among other things, from the qualifications required of managers espoused in for example the weekly SAS Magazine. Also at the courses held by the Leadership College, the importance of the social qualifications of managers now was being discussed.

The set of rules was being changed. Formerly SAS was an organization managed from the top with manuals for everything. But now in some people's opinion, something close to anarchy existed in some areas. "Pyramids have been demolished" – but in some cases the pyramids have been built up again, according to some interviewees.

In some cases the pyramids have been absolutely flattened, and they are still flattened. In other cases they have been flattened but are not flattened any more. They have consciously been raised higher than they actually needed to be (male manager).

The decentralization of responsibility to each individual employee had the effect, according to interviewees, that many people experienced tendencies to become his/her own boss. The effect of this was described as follows:

It is obvious that when messages are received that everyone is his/her own manager. Then those who are managers ask, 'what then is my function?' Now the message that everyone is to be his/her own manager is, of course, a slogan. It is a slogan just as so many others, but we also need slogans (male manager).

However, the 'tyranny' as regards titles and hierarchy still exists in SAS, according to many. Thus titles can give different status. For instance, being a manager gives a higher status than being a specialist. For the sake of clarity, we should mention that in Denmark, 'manager' as a concept and a title is used exclusively as a designation of a salaried employee with personnel below him/her, compared with the USA, for instance, where the title is used more widely.

Structural changes are never absolutely painless some employees gave vent to their disapproval through what may be called passive aggressiveness, i.e. resistance which was not expressed directly, but expressed indirectly by way of decisions being held up, shelved, or not being approved and various other manifestations which are symptoms of underlying problems.

Many employees felt that organizational changes took place too rapidly and that it was difficult for the individual to keep up with what was going on. In certain instances the decentralization made a number of demands on the employees which were not so easy to live up to.

It is not surprising that it can be difficult to make an organization more effective through demanding more of its employees. One difficulty within this company followed from the contrasts between the production logic, focusing on cost-effective, reliable flight operations, that had traditionally dominated within SAS and the market logic, focusing on a service concept in which the wants of the individual customer is flexible taken into consideration. The conflict between these logics was intensified during the 1980's and many issues associated with it had been pushed aside rather than adapted and integrated (Edström, 1988:47). To sum up the effect of the changes, SAS was characterized both by a successful, overlapping change and also by tensions and problems. These were in part related to the difficulty in finding the right organizational structure.

We still have all forms and I think we will go on having them. It is not that the organization is static – God knows – here and there changes are made. Some departments make changes several times a year. The data department, for instance, attempts to find a role that is suitable within the surrounding world and turning such a colossus as SAS around is really a major process. But otherwise, hardly three years pass without some major change being made within the organization (male manager).

Later on we will discuss in more detail the consequences of this which affect the theme gender/management. The new corporate strategy and the overlapping organizational change within SAS gave rise to, among other things, two results which were of importance in part for women's 'objective' possibilities of becoming managers and partly (perhaps) for a larger urge on the part of women to apply for management positions.

Firstly, cutting down of bureaucracy led to different demands being made on qualities of leadership. Therefore specialists within various fields were no longer automatically appointed managers. The kind of knowledge and experiences – often associated with technical jobs – that were earlier demanded or given priority to were seldom possessed by women. However, the social qualifications, etc. that were now demanded, gave women an increased possibility of putting themselves forward as applicants, also the organization could now make use of the qualifications that are sometimes characterized as female qualities.

Secondly, the change in SAS from an organization which was managed traditionally with functional organization, bureaucracy, product-orientation, and technical rationality into an organization which was managed with less bureaucracy, less hierarchy, and was decentralized and service-oriented and thus based on a market and service concept, in which a flexible adaptation to the wants of individual customers are viewed as central, has meant (according to interviewees) that it became more attractive for women to become managers.

It is important to note that this development also affects the cultural level, i.e. the deeper understandings and meanings of management. Service is often associated with something female, at least in another way than production, and the idea that this ideal should permeate the entire company may encourage a somewhat more 'pro-female' view of the activities and crucial elements of the company thus mentally opening up for women approaching more important tasks and jobs. Cultural change in this sense has a clear gender connotation.

8.4   Staff conditions

8.4.1 Recruitment

Most employees of SAS have grown up within the SAS-culture. They come into the organization as young trainees and have attended their training courses within SAS. Most of the managers interviewed have a background of "street smartness", an expression used by one of those interviewed. This means that they have started from the bottom and learned the system on their way up. Previously SAS had not had a tradition of employing people with higher education apart from pilots and engineers/technicians. However, according to Personnel and other managers, SAS has now become a high-status company because of its espoused market orientation and perhaps mainly because of the publicity surrounding SAS. There are many applicants for the available jobs.

When engaging a new employee, SAS is interested in whether the applicant has skills which can be used in various departments in the company. For instance, SAS tries to find employees who can sometimes be used within an administrative department and other times for checking-in. Some feel that this is an utopian view, as very different basic attitudes are required if the employee is to be in the front line or working in the 'backroom', i.e. without contact to customers.

In general, it is important that the employee is "service-minded", mainly, of course, within the service divisions, but some believe that this is communicated also to the administrative departments and that SAS is looking for the same type of person for both situations. Service-mindedness seems to point to a capacity and willingness to perceive and respond to the wants of the individual passenger – especially if he or she flies business class – thus overcoming bureaucratic behaviour.

Some managers choose new employees according to whether they like them or not. In addition to this, they choose the new employees who are qualified for the job and have the 'right' attitude. For instance, in the economically independent units those must be employed who like to do business. Other managers to a greater extent seem to pay attention to 'good chemistry' between themselves and the applicant, and they attach more importance to this than to the applicant's qualifications. As one male manager said:

We have the standard principle of focussing 100% on 'chemistry'. If the 'chemistry' is not OK, then it will not work. If the 'chemistry' is OK and some of the qualifications are not quite as they should be then we say: we'll see whether these qualifications can be gained over a period of time.

The 'chemistry' is not defined in detail, but cooperation among all employees is so highly regarded that some managers have all their six to seven employees interview all applicants in order to get the old employees' evaluation as to whether they could cooperate with the new employee. If they can cooperate, then the chemistry is as it should be.

The reason for this very selective choice of employees is, according to a male executive, that "the whole environment would break down" if someone was wrongly placed. Above all one must fit into the SAS culture. However, first impressions must not always be decisive. For instance, the procedure may be that the manager first talks with the applicant, then the employees talk with the applicant, and finally the manager talks with him/her once again after which a decision is reached. Some managers prefer to make job profiles for all applicants which are to supplement the personal impression. Other managers use such profiles in applications for management positions. A female manager suggested that 'chemistry' simply means choosing somebody resembling oneself, which is also called homo-social reproduction (Lipman-Blumen, 1976).

People are also recruited from the families of employees. Many have their wife or child employed for 'unskilled' work or as trainees. As a male manager suggested, "one enquires within other departments, when new employees are needed saying, 'can't you use my son?' or 'can't you use my wife?'".

8.4.2 Staff turnover and social climate

SAS is said to be a place of work that is in high demand. People do not voluntarily leave SAS. For instance a number of 40-year anniversaries at the workplace are being celebrated at the moment, i.e. these are people who have been with SAS from its start.

It has not been possible to obtain information on the average term of employment over the whole organization. However in SAS-Data the average age of employees is 40 and the average term of employment is 12-13 years (1988). People seldom leave SAS. "It is almost impossible to make them leave" (one of those interviewed). The average term of employment of employees of SAS among those interviewed by Christensen et al (1984) in a study of the organization was 18 years.

Despite this, dismissals do take place. However, there must be a good reason for somebody to be dismissed, such as the person concerned being absent without cause or refusing to do some specific job. Problems of cooperation may also cause dismissal in some instances. However, since dismissals are an important matter, one manager alone cannot reach a decision to dismiss an employee. Such a decision must be authorized higher up in the hierarchy.

Social life is important within SAS. A large number of clubs exist and almost all employees of SAS are members of such clubs with interests as diverse as athletics, badminton, basketball, table tennis, bowling, bridge, archery, diving, philately, etc.. One of the managers interviewed estimates that more than 75% of the employees of SAS in Denmark are members of some form of work-based association or club. All these spare-time activities mean that most employees of SAS meet socially and in their spare time.

Picnics and Christmas lunch parties are held as in other companies. What makes it a little different and more fascinating is that in SAS, the celebration can be held in a different country, such as a Christmas lunch party in Rome. Employees can use staff travel concessions.

The climate in the various departments differs but the general impression is that people like working for SAS. On the basis of the limited material of this investigation it cannot be ascertained whether this is due to the working conditions, the social climate, the many spare-time offers (clubs), an unusual staff policy, the size of the internal labour market or the unemployment in society in general (in Denmark since the 1970's) and the resulting lack of alternative possibilities. The shift in image in SAS has meant that many applicants apply for a position whenever new trainees are taken on. Thus SAS can 'pick and choose' among young people with an upper-secondary school leaving examination and high marks in languages. SAS's popularity among job applicants may be due to its image but it may also be a result of the generally restricted admission to institutions of higher learning that exists in Denmark.

8.5 Composition of the sexes within the organization and as regards management positions

SAS-Denmark has approximately 7,800 employees of which 2,500 are women (i.e. 68% men, 32% women), of these employees 488 men and 78 women hold management positions (86% men, 14% women) (1988-89). Thus, at the managerial level men predominate in management positions when compared to their percentage within the organization.

No statistics are available to show the number of female and male managers at various times in SAS's existence. However, the general impression is that the number of female managers has increased since 1982. This is attributed by some to the 'cultural revolution' in SAS when a new generation of executives came to SAS which was more tolerant and open to female managers. Some importance may also be attributed to the fact that SAS no longer takes on specialists as managers, but rather hires those who are perceived to have social 'insight' and are capable of delegating work and leading others.

We find in our study of the Business Service Division and the personnel department, that a similar disparity in the male to female ratio exists. This has, however, been remedied somewhat during the past years (1985-88) as one or two female managers have been appointed. BSD consists of two main areas, the revenue information department with a female functional manager and the administrative finance department with a male director of finance.

The revenue information department has approximately 405 employees of which 69% are women. At the management level below (the female) functional manager there are eight male heads of departments. Therefore eight out of nine (or 89%) of the managers are men, whereas only 31% of the total employees in the department are men. The administrative finance department has 145 employees, approximately 33% men and 67% women. At management level there are three women and three men. Therefore men hold 50% of the management positions.

The personnel department has just over 200 employees of which 66% are women. At management level there are two women and seven men or 78% men and 22% women. Perhaps one would expect to find the female managers among the seven personnel managers who are within the seven divisions, but only one of these is a woman. In SAS we find that it is trade union leaders who have often been promoted to personnel managers; these are "really tough guys", according to one of those interviewed.

The fact that the discrepancy is so considerable between the percentage of women in the organization and the percentage of female managers may be due to tradition. If we look at the division of labour between the sexes in the various departments of SAS it does not differ from that within society in general. For instance, there are very few women in the technical division (6%) but many among airline personnel (stewardesses) (67%). In addition to this, women and men have jobs that are typical of their gender. For instance, by and large all key-punch operators are women as are those who attend to customers, service etc., whereas everything which relates to technical aspects, maintenance, plane repairs, transport, stores, etc., is carried out by men.

The division of labour applies not only between the various divisions but also to some extent within the various divisions. For instance, in the key-punch operators' department within BSD there are 100 women and two men. Men have been given employment in this department, but they have not stayed for very long. Either they sought employment outside SAS or they found other work in the airport, as they "did not want to keep this boring job", according to one of those interviewed.

In principle, in BSD gender is not considered when employees are placed in various work functions. Gender becomes an issue, however, when the composition of the team in which they are to be placed is evaluated. If there is a majority of women in the team, men are preferred in as new employees where they have the same qualifications as female applicants and the opposite is true where men are in the majority. A number of people stated that they endeavoured getting a fifty-fifty distribution of the sexes and hoped to have at least a quarter of whichever sex is in minority, if this is possible. The taken-for-granted assumption behind this is that in the teams consisting only of women there is a tendency that the conversation among these employees will be specifically 'female'.

There is too much nonsense and gossip and far too much talk about knitting patterns and recipes. It may not be a positive thing to say, but also talk about children (female manager).

The assumption among more interviewees is that in teams where there are only men there is an altogether different kind of conversation and a rather tough environment. One can, of course, discuss whether these opinions reflect sex stereotypes or whether they are true. Nevertheless, many feel that a combination of the two sexes gives a more settled environment and the best working climate.

The most male-dominated division is the technical division, but this department claims to be very interested in opening its doors to more women "to ensure that we get qualified labour" (technical manager). The lack of suitable applicants has made the technical division look with a critical eye at its own prejudices and belief in sex stereotypes. They are not afraid of admitting their own prejudices. The technical manager describes his visions for the future as follows:

One need not be a prophet in this country to see in a few years, if developments continue in the way they have in recent years, that we will be in competition for the qualified young people seeking jobs in the labour market. Smaller classes are on the way and there will therefore be competition for young people with qualifications. We have to realize this now. Unless we get rid of the old prejudices as regards the pattern of sex roles in employment we will not be able to cope in the competition for qualified labour.

However, despite these enlightened claims a recruitment policy aimed at getting more women into the traditional male jobs in the technical department has not yet been formulated. The department is 'thinking about it'. Girls are encouraged to apply for jobs, women employees are interviewed, etc., and an attempt is made to influence the managers of the technical division, who also pose a prob-

lem, through courses and information. More effort is made in interviewing female applicants than male because the department is interested in finding

some girls with stamina, some mentally strong girls who wish to join and contribute to
breaking down the norms that apply, and some girls who are particularly strong for a
technical division that is really dominated by men (male personnel manager).

This same manager points out that in circumstances where female and male
applicants were equally qualified for the job they exercise positive discrimination in favour of the woman. It is emphasized that some years ago when a number of base managers were needed an attempt was made to appoint a woman but
there were no applicants.

The climate is experienced differently in the different departments. Special
characteristics are thought to have been created in part by the employees,
whether men or women are in majority is believed to be of importance, and also
created in part by management. For instance, BSD is mentioned as a division
that is believed to have been influenced by having a female manager as head of
the division.

People coming from outside BSD were amazed at the atmosphere. They said
it was caused by the female manager. There was far more openness and it was
possible to improvise much more. Everything was less rigid and they felt it was
exciting to join BSD (female employee of a different department).

Obviously, one can discuss the validity of such a statement both in terms of
the precision of the observation and the attribution of the cause behind the stated
atmosphere. It seems, however, that people attach special importance to the gender of the manager in creating a specific type of environment. The female manager appears to be a symbol for openness and more freedom.

This tendency to connect gender with certain distinct orientations appears to
be typical for SAS. Interviewees seldom hesitate in describing males and females in quite different terms. SAS in this respect differs strongly from BSW
and, as we will see in the following chapter, the Ministry of Foreign Affairs.
Whether the statements reflect widespread stereotypes (many of which are positive) or they tell us something about 'true' differences between male and female
employees is hard to say. Most likely, both elements account for the opinions
and observations of the interviewees.

8.6   Recruitment for management positions

8.6.1 Visibility – the gendered division of labour

As in the majority of other organizations within SAS, women are to be found at
levels where it is probably more difficult to become visible and more difficult to
show results. The pool for recruitment is considered to be generally smaller

among women for management positions, and there are relatively fewer women applicants.

For instance, we see how many women are employed in the punch-key operator department where it is not easy to become visible, with little opportunity to exercise discretion, demonstrate capabilities etc. In addition to this, many of the female employees are hired as temporary office workers. According to one of the temporary workers, many of those employed in the department stated that they wished to work there so that they did not need to concentrate too much when they were at work and therefore could better concentrate on their family and private life. Then when their children had grown up, they would start afresh. These women, and probably many others do not consider a management position at all, they are not interested in it, they have other interests and would perhaps not be suitable for the job. In addition to this, as throughout society, women are found at the more 'invisible' lower levels of work where it is not easy to be noticed as they have no independent results to show. For managerial positions it is necessary to be noticed, for most managers are hand-picked, i.e. they are encouraged to apply for a top position because they have been noticed.

Thus in many departments the work is divided between employees according to sex stereotypes even though in certain departments within the divisions, endeavours have been made to compose the teams on the basis of an equal distribution of the sexes. The division of labour by sex can explain only in part why the percentage of women in management positions falls below their percentage within the organization. Women are also in a minority of management positions in parts of the organization where women predominantly are employed. One example was within revenue information where remnants of the 'old' SAS still existed and where specialists were chosen as managers.

Where women have jobs with few possibilities of development it will (according to Kanter, 1977:135-136) affect their ambitions, i.e. they tend to limit their expectations and ambitions, and may have less self-confidence. To a greater extent they regard their jobs as allowing them to have a more meaningful sparetime and the work loses its importance as a means of realizing themselves. The opportunity structure will therefore shape the worker's behaviour as a kind of self-fulfilling prophecy.

8.6.2 The dynamics of chance. How does one become a manager?

Most managers are recruited from within the organization and have been trained by SAS. Managers are expected to have gained experience within SAS, they are, so to speak, expected to have an employment record with the company.

They must know what to do, for example, in the event of a strike or if the airport is closed on account of fog. They must know what it means when 200 passengers are screaming and yelling at you. If you are to be a manager and make decisions that have an impact in this situation with your employees, then you must understand the conditions they work under (female manager).

Formerly a number of managers were appointed because they were good at selling tickets or repairing aircrafts:

Formerly, if a station manager was needed it would be one who had grown up at the station and knew everything about the system, but now we are experiencing a tendency to select a manager and then this manager has under him a number of specialists (same manager).

All management positions must be advertised. There is staff participation in the appointment of all managers, but the staff does not have the final say. The representative of the trade union joins in the interview phase, in the evaluation, and in the recommendation. However, generally the points of view of this representative are identical with those of management. Women represent the trade unions just as often as men.

Considerably larger numbers of men than women apply for management positions. However, the balance is changing as ideas about the qualities required for management are modified by changes within the organization.

When asked how they themselves have become managers a clear pattern emerges in the replies and that is consistent for both women and men. They say that it was a matter of chance, a question of being "in the right place at the right time" and being able to take up a challenge. However, what this means is rather more problematic. For some, being in the right place at the right time means that they had grown tired of their previous work and were now interested in other challenges. Therefore they were ripe to attempt to get a management position and to accept it was challenging.

I have had an incredible ability to be at the right place at the right moment. And also then I have never said no to challenges (male manager).

Arguably, a common factor was that many of the employees were seeking not so much a management position as for a new field of work. It is also important that a superior is aware of the person in question as a potential manager. Also, the management style of the person is important and how they have co-operated. In a few instances it has been significant that the person concerned was a woman. In one instance the manager herself felt that her chances of becoming manager were not impaired by the fact that she was a woman: "it was not detrimental to me that I was a women, on the contrary".

This woman manager, aged about 40, employed in one of the top positions had been appointed during the period when the organizations was under the influence of Carlzon's view that a synthesis of male and female qualities gives the best management. Therefore it was probably obvious to implement this idea by choosing a woman for a top position. The appointment backed-up policy statements and illustrated and reinforced the cultural changes advocated.

After the decentralization women experienced an increased chance of applying for leading positions as a result of which the earlier very marked division of
labour between the sexes began to soften. The possibilities of getting a management position have increased after the change of the qualification requirements
from technical to social qualifications.

8.6.3 The wording of advertisements for management positions

It has already been mentioned that more men than women apply for management
positions. A rather widespread perception within SAS is that this is related to the
wording of the advertisements such that they appeal to men. A female manager
thinks this is because men describe their own jobs.

I feel our advertising has been directed at men. This has not actually been done consciously by the recruitment department, but rather when a job has been vacant, it has been
a man in one of the divisions who has prepared the job description. As a rule it has been
his own job that he described because he was perhaps going elsewhere in the system, and
for this reason the advertisement has appealed to men.

The point here is that the job may be exaggerated to include dimensions that it
does not really have. One needs not necessarily be able to fulfill all the requirements of the advertisement to be able to cope with the job.

Men know this and apply for the job even though their background does not really justify
them doing so. Women, on the other hand, do not know the rules of the game and do not
apply for the job. They think that one needs to fulfil all the requirements, perhaps even
more so – 150% (female manager).

Another female manager describes it as follows:

If a man can cope with a small number of the requirements specified in the advertisement,
it becomes a challenge to him. If he can cope with everything he will not apply for the job.
With women it is different. They apply for the job only if they can cope with everything.

Women check all 10 out of 10 qualification requirements before applying at all. Men
check four of them and as far as the rest is concerned they will make it up as they go
along. We women have not been trained to be certain of ourselves.

Many point out that, in general, advertisements are exaggerated and one never
expects anybody to live up to all the requirements contained in them. The female
network Scanweb is aware of the wording of the advertisements and has decided
to try to make them more 'female'. The question is how the advertisements
should be expressed to encourage women to apply for a leading position or, in
other words, whether a sufficient intervention can be made to make more
women take an interest. This is an issue which will be discussed fully in section
8.11.

8.6.4 Internalized barriers

The fact that women are less likely than men to apply for management positions can also be related to what a female manager calls "women's addiction to security". In general she feels that women are "naturally timid". In SAS, perhaps in particular among the women interviewed, this is an agreement that the problems rest with the women themselves. The sense of inferiority in women and their lack of self-confidence are mentioned by both female and male managers as a serious obstacle for women in their attempt to get on in the system.

We have not yet got used to seriously thinking that powerful people with broad shoulders and hair on their chests could also be displaced by girls who are capable of coping with decision making and capable of thinking strategically (female manager).

This manager feels that there are clear expectations when it comes to filling the role of managers, a stature of a human being with many subordinates. She defines it both as a problem of attitude amongst those who decide who are to be managers within the organization, and also as a problem of sex stereotypical thinking by the women themselves.

Some female managers feel that women must be more competent than men in order to become managers.

As a girl[2] one must be sure of oneself, so sure of oneself that many men resent it for suddenly the girl becomes an equal opponent and men do not always find this comfortable. For them it is much better to be defeated by another man than by a mere girl. This must be degrading for a man as his superiority is inherent in our cultural upbringing.

Many women also feel that they are regarded as women (or girls), much more than men are regarded as men.

Perhaps you need not be more competent than men, but at any rate you must achieve success reasonably quickly. You are then left in peace for a while and you can work on matters that may take somewhat longer – or you can make a few blunders.

According to several of those interviewed a major problem and one widely believed is that many of the women potentially able to apply for management positions do not do so because they are afraid. Not daring to apply can then be seen as a problem within the women themselves. If this is the case, then the strategy to overcome the problem will be 'self-confidence training' for women. Many such courses exist in the USA.

Actually, I think that many girls could achieve more, if they would be a little more 'pushy'. Actually, I think that it has got much to do with a lack of self-confidence and a sense of inferiority. I only have to look at my own inner feelings (female manager).

I think that not enough women dare to achieve (male manager).

The women themselves are their own worst enemies when it comes to achievement (female manager).

According to Rothwell (1985), this argument, that women are their own worst enemies or that the seeds of their lack of advancement are to be found within themselves is accepted by many female managers. They are conscious of the ambiguities that exist and this is a factor that cannot be ignored. However, the eagerness with which male managers seize upon this explanation, says Rothwell, indicates a "blame the victim" syndrome and also an unwillingness to look at the social conditioning which contributes to creating these attitudes and which they themselves take part in. Apparently men and women have widely differing opinions of the ability of women to take up a career. The same conclusion is also indicated by a Swedish investigation. Asplund (1988) obtained different answers from female and male employees to the question of whether women and men have the same opportunities in developing a career. Only 30% of the women answered yes, that women have the same opportunities as men for receiving training within the companies, while 70% of the men felt that women had the same opportunities as men.

Asplund (1988:33) also investigated the explanations given for the fact that women do not advance at the same rate as men.

Women felt that the following factors were the most important ones:

– Women do not have (or cannot get) an education that leads to promotion.
– From the start women are assigned tasks that do not lead to promotion.
– Women do not receive from their managers the same attention that men do.

Men felt that these factors were the important ones:

– Women do not receive sufficient support from their families.
– Women do not dare to take risks.
– Women do not really want to be promoted.

Here we find (as also stated by Asplund) that the women emphasize factors that are related to the work and the role of the manager while the men emphasize the psychology of the problem and seek explanations in the personal situation or in the psyche of women.

A more detailed investigation was carried out as to what was behind the phrase current in SAS that 'women do not dare'. It was studied by turning to a number of employees who could be said to come into this 'category'. Here the picture became somewhat more varied. It seems also to depend upon a different way of sorting out priorities. It may also be a problem of a specific generation. The women interviewed were those who were raised to have marriage and family as an objective. This was the female career that was valued some decades ago. However, at some point (female interviewees said) often when the children have grown up and these women feel rather superfluous, some of them start asking themselves whether they have really achieved what they wanted. Some among these women do not wish to attain a management position, but they may choose to change from part- to full-time work. For others the result of this confrontation with themselves is to make different demands on their jobs. These women would like to get a more responsible position. Obviously, there is a difference between those women giving high priority to the traditional family orientated life and those actually wanting a leading position but not having the courage to apply for it.

One of those interviewed in SAS stated how she felt that she had been the supporting person for almost all her life, first and foremost in relation to her children, her husband and the home, but also as part-time secretary. She decided that now she wanted an independent job. She saw an advertisement for a more qualified job that suited her but did not dare go after it. Then one of the female managers that she knew through Scanweb called her and asked why she had not applied for the job. This push forward gave her the confidence to apply for the position.

It was important for her to change her attitude to job advertisements. Earlier she would not have dared to apply for a position if she could not live up to all the requirements, but she applied for this job in question mainly on the basis of wanting the job.

Important for these women applicants, who are said to be afraid to apply for the position, is the choice that they make when they discover that their earlier and important function in life is draining away.

Other possible reasons for the small numbers of female managers are those already mentioned, viz. that women believe they cannot live up to the requirements of the advertisement and they underestimate their own abilities.

Firstly women make demands on themselves and feel that they must be able to meet the specified requirements 120%. They do not emphasize enough of that which they can do. They do not make a great display of it as do men. Then at the interview they accept the fact that they will only answer questions instead of entering into a dialogue with the interviewer. Women very rarely sell themselves well as it is very difficult for them to do this. One must really know them beforehand so that one can remind them that they have this or that qualification and that they are able to do this or that (female manager).

This statement is supported by a number of male managers.

Women are probably more frightened of professing their ability to meet the conditions that are set. Probably it is more in men's nature to reply that they can manage it all even when they can live up to only about 70% of the advertised qualification requirements and those discussed during an interview. Women believe that they must be able to meet the requirements 150% (male manager).

The above applies not only for women who are not sufficiently confident of their qualifications. The female head of a division had held her job for three years at the time of the investigation, yet according to another female manager, many men were heard saying, "Well, let's see how it will work out".

Obviously in a male-dominated organization the first time they engaged a woman for an important job it was felt to be a bit of a lottery, but I have never doubted that this particular woman would be able to manage well. However, I have heard many statements like, 'Well, it won't last long' (female manager).

My impression is that of the women I have spoken to all were actually proud of her and I do think they had reason to be (female manager).

In spite of this, the female manager quoted believes that other women may have more difficulties in accepting that women advance in the system. She believes that there is often more disagreement at places of work among women themselves and more jealousy. The reason is not that women are different from each other, but that women of her age, 40-50 years, have not had the same educational advantages as the young women. They believed they had to accept the service jobs offered to women. She feels that young people are different today and do not choose similar service jobs. Now many more women have jobs within traditional male trades. "I believe the envy is an expression of bitterness."

This female manager thinks that women of her age feel bitter because they see younger women who are trained in the field of business administration pass them by and because they themselves did not have this opportunity (cultural orientations discouraged them from seriously considering career-oriented life choices). She believes that the older women should be helped to understand this.

8.6.5 'Good advice'

Female managers often have good advice for other women wishing to hold management positions; put differently, they are fully aware why women fail to advance in the hierarchy. One opinion is that "you must go for the job". According to one female manager, many women tend to guard against defeat by convincing themselves that it is not so important if they do not get the job.

But one must watch what one says for how do we know how we influence ourselves? In our own minds we guard against defeat. I announce outright that I applied for the management position. Everybody understands that I do want to get the job. Obviously, I will be terribly annoyed and become stubborn and cross if I don't get it. That is quite obvious.

Her point is that you have to watch the words you use. What you say to yourself could easily become a self-fulfilling prophecy.

If when lying in bed at night you use your energy to convince yourself that it is in fact not the end of the world if you do not get the job, then you will have undermined your endeavours to get the job. You must want to get the job and you must know what you want to do with it.

Another female manager says that it is useless to moan or cry. It is necessary to create a number of preconditions so that women may have a chance, among other things, male colleagues must be influenced. But as she says,

Nothing is free or acquired without their own effort. The world may be unjust. The reality may be that men meet over a beer and talk with each other, so this is where one must start. Of course I am influenced by the fact that I am surrounded by male managers, but I feel one must use one's own strength in relation to the strengths of others. It is not really a question of changing oneself but of adapting. Perhaps this is too strong a word, but it is necessary to be much more conscious of oneself and one's own importance.

Therefore, she suggests, that we should become conscious of the fact that we live in a male-dominated culture and that we cannot avoid being influenced by the world we live in. She compares it to moving to a completely different culture, such as the French culture. The result would be that of becoming more French in one's ways. She believes that this should not result in our losing our own values.

8.7   Female managers compared with male managers

Among the managers interviewed, none feels that the female and male managers are alike. Among the subordinates interviewed, however, the opinion is that the differences between female and male managers are not very great. Often, however, they have not experienced different managers, and they have only second-hand experience. One of the male managers who participates in a management group consisting of half men and half women clearly feels that female and male managers are different, and that men are probably more direct and straightforward whereas women contribute with new ways of thinking.

A male manager in the personnel department feels that women share a different view point than that of men, "women look at problems in a different way. They can point to different models for solving problems. They also have intuition". These 'characteristics' can, he feels, be effective in management jobs on the condition "that females remain females, that they do not start being managers on men's premises". None of the men interviewed said, they would be opposed to having a manager as their superior or their colleague. And yet a female manager who has only been in charge of women is often asked whether she believes that she could also be a manager of men. She is convinced that she could. Yet who would ask a similar question of men?

Female managers have in fact not felt that they have had difficulties in being accepted as superiors by their staff. On the contrary, they have felt that they have been supported. It is, however, one thing to find support but quite a different matter for a woman to become a manager at the cost of a number of men. This can give rise to problems of a different nature, for instance, difficulties in preserving social contacts.

I have experienced difficulties in maintaining social contacts with some of my colleagues who have had a career that differed from mine. In several instances over coffee at a private dinner there would be an obvious wish to talk about all the frustrations and the bad personnel policies that are inherent in the system. It is justifiable to discuss this, but if it recurred too frequently I have chosen to take it as an expression of some kind of personal frustration in relation to what I have achieved (female manager).

Those who have not themselves had experience as competitors for the job have acted differently. Another female manager states, "I have never experienced any active resistance or any active negative attitude. But the undertones that have been there have been such that I cannot really put my finger on them".

Hearn & Parkin (1986/87:43) refer to an investigation that looked into the reactions of subordinates in groups with male and with female managers, respectively. Here men's reactions to groups with female managers were in particular interesting. They varied from hostility, dependence, confusion and, most of all, uneasiness. In the above instance it is more precisely competitors for the managerial job who have reacted negatively to the appointment of a female manager.

According to employees there is a greater understanding among female superiors that there may be problems within the home, that children may become ill, and that it may be necessary to take time off.

The impression that women have a well-developed intuition is widespread among both male and female managers,

Actually I believe that women have some kind of intuition that many men do not have. And I do not think that it can be taken away from women, it does not change. I also think that women are goal-directed in a way that differs from the goal-orientation of men. Men go like clockwork, at least that is how I see it. They do not allow themselves extra scope. I think that in general women involve more people in the work process than do men. I think that women have a kind of courage in trying something else apart from the merely traditional (female manager).

In this connection she mentions that their courage may concern believing in a project without getting a lot of proof that it will work in advance. Such a project may produce a result that will be better than the project where a lot of resources had been used on analysing it beforehand.

I believe that as women we are much more willing to say, all right, we will reach a decision in this matter now. It may be that this decision will turn out to be wrong in two years, but by then we will reach a new decision. I think that men are sometimes tremendously afraid of coming to the point and taking the consequences because they are not sure if it will go wrong in the final instance.

A very large number (three fourths) of the female managers interviewed have in different ways expressed the same point of view, viz. that they are willing to and perhaps actually interested in 'going down the ladder' again. They believe in job rotation, where one is, for instance, a manager for a number of years and then takes a more mundane job for a number of years to "gain strength" as one woman puts it. She believes it would be best if managers were employed for a fixed period. Then one could say, "you will get three years. Show us what you are capable of doing".

None of the male managers interviewed expressed similar points of view, nor have the female managers heard male colleagues state such points of view. Some of these women think that since most men are dependent upon the salary they have achieved they cannot suffer a drop in salary, and also that status means more to them than it does to women.

A male manager believes that some fear losing face if they lose their title to become specialists. He gives a number of examples of those men who would be willing to take a drop in salary in order to maintain their status. These norms and attitudes of men are not unique to SAS but are found everywhere in the surrounding society.

I believe it is concerned with titles. I have heard several examples of men who did not dare go home to tell their family that they had changed over to a different job even though they had actually obtained a higher salary.

One female manager regards it as great freedom, giving scope of action not to need the salary she receives at the moment. She has not increased her consumption, instead she saves money in the expectation of 'going down again'. She has no wish to advance further in the hierarchy, since she does not find it worthwhile. She gives some concrete examples of jobs she would take within SAS at lower levels.

Several female managers see their right to hold management positions in terms of what they have to offer. If they had nothing to offer they feel they would not hold the position. Several of them describe their goal as follows:

I want to leave the department when I think there is nothing more I can do, that is to say, when I think I have accomplished what I think is necessary in order to make the department function.

That several female managers are willing to step down in the hierarchy at some point is related by them to what they call a female characteristic, the demand for perfection. It is described as follows by a female manager,

Our level of ambition with respect to our own effort is far, far higher. We are not nearly as capable of entering into a compromise with regard to our own effort as are our male colleagues.

The job is harder than she expected, but she thinks this is because of her high expectations of herself.

8.8   Problems specific to female managers

8.8.1 'Keep the balance'

Some female managers who have been in a group where they were the only woman explain the strategies that they used so as to be treated on an equal footing with men and thus get their projects through. Many of them found that some men used a condescending technique (ridicule, for instance, or questioning the very presence of the woman). Several say that they reverse the mechanisms so that it hits out at the one exercising them.

Generally they (the men) get an unexpected response. They do not ask ridiculous questions again. I do not work myself into a temper over it, but I do become rather irritated and when I have responded to it, it is over and done with. I try to find a response that is humorous but does not ridicule him completely. Then he can take it. Often this is the method I use. Otherwise he will get angry with me feeling he has been exposed to ridicule (female manager).

It takes its woman to find this balance such that at one and the same time she repudiates rudeness on the part of a male colleague yet sees to it that he saves face. Another female manager says she has had no problems being accepted as a manager but does toy a little with the experience she has had because of her sex. Perhaps here it is the other party who comes off worse.

When pilots come to file a complaint they approach the secretariat and say they want to speak to the manager. They see me and say hello. When I say 'hello, what can I do for you?', they say 'we want to talk with the head of the department'. Then I say 'yes' (I do not tell them straight away that it is me). Then they again ask for the head of the department. I say 'sit down, I am the manager'.

She also relates that at meetings where, as a rule, she is the only woman, when a male employee has joined her, other automatically approach him first. "Only then do they realize that she is the boss and approach her. Several of them say, "well, we thought you were the secretary".

She feels that women have a great advantage when participating in meetings where only men are present. Women can more easily say things with a smile yet in a strict and direct manner to a man without it being resented whereas it would not be acceptable if a male colleague did the same.

Another female manager is more direct and tells men not to react on account of her sex. She suggests that they concentrate on the issue at hand instead. This usually has an effect. However, the message must be given in the right way:

It may be perceived in the wrong way if you communicate with a smile. If you want to be taken seriously and get your message across you must stop smiling apologetically, as women often do. It is up to you to stop the game and say, 'I must concentrate and explain precisely what I mean'. You can invite trouble and risk him becoming aggressive. But that cannot altogether be avoided, so one must be ready for any confrontations that arise. One cannot have one's cake and eat it.

Finally, one female manager feels that her male colleagues have reacted with irritation when she has presented issues openly. She feels that she has not yet learnt the correct strategy and that she has "not had her rough corners knocked off".

By and large everyone agrees that women and men negotiate using different rules during meetings, etc.. An analogy that has been used by a number of people is that they are playing different games.

8.8.2 Techniques of negotiation

Many female managers think that women and men use different techniques in negotiation. Once this is realized one female manager thinks that it is a question of using the technique that is most successful which is not the technique used by women. She says women tend to show their hand, whereas men do not. This phenomenon has also been described in *Games Mother Never Taught You* (Harragan, 1977).

I am the type who says things as they are. I show my hand saying, 'this is my position, what is yours'. Men do not do this. Men as in card playing take one trick at a time. 'We have this one, we will finish our negotiations about this issue – settled. Next item … backwards and forwards … now this is settled. You have won once, I have won once.' And it continues like that until one or the other has most points, as in a debate. Always.

So when I say 'firstly, secondly, thirdly, fourthly' (the last point being in general the weakest, and to be considered last) then men will straight away pick up the last argument and have it out. Thus the man gets the trick and you are left with three strong points but must be incredibly tough to start all over in the discussion. You end up with having to take one trick at a time, after all, so you are wiser to start with the strong point and win the discussion.

As was commented upon by one of the female managers it is a question of men and women representing two different cultures and as a result negotiating or conducting meetings differently, "women typically conduct meetings in a collective manner whereas men do it in an individualistic manner".

What is described is a clash between two different cultures in which the procedure adopted by men becomes the one that dominates. The latter should not solely be understood as morally inferior. Effective management may partly be a matter of the exercise of a continuous influence in which suggestions, ideas, etc. are being communicated and rooted in various, not least informal situations and on various occasions (Kotter, 1982). Dealing with problems, that have not been prepared for in (formal) meetings, often takes considerable time (and many people may be involved). But what is more important is that men are in the majority in most meetings and their rules have been accepted within the companies, where the male culture prevails. The fact that women do not play their cards concealed may also put them at a handicap when it comes to preliminary meetings and lobbying. Women often go to meetings unprepared and speak their mind directly without having previous private or informal agreements as do men.

One female manager feels that this is a sure way of getting nothing through,

Men are used to lobbying. They almost never go to a meeting to present a suggestion that they have not talked through with at least two or three others beforehand. In Scanweb I have stated, you must find allies before going to meetings. Either men or other women. 'But this is not fair. It is lobbying.' There is nothing to do about that. One wants, after all, to have one's proposal accepted.

If a woman does not like this kind of put-up job, then she does not want to accept the rules of the game and then the most obvious solution is not to join the game in the first place.

Why put on airs. If you sit at a table with a group of 10-12 men in pin-striped suits, and you are the only woman and then you present a proposal that demands they reach a decision on straight away. I usually say, 'but you catch them with their pants down. Then they have no defence and they don't know what to do'.

She suggests instead of "catching them with their pants down and raising aggressions towards oneself", to find allies among them beforehand.

Then they can take part in a dialogue based on an actual proposal. You can present what you want but you need not present everything. You must be sufficiently flexible to realize certain proposals are perhaps not a good idea at that time.

It appears that broad agreement exists on the fact that female and male managers represent two different cultures with their own rules. The rules of male culture are the ones which achieve the best results. The female managers who have been quoted have already realized the clear advantages of using men's rules.

8.8.3 Female managers in relation to men

A female manager has experienced a somewhat special form of the dominating technique, viz. where men begin to flirt in a situation at the point where she is about to get her issue through. In this situation she feels that men are using the stereotypical perception that they hold of women and they 'forget' who they are dealing with. It is a situation wherein one is perceived as a representative of the female sex and not as oneself with one's own specific personality,

This is most often experienced in the situation where I am about to win my point, but some of the men would like the matter to be seen from their point of view. Then they begin to flirt. They sometimes attempt to just wipe out the opposition, but as a last resort and almost always when I am on the point of getting the upper hand, then they will try flirting. This is definitely not a method that they like themselves.

She does not think that this special kind of attention is conscious. It is simply a result of their not being able to see another way out.

It is more a question of the tone of voice. Such as, 'perhaps we should try out the proposal made by Mrs A. It could be done, you see, and it will do no harm. We can always change it afterwards'. Or they start making a demonstrative show of it all: 'How great, the only

real man in this group is in fact a woman' … or other stupid comments of this nature. I
think they feel that they are cornered.

One of the female managers participates in a management forum where she has
been the only woman for four years. In the beginning she experienced tremen-
dous opposition, but now she is used as a sparring partner.

In the beginning in that group I experienced a great personal crisis. What happened was
that when my turn came to say something, nobody wanted to listen. I was unhappy about
this and through being unhappy became angry. At time I showed my anger. I felt it wrong
that they would not listen to me as a human being. My management problems were similar to theirs that were discussed at those meetings so I told them, 'if you don't listen to my
problems, then you will yourself have a problem, for it also concerns your employees and
your department'.

I discussed it with them singly. Perhaps I should have done so in the forum as a whole.
However, I did not, but spoke with each one of them individually and tried to tell them
that they needed me, that I was convinced they needed me on the forum. Now it has
become clear that they do need my opinions.

Several of the women managers interviewed have replied in the negative to the
question of it being an advantage to be a woman and a manager. They feel that
the attitude toward female managers is more critical than toward a man. This is a
point of view supported by several international investigations. (See Chapter 4.)

When one is a female manager, I believe one must be better than the men in order to be
heard. I see an advantage being a woman in my daily work, but I think one knows that
men are more critical of a female manager. That is my experience.

Any extra attention that I attract is not related to my being a good manager but to my
being a woman.

Some women think the future looks brighter and feel that being a female manager will gradually become an advantage mostly because women have some
characteristics that the men realize are good. Intuition is mentioned as an example. A number of female managers do not regard themselves as particularly feminine, but feel that perhaps they are tough. This is a feeling that may easily arise
when one has to assert oneself in a culture that is not originally one's own.

As stated earlier (Chapter 5) women may be judged differently from men,
even by themselves, whenever they demonstrate 'masculine' qualifications.
Then in their own and others' opinion they can be regarded as being 'too tough'.
The point is not whether they are best described as 'tough' or not, but that the
same behaviour in a man may be judged and characterized differently, because
in this way the woman goes beyond her usual gender role.

The traditional 'world' of management can be compared to a tribe with special norms, values and rules of behaviour. The tribe consists of insiders who are
all alike, wear the same clothes, etc.. According to Symons (1986:381) admission to the tribe is particularly difficult for women since they risk being regarded
as a threat to the clan because of their difference. However, being admitted to

the territory is one thing, but being regarded as a worthy member of the tribe is quite a different matter. Where women are concerned they are in a field that has traditionally been dominated by men.

8.9 Scanweb

One of the founders of Scanweb was a female head of division. Her reason for becoming involved was based on her feelings at a conference she participated in where very few women were present. She expressed it as follows in a folder:

Once upon a time there was a conference of executives in SAS
Actually, it happened not such a long time ago
It was in the spring of 1985 to be precise
A large number of managers met
From near and far
There were managers at top level
Where the important decisions were being reached
Six women participated in this conference.
The total number of participants was 156!!

Thus Scanweb was born. In 1985 a group of women who were representatives of the divisions of SAS in Denmark, Norway and Sweden met. They established a formal cooperation across all regions and divisions. At the end of 1985 the joint Scandinavian group took the initiative in forming regional Scanweb groups.

In addition to Scanweb's wish to create a network for the women of SAS, their objective is to make SAS a better company to work for. Their vision is "that the management of tomorrow should reflect the needs of SAS and its employees". This can be realized, they say, among other things by employing more female managers since "a combination of male and female qualities provides the best management" (the folder about Scanweb). The women within Scanweb feel that managers of tomorrow must possess female characteristics. They also feel that the management of the future must be "capable of meeting the challenges of tomorrow, and attach equal importance to abilities and to social understanding. Planning and intuition must go hand in hand" (the folder).

The purpose of Scanweb is to work for a balanced composition of women and men within management. SAS is asked to employ more female managers, strengthen the female qualities within the existing teams of managers, and set up job rotation in its management. Scanweb wishes to help extending the recruitment base when positions are to be filled, so that it becomes possible for more women to attain management positions and also, once there, to cope with their responsibilities as managers. The recruitment base is to be extended "by supporting and coaching women who will then apply for management positions", "by pointing out that women have a choice", "by pointing to the available but underused management resources" (The folder). Female managers already employed are supported through Scanweb. In addition to this, the network contributes to overcoming the myths and changing the traditions that have so limited women's possibilities in taking on management positions.

The Scanweb project is supported by the top management of SAS, in particular by Jan Carlzon, because he is said to want a different type of manager, and a management with female characteristics. However, there are many managers within the organization who do not take it seriously. One female manager says,

Perhaps some of our managers at the middle level may feel threatened by it. If women want to go far within the hierarchy they must pass the middle management level. Then they will most often do better than the men as they have to be more capable to get to that level than the more numerous men who have reached it.

In 1988 all women in SAS Denmark (2,200) were invited to a large meeting about Scanweb. About 150 turned up to the meeting. At the meeting the representative of the basic group told those present about Scanweb and the work carried out within Scanweb, and they were encouraged to start project work themselves at a decentralized level.

The network structure that was formed was based on the name of Scanweb. In the middle there was to be a kind of 'spider' to gather up all the threads. This consists of four individuals with three main tasks: to coordinate, to inform and control, and to set up local interest groups or dialogue groups which were to pass on information from the basic group to those interested. The basic group of four was also to be in charge of PR-activities.

It was suggested that communication should take place via PCs with a special code so that everybody having access to a screen could get information and up-to-the-minute news from Scanweb. The comments by those attending the meeting on Scanweb were very positive. Some women commented that it was very important that the women who had become managers were supported because it is still true that "women must be at least a little more capable or even much more capable and much stronger in order to make their mark in management positions, within SAS".

Furthermore, the comments emphasized that the problem with the lack of female applicants also was due to the job profiles which were aimed at men. Therefore it was suggested that a trans-divisional interest group should be set up to deal with the preparation of job profiles.

One female employee claimed that for many women the problem is,

that when one reads a job advertisement most women say to themselves, 'am I capable of doing this, or capable of doing that'. They consider each point. This way of thinking is their experience in everyday life. Later it often turns out that the man who was appointed was not as capable as the woman in the same department.

A female purser on the flight deck suggests that a consultation office should be established for women who would like to apply for management positions at all levels. Here they could obtain an evaluation of their suitability for the job. The problem is, she says, that women say "no, I am not good at that, or that", while men say, "I can do this and that". Another woman in the audience mentions the following in connection with a job profile.

Any woman should be capable of applying for this job, but what worries me is how the people who are to read the applications are dissuaded. What is the point of women applying for the job if those considering the applications are simply overcome at the idea of a woman applying for the job.

The Scanweb meeting took place in a department under the technical division. This was intended as a provocation as this department is the most male-dominated division in the Danish region. However, the technical division showed an interest in the meeting as they felt that in the future there will be a shortage of labour and it will be necessary to consider other sources than those that have been in focus so far.

The technical division stated that they were interested in women with stamina. This does not mean, however, that the division wants women who are just like men.

But we are interested in finding girls who can act as 'bulwarks', who can destroy the norms we have established within the technical division, dynamic girls who are prepared to battle for a change in the attitudes of our managers and the attitudes within the technical division in general (male personnel manager).

It seemed that the division was looking for new female employees of a rather unusual kind.

What we need are girls who because they differ from the norm can add those elements that are essential to a technical division. We need girls with their intuition and their sensitivity and we also need the feminine traits that the girls bring with them (same manager).

It is explained below just how these feminine traits are thought to add something important to the technical department.

Imagine a smoking room with 42 men. Then three female aircraft repairers, of which none have been employed in the department for 30 years, arrive. Suddenly signs appear on the toilet, 'Ladies only'. Then people wash their hands before going to lunch and their boiler suits are changed every Thursday. People look better and are clean and well-groomed. People comb their hair, etc. (same manager).

Here we find femininity has been reduced to a question of making men change their behaviour and appearance in relatively trivial ways. It may, however, be a necessary transitional stage between that of no women – (to women getting the role of sexual objects) – and finally to equal treatment. Women here are still seen as clearly constituting a minority.

At the meeting it was stated positively that small project groups would be started up. The basic group of four would only assist in the starting up of these groups, however, and the initiative was to be decentralized. A PC mailbox was established where one could call up the latest news and where one could find information of interest in establishing a group on a given subject. The whole project almost came to nothing as there was no real initiative. The basic group found out that something more effective was needed if Scanweb was to work. Therefore, an external firm of consultants was approached which suggested day meetings to deal with specific themes as well as a large-scale conference,

where some important people from abroad are to speak not only about female managers but about management in general and where, of course, Jan Carlzon and other top managers must be present (female employee).

The purpose of this is to influence people's attitudes and point to the fact that "a lot of women are very active. By getting professionals to assist us and tell us how to do it, the whole issue can be promoted" (Scanweb member).

The reactions to Scanweb have been somewhat mixed. On one hand, it fitted very well into the philosophy of Carlzon who contributed by giving it official status from the start, something that had not been planned. On the other hand some people made fun of it and did not take it seriously. Most of the female and male managers who have been interviewed supported the idea. This does not mean that all female managers are necessarily members or even plan to work actively for the network. Some do not like the idea of establishing, what they named a lodge. Most of the female managers interviewed have, however, at some point been involved in the project.

In the beginning, the group of four behind Scanweb acquired the image of men with their own little lodge-like association and it was claimed to be a very exclusive association. They disliked this image, as one of their objectives was to get other women to join in and for themselves to function as a network for those involved. This exclusive masculine image was created in particular by other women.

Symbolically, it should not be possible to associate the name of Scanweb with a lodge. According to Gilligan's investigations of the thoughts and fantasies of women and men, web represents a female way of structuring relations and in her opinion is associated with a different self-perception. The top of the hierarchy becomes the outer edge of the network and, conversely, the middle of a hierarchy becomes the centre of the network. Therefore, in the opinion of Gilligan (which is perhaps somewhat stereotypical), each sex fears the other's imagery whereas females feel safe in a 'network' and males prefer a 'hierarchy'.

Thus the images of hierarchy and web inform different modes of assertion and response: The wish to be alone at the top and the consequent fear that others will get too close, the wish to be at the center of connection and the consequent fear of being too far out on the edge (Gilligan, 1982:62).

Scanweb has by some people been described as a lodge which was not related to its name but to its function which could be difficult to distinguish from a lodge when looked at by an outsider. The problem was, among other things, that many women would have liked to join but were unable to be admitted on account of the structure then in existence. The basic group wanted to stand on its own feet before passing on the idea to other women. The result of the criticism, however, was that the small 'association' was ended and (in principle) all women of SAS could become members of Scanweb if they so wished. However, not many activities were begun. In Sweden Scanweb attracted a women's lib image, men became afraid of it (according to a Swedish female manager), and the name of Scanweb was changed to "The Take Off". It became largely concerned with personnel development, in particular for the group of secretaries (jogging, assertiveness-training, make-up courses).

8.10 Discussion

The following dimensions seem to be of particular importance if one is to understand SAS from a gender perspective. They also explain what makes it easier and more difficult for women to achieve and function in SAS management positions:

- The past history of SAS, the dominating factor having been the origin of growth of the company as a 'machine bureaucracy' with a pronounced hierarchy and its main emphasis on technical values.
- The changes first and foremost during the 1980's, creating turbulence and new ways of thinking, primarily in its business aspects and customer orientation, but indirectly in all areas of the company.
- The results of these changes, such as the working method, the priorities, values, etc. that are characteristic of the organization at the time of the investigation.
- The relatively low level of training and education that is characteristic of large groups of the employees of the organizaiton.
- The long-term employment history of most SAS personnel. It is normal for personnel to be employed young and for them to make a career internally. Therefore the socialization within SAS is relatively strong as compared to organizations with a more extensive turnover of personnel or other organizations where those employed are somewhat older and have had experience in various places of work.
- The pronounced division of labour according to sex where there are men as pilots and technicians and managers at higher levels and women in service jobs and generally overrepresented at lower levels.

Historically, as described earlier, SAS has been dominated by a way of thinking which concentrated on production. What this has meant in concrete terms is described by Edström (1988:43) as follows:

Since the birth of aviation, safety has been of major importance. It has motivated large investments in education of engineers and pilots, careful control and follow up of indications on errors, and regularly check-ups of airplanes and engines. Detailed instructions and rules for maintenance as well as harsh sanctions against risk taking affecting safety were other significant ingredients. Quality, carefulness, control and planning were the values that dominated the organization. These values also permeated the relations between the people involved, for example the relationship between manager and co-workers. Management was centralized in order to assure a unitary behaviour in the entire system. Management was founded on expert knowledge with a strong emphasis on instructions.

Even though this working method and the priorities and way of thinking that follow from this view of the organization first and foremost characterized the technical and operative parts of the company and management, it indirectly influenced administrative and market/sales-oriented units. Traditionally, and this applies also in SAS, women seldom have chosen (or been encouraged to choose) the type of training or occupations that constituted the former core of the company, such as engineers and pilots. This meant that the number of upper management positions that women could apply for was limited.

Of more importance, however, were the consequences this had on the cultural level, i.e. expectations, perceptions, values, attitudes, etc.. The climate within the organization was influenced by the nature of the company. Thus expectations and perceptions of managerial behaviour were more in accordance with a typical male sex identity and male behaviour. The role of manager is therefore related to being technical and being a specialist and holding views in harmony with specialist-technical thinking. This favours male dominance in the general way of thinking and in the employment of people for management positions.

Both structurally, which demanded the right educational and occupational qualifications for certain high positions, and culturally, which moulded the thinking, the expectations and the symbols related to the role of manager, this historical mode of functioning at SAS made it more difficult for women to have access to high positions within the company. Also it is possible that it reduced women's interest in getting these positions. Traditional cultural patterns created or reinforced a feminine gender identity which was experienced as alien to higher management positions.

Two consequences resulted from the considerable changes that took place in SAS, when the production logic no longer dominated the company. One primarily concerns structural conditions, the other concerns the cultural sphere (values, meanings, perceptions, etc.).

From the structural point of view, the centre of gravity has shifted predominantly from production logic to the market factor. A certain decentralization of the organization has been effected, which has meant that more positions at a high level are open to those who are not technical experts. The service and market aspects of the company now have a greater impact which means that the competence and experience held by many women is more valued than formerly. From the point of view of qualifications, the higher levels of the organization are thus more open and accessible to them than earlier. This has contributed to a larger share of female managers than earlier.

When positions at a high level become accessible to women and are taken up by women, then the symbolic linking of the management role with the male sex becomes weaker. Previously this linking followed from the fact that management positions were associated with male holders and with the occupational background and qualifications that were typical for men but atypical for women. Thus a cultural change results from the structural change. The way of thinking as well as assumptions and expectations toward management became more flexible. The association of management and maleness was weakened. This was facilitated by the increased value put on the service functions in which women were well represented, while those parts of the company strongly dominated by men, primarily engineering, to some extent lost prestige and influence.

The relationship between the structural change and the changes in cultural understandings of gender and management is not, however, solely a matter of the former encouraging the latter. That a larger part of the higher functions and positions become available for women to strive for is not a simple 'objective' issue (as tends to be claimed by structuralists like Kanter, 1977). The opportunity structure does not simply exist and is mirrored in perceptions and expectations, but is in itself constructed by ideas and actions of people, including women who may or may not think in terms of career and promotion. The cultural change and the increase in experienced confidence and importance of service personnel may have affected the mental 'opening up' of managerial positions as increasingly available for persons with other backgrounds than those traditionally promoted to jobs on higher levels. In this sense, not only a structural change from above, but also changes in meaning patterns from below are contributing to redefine the view on management and managerial jobs. Such a redefinition created new or at least modified opportunity structures which thus, in the next step, further reinforced cultural changes in relationship to gender and management. Our point is thus that opportunity structures not only interact with and affect culture but must themselves be seen as a cultural constructions.

SAS changed its way of functioning and the consequences of this affected women's possibilities – primarily in a concrete sense, but also secondarily as regards a broad set of meanings and attitudes, including those of gender and management. It is interesting to note how a rapid, forceful, and dramatic corporate change can have side effects. Such changes as experienced in SAS can lead to a general weakening of fixed perceptions. New ways of thinking, awareness of problems and willingness to undertake change are now important in the company. Even those fields not directly exposed to change can find their earlier fixed mental structures beginning to shift. Once certain perceptions are shaken, others can also be affected. One could say that the winds of change in general blow strongly and affect even those that are some distance from the centre of the storm.

The changes in SAS during the 1980's in business thinking, in strategy and organizational structure, in image, and in management do not necessarily in themselves affect gender relations. The only direct consequence of these changes in terms of gender and management is that the number of high-level positions open to female applicants increases somewhat. The fact that women can apply for top posts does not mean that they will do so or when they do that they will necessarily get the job. Within SAS, the question of sex importance has not been of any major importance during the process of transition. Neither the percentage of women holding management positions nor the abstract relationship between 'masculine' and 'feminine' managerial qualities has affected to any extent the strategic changes adopted by SAS during the 1980's. Presumably, the management of SAS did not think about the possible consequences until they occurred after a period of time. One gets the feeling that it is a low-priority area even though Carlzon's (1987) book on SAS refers to the sex of those in management positions. However, these changes are in harmony with the beliefs of Jan Carlzon and as mentioned earlier they have to some extent been supported by him.

What is most interesting and important is the indirect effect of the change within the company. This new way of thinking and the openness to change also affects the outlook on gender within the company, though not to a revolutionary extent. Here we have a small number of female managers at a high level who are conscious that only 6 out of 156 participants in a SAS decision making conference are women, and who find this extraordinary and so set up Scanweb. Thus we see that a certain phenomenon is no longer taken for granted or blindly accepted. This tendency to seriously question a phenomenon that was earlier accepted and thought unchangeable and to now see it as something extraordinary and problematic and furthermore to take action to change it, shows that a new insight is more likely in a turbulent than in a static environment.

Obviously the questioning arising from this problem and the consciousness it aroused is not an isolated phenomenon. Throughout the 1980's this type of question has been given great attention within society in general. A considerable change in consciousness has taken place and a number of definite changes have occurred. The modernization of perceptions about the sexes and the relations between them which is a characteristic of more advanced societies, and even to some degree have influenced some organizations, has certainly characterized SAS more than many other companies. One could say that within SAS the general, societal modernization process accelerated at the local level, compared to the situation before the 'cultural revolution' within the company. This compares favourably with many other organizations.

The two factors mentioned, the structural consequences of a radical process of change and changed cultural ideas within the company, thus contribute to making it somewhat easier for women to reach higher positions in SAS. However, our examination indicated that it is still unusual for women to hold management positions. Developments in this respect are not particularly rapid.

Factors concerning the speed of change deserve a further examination but first it is necessary to qualify previous comments on the scope and depth of the organizational change in SAS. Descriptions of such changes easily focus on what has been altered but overlook what has not been changed. This applies to the descriptions of both those interviewed and those doing research. Qualitative changes of a complex nature cannot be described using quantitative terms. Thus SAS is easily portrayed as a dynamic, decentralized, market-oriented company. This is probably a correct picture, compared to the conditions prevailing in SAS formerly, but in relation to many other organizations, such as more flexible high-technology companies or those where different project tasks dominate, SAS is a company that may be described as relatively centrally governed, hierarchical, formalized.

The task of the SAS company is to offer services on a mass basis. The basic air transport activities are necessarily governed by technical rationality, based on care, control, planning, and safety measures. The majority of the activities are routine activities. Basically, SAS can be described as a machine bureaucracy (Mintzberg, 1983), although with many organic and 'soft' characteristics.

The above-mentioned aspects obviously do not offset the fact that the organizational changes have had certain very clear consequences. The purpose here is to discuss the scope of these effects and relate this to what has characterized SAS (and similar companies) in the past and continues to do so also in present.

An organization is always strongly influenced by its history. The importance of history shows itself partly at an overall, aggregate and total organizational level and partly in the manner of socialization and earlier experience of the staff of the company. The inertia and the preserving effect of history and tradition vary. The deepest and most stable is what cultural researchers call basic assumptions, i.e. the idea of the basic nature of human beings, the activities of the organization, its relations with the surrounding world. All these conditions are taken for granted and normally not accessible for conscious reflection (see for instance Schein, 1985).

Certain forms of behaviour are easy to change. Attitudes usually go deeper and are therefore less easily shifted, while values and assumptions often go deepest of all and since we are unconscious of them and take them for granted are the hardest to change. A person's self or identity is influenced by history to an even greater extent. A person's sexual identity is one part of his/her identity. A central aspect of the person's identity is the feeling of coherence, confidence, security, and self-assurance in his/her life (Erikson, 1955). A person's assurance of his own identity makes it easier for him/her to resist certain frustrations and difficulties and reduces uncertainty and fear.

A person's identity may be understood in terms of many different aspects and dimensions. What is of most interest in our context is the work identity of a person. In part it is shaped by the identity of the person as a whole but also by background, experience, etc. within previous work situations.

Thus a person's work identity is shaped by a number of different factors. Their life before entering the labour market is important. It includes one's experience while growing up, parental models and influence from other important adults. Education is of central importance, and so is the occupation as a source of self-perception and identity. The socialization that follows after one has started working and the experience gained at various places of work are also essential. What expectations and values does one encounter? What picture of oneself do the surroundings provide? How is one's self-perception influenced and possibly changed? What models and ideals are available?

In a company such as SAS where the majority of the employees begin their working life with the company when they are young after a relatively short education and without experience from other places of work, the socialization within the organization is very important in the development of their identity. Not only the most recent years of socialization, but also the cultural outcomes of the socialization of the past 10, 15 or 20 years will be communicated to the contemporary SAS employees.

On the basis of this, we are better able to understand what many of those interviewed refer to when they say that women do not 'dare' apply for management positions. An understanding of the phenomenon requires a more extensive illustration than one which is kept within the framework of the organization, but here we shall not do more than underline the importance of the organization. Female employees of SAS who have reached an age where management posts become possible, i.e. 35-40 years, have in many instances a socialization at the place of work that is characterized by the traditional division of labour according to sex. The large majority of all management positions at the higher levels have been occupied by men, and therefore typical male experience, competence, orientations, etc. were related to the management role and vice versa. This will affect attitudes and perceptions and also women's and men's own identity. While attitudes and expectations are far from easy to influence and change, the cultural socialization which has been internalized goes considerably deeper.

A certain discrepancy between the identity developed by the socialization at the workplace and (women's notions regarding) the management role has thus become salient for many female employees of SAS. Thus the previous male dominance within the company contributes to the uncertainty, the ambivalence and the low self-confidence of many women when it comes to applying for and functioning in management positions. The male dominance has decreased and the present dominance reproduces only partially the traditional blocking of women as managers.

To some extent the possible effects of the relatively low educational level that is a characteristic of SAS employees (with the exception of the groups of engineers and pilots who are almost 100% men) contribute to the lack of accordance between the identity of many women and their attitudes to management positions. We found that the majority of potential female managers have no qualifying formal education like an MBA to fall back on. As indicated before, this applies also to many male managers and is a general feature within SAS. This means that the symbolic confirmation and self confidence afforded by higher education is lacking. Higher education will often teach the employee useful, technical knowledge and other subjects of value, but of even greater importance in our context are the socialization skills, the acquisition of cultural capital and a general confirmation of one's identity that result from such higher education. In higher education one has colleagues who believe that a career within trade and industry is a natural continuation of their life. Higher education thus provides social and cultural support for a further management career. This differs from the lack of support one has when starting in SAS when one is young and has only colleagues with varying and on average probably not very keen career ambitions.

Therefore, our thesis is that higher education provides a better basis for women to attain higher job positions. The same applies to men. However, education may not be as central to men's attainments. The existing social and cultural conditions make it easier for them, as compared with women, to get management positions. Therefore their need for symbolic support by way of a qualifying education is not so great.

The generally low formal educational level in SAS also plays a different role (at least compared to organizations such as BSW and the Foreign Ministry). There exists a lower degree of 'modernity' and 'sophistication' relating to the sexes and the equality between the sexes than exists in those parts of society where the educational level is higher. We shall later revert to the question of how much the conditions promoting modernization by way of a 'cultural revolution' and its 'offspring', Scanweb, have counteracted this.

It is likely that more educated groups which are influenced strongly by great cultural capital can see more quickly that the way of thinking about the sexes is influenced by conservatism and prejudices. These educated groups see that modern, enlightened individuals favour equality between the sexes, at least to some extent. Older and less educated groups are probably often behind the others in this process. Within the highly educated group one may assume that those with 'cultural capital' are more in favour of social progress than those with 'technical knowledge capital'. Teachers, humanists, social scientists, and psychologists belong to the first group, while graduate engineers belong to the second, while economists and administrators perhaps belong to the middle.

As the cultural capital is not so great within SAS it may be assumed that equality is also lacking here when compared to other sectors of society where consciousness and progressiveness of participants are greater.

8.11 Summary

One reason for choosing SAS for this investigation was that to the public at large the organization appeared to have a progressive image with its new ideals of management, its interest in emphasizing the female aspects of the management role, and also its talk about a new horizontal organizational structure, etc.. It appeared interesting to take a closer look at all of these conditions in SAS with a view to finding the possible barriers that exist when women apply for and function in management positions.

Prior to the investigation we assumed that the composition of the sexes within SAS-Denmark would be equal, i.e. that an equal number of women and men would be employed in the company. We found however that only one third of the employees are women as opposed to the employees of SAS-Sweden, where half of the labour-force is women. The uneven distribution of the sexes in SAS-Denmark may reflect the pronounced division of labour by sexes that exists. In the technical division men are much in the majority, for instance. This division has made some attempt to attract more applications from women.

The division of labour by sex is important for women in general in SAS because it makes it more difficult for them to become visible and acquire the necessary qualifications to be able to cope with a management job. Their lack of visibility means that women are rarely hand-picked for management jobs. For many of them the work is a means of getting a salary rather than a career. This also applies to many of the men. As most of the employees of SAS have been SAS-trained and are expected to be generalists, a lot of them should be potential applicants for many management positions. As already mentioned, 'specialists' were earlier more often appointed managers, i.e. these were mostly men who had shown their expertise within a specific, narrow field. Even though SAS has dropped this policy, it takes some time before the old expectations of norms for sexual roles are overcome, contributing to the result that in SAS first and foremost managers are men.

Many, both men and women in SAS, have stated that women must be more competent than men in order to become managers, and they must also be highly visible. Their experience is that women must produce better results. Therefore, probably it is not only an internalized barrier within women themselves that exists when they say that they must comply with all the qualification requirements of an advertisement, "even 150%", before they take the chance and apply for the job. Perhaps it is true that men can apply for the job when under-qualified as they are expected to be able to cope with the job, whereas women are not expected to apply unless they are over-qualified for the same job. It is not so difficult to understand why women are often uncertain and ambivalent when it comes to applying for management positions. It may be an outcome of a mixture of psychology and realistic evaluations of the situation. The female managers refer a great deal to the wording of the advertisements and Scanweb has attempted to influence the wording of advertisements so that they appeal also to women. In actual terms this means that the advertisements are made less high powered.

Another reported difference between women and men in SAS-Denmark concerns the way that the rules of the game within the organization affect them. There is a specific set of rules to be learned, first to feel free to apply for management positions and then to be able to cope with meetings. Another reason that women do not apply for management positions relates to their internalized barriers. Women tend to be more perfectionistic, to over-emphasize formalities, etc.. This 'exaggeration' of the difficulties of the job may result in a lack of self-confidence that is reinforced by the lack of the symbolic support of higher education which is usually regarded as proof of a certain competence. It seems that many employees of the parts of SAS-Denmark that we have studied, both women and men, are locked in a number of more traditional sex role patterns (than we found, for instance, within the National Board of Social Welfare and the Ministry of Foreign Affairs).

Scanweb has attempted to question these traditional ideas of the place of women and men in the work place. The network of women has actually been useful to the women that have participated in the group. Connections have been formed, and since they have been aware of each other it has been helpful in finding candidates when management positions were to be filled. Scanweb has also confronted the barrier or defence mechanism, entitled 'dare not'. A female manager mentions the essential point that women's tendency is to guard against defeat by stressing the fact that it does not matter so much if they do not get the job. This is a form of female masochism which causes one to blame oneself, when things do not work out as one had hoped. This attitude does guard oneself against defeat but it dissipates one's energy and could even prevent one from making future applications.

In this organization it is seen clearly that many women and men come with their own gender cultural background. Both women and men emphasize the fact that women have a different view of things to men. The paradox is that whereas in the interview situation men say they look for and want female characteristics in management, yet when they become managers women describe how difficult or impossible it is to play according to their own female rules. They have to play by the male rules in order to be taken seriously and get anything through in committees. There seem to be very clear differences between the sexes. Men do not like the way women negotiate. They feel that women violate the rules of the game when they present proposals at meetings that have not been 'agreed' between members beforehand. It should be mentioned that the male managers interviewed were not necessarily the same men whom some of the female managers interviewed have met with during meetings.

Another difference noted between female and male managers is that almost all women were relatively relaxed about a shift in status. Actually most of them declared that they were willing to "go down the ladder" again. None of the men expressed a similar attitude. This is probably also related to the social expectations men have of themselves. If they were to leave their management position this would be regarded as a defeat and not a free choice. However, it is easier for women to retreat as it will be accepted as understandable if women do not, after all, want to be managers. Some women and men might be of the opinion that they were not able to cope after all. It appears that female managers regard their work as managers as a kind of mission. They are open for the possibility of quitting when they have solved the task specified.

Scanweb was set up when the female managers realized how few they were, and what a problem this was. The purpose of Scanweb was, among other things, to create a network for all women in SAS and also to help to find a new kind of manager with certain qualifications that resemble those described by Carlzon in his book (1987). Scanweb has not managed to become known to the great majority of women at SAS-Denmark. Possibly this was because the early Scanweb members were an elite and focused to such a great extent on management positions. Perhaps they have not had a genuine interest in focusing on the majority of women. In Sweden where Scanweb changed its name to "The Take Off" it had to a much greater degree success in getting women interested. In Sweden the Scanweb members have chosen to use their resources to help personnel development and have a firm basis in the trade unions. They have made an effort to 'lift' the group of secretaries by offering various courses with the aim of "development of women", such as education, self-confidence, assertiveness-training courses, appearance (composition of colours, etc.) and exercise. The support has been great. This involves in some cases a reinforcement of 'typical' female ways of behaviour and therefore can hardly contribute to reducing stereotypes as regards the sexes.

In Denmark, on the other hand, an external firm of consultants was given the task of planning a number of days with specific themes for women and men, on "women in management", etc.. If the strategy is to get more women in leading positions and able to cope, etc., this is a way of making propaganda for women. If the strategy is, on the other hand, to create a network (cf. the name) for the women of SAS-Denmark it seems rather strange to arrange mass meetings which are known in advance and which only attract those with an interest in problems of career and management. It seems that in Scanweb the aim is primarily to be close to Carlzon's thoughts and get more female managers. It is not the more ambitious aim that was once presented of creating a network for all women of SAS. The question is whether a large group of women will be overlooked by following the new strategy?

There may be two possible strategies for assisting and increasing the number of female managers. One is to give women in general more support through courses, in-service training, seminars, etc. and hope that as a result they will want to apply for management positions. This strategy is an indirect consequence of efforts to accomplish a general improvement of women's situation, through mutual support, etc.. The other strategy was the one chosen by SAS-Denmark; focusing on management jobs. They use the tactic of persuasion, convincing upper management that good potential female candidates are available already who can by various means, such as learning to sell themselves better become managers. The latter strategy will probably work for a small selected group and make it easier for potential female managers to be selected for management positions. However, the first strategy works for the great majority of women and may contribute to creating an environment at the place of work more conducive to the promotion of women managers and thus have an indirect influence on general management and help in the recruitment of women for management positions. Of course, this approach is much more demanding and perhaps uncertain in pay-off in terms of women getting more managerial jobs.

Notes

1   No doubt there are others in addition to female writers and managers who advocate these forms of organization; actually the female managers in no way set the trend in the reorganization within SAS. It must be seen as an open question whether most female managers favour flat organizations.
2   In this organization a common expression for women was "girls", whereas men were referred to as men. Women as well as men used the expression "girls". This was only salient in SAS.

9   The Danish Ministry of Foreign Affairs

9.1   Introduction

One of the criteria for choosing the Ministry of Foreign Affairs (MFA) was that it seemed to be strongly male-dominated. There were very few female managers. Another criterion for choosing MFA has been its high prestige in the eyes of the public. For this reason, there is always keen competition to be recruited by the ministry, to get one of the attractive foreign postings and later in one's career to achieve a managerial position necessary for ambassadorial appointments.

Although the organization has a very equal distribution of the sexes in terms of the total number of employees there is a very pronounced gender hierarchy. The large majority of clerical employees are women (approximately 70%) and men constitute 86% of the graduates (university graduates, heads of divisions and above). Altogether there are 410 university graduates in the Ministry of Foreign Affairs (56 women and 354 men in 1988). Of these, 136 are in managerial positions (4 of whom are women). Women thus have about 3% of the managerial posts. The 410 are employed in what is called the ordinary service. This requires that the employees participate in a job rotation system and are available for transfer. This ministry differs from other ministries and the large majority of organizations, in particular on account of the long-term stationing abroad of personnel.

Besides the employees in the 'ordinary service', there are other employees in the ministry who deal with special tasks (e.g. in the Department of Danish International Development Aid – Danida). By and large we have chosen to disregard these special groups in our investigation as they do not take part in the 'normal' rotation and stationing arrangement.

In the ministry there are three departments; the Department of Foreign Affairs, the Department of Foreign Trade and Industry and the Department of International Development. The interviews primarily took place in the two departments where there were female managers at the time of the study, and these were the Department of Foreign Trade and Industry and the Department of Danish International Development Aid. A total of 16 were interviewed (9 women, 7 men), of these 6 were heads of divisions (managers) the remaining ten were (non-managerial) graduates (of whom some were heads of sections). The interviewees are all university graduates.

First we present a general introduction to the organization. After this, we describe the circumstances relating to recruitment of new employees, their terms of employment, overseas postings, etc. We provide a description of the recruitment of managers and the course of their career. Finally, we describe the special problems and difficulties met by female managers and other women. This is followed by a general description of the working environment and a discussion of the circumstances that may explain the low number of female managers and the unequal distribution of the sexes within the organization as a whole. As with the study of the National Board of Social Welfare, our investigation concentrates on the group who are university graduates, since managers (heads of division) and those at higher levels are recruited almost exclusively from this group. The rigid principle of promotion could be studied but that is outside the scope of our investigation. The remaining personnel is mentioned only marginally.

As we wished to speak primarily with the female managers, we mainly interviewed in the two (out of the three) departments where female managers are employed. The Office of Administration found male managers who have been complementary to the three female managers as regards their position and number of subordinates.

In addition to this, six graduates (potential managers) have been interviewed who were directly responsible to the interviewed managers. Although their formal titles are heads of section and deputy chiefs respectively, leadership and management is not central in these jobs, it is restricted to some responsibility for one to three subordinates. In addition to this, three graduates employed in the Department of Foreign Affairs have been interviewed. Finally, a few graduates and a manager from the Office of Administration were interviewed. There are no female managers at levels higher than head of division. Nor have any male managers at higher levels (deputy undersecretaries of state, undersecretaries of state) been interviewed. The career structure for the professional class starts with the recruitment of university graduates.[1] From the level of manager (head of division) it is possible to be appointed ambassador. In the following we concentrate on the titles graduate, manager, senior/top managers.

9.2   A picture of the organization

9.2.1 General

The Department of Foreign Affairs was established as a government system in 1848. The third department (Danida) was established as a sub department in 1960 and as a full department in 1987.

Politically the Ministry of Foreign Affairs is headed by the Minister for Foreign Affairs, administratively by a permanent secretary. The activities of the ministry are divided into political, service and assistance and administrative tasks. The ministry is divided into three departments. The first department is the Department of Foreign Affairs which is responsible for the organization of the foreign service as well as the representation of foreign countries in Denmark, general questions relating to foreign policy as well as information, co-operation with the foreign press, etc.. The second department is the Department of Foreign Trade and Industry. The following matters belong under this department: questions relating to the EEC and other questions relating to foreign economy and trade policy as well as tasks relating to export promotion. The third department is the Department of International Development which is concerned with cooperation in the field of international development and aid to developing countries.

Each department is subdivided into three sections, these sections are in turn divided into divisions. Each division has a staff of 10-20, and may have three or four working groups. Here, one or more members of staff under the management of a more experienced head will be responsible for a given field. (For the organizational structure, see Table 1.)

Table 1: The organizational structure in the Ministry of Foreign Affairs and the corresponding title in the hierarchy

Minister			
			CEO
1. Dept. Foreign Affairs	2. Dept. Trade & Industry	3. Dept. International Development	Secretary of State
Sub-departments			Deputy Secretary of State
Divisions			Managers (heads of division)
Sections			Heads of section University graduates Clerical staff

The organization has a total staff of approximately 1,250 (1988). Of these just over half are commercial and clerical employees (who are not university graduates) and women constitute approximately 75% of these. As mentioned before we are concerned primarily with managers at middle management level (head of divison). The lower management levels such as, for instance, those in charge of clerical staff, heads of small sections or working groups are thus not regarded as managers in the investigation.

There are approximately 410 civil servants who are university graduates (including managers) of which 14% are women. Women's share of the managerial positions is 3% (4 women out of 136). Of the graduates 20% are women. 8% of all the women, 40% of all the men in this category are managers. As the university graduates constitute both the group of managers and the only potential managers, we are primarily concerned with this category.

After Denmark's entry into the EEC in 1972, tasks have increased considerably because of a greater need for coordination of the political and economic cooperation within the EEC. Therefore, according to one male manager, there is some flexibility in the second department, over EEC questions, etc. as compared to the traditional structure of the departments and the accompanying bureaucracy found to a greater extent in the first department. This manager says that it is necessary to work across the sub-departments and it may also be necessary to approach the minister directly when the situation demands. However, the usual procedure is that a matter goes through the "machinery" (a metaphor used by several of those interviewed), from graduate to head of section, head of division, deputy secretary of state, secretary of state, etc..

The typical procedure is the hierarchy. Most of the matters we deal with are fortunately in terms of time of such a nature that we can reasonably quickly get them through the hierarchy.

For the EEC matters we obviously use the hierarchy. They must go through the whole machinery. However, in a large number of instances, where the matters are more individual, a more flexible arrangement is probably used, an arrangement which spreads out the pyramid – if that expression can be used.

One of the managers interviewed explains that the fact that it is a bureaucracy and that it is structured as a hierarchy is related to the fact that there is one minister for a very large field. This is the reason why a number of traditional working procedures are maintained. When the work process has been rendered hierarchical, this, in his opinion, provides the necessary control needed throughout the system.

Most people think that hierarchy is a sensible way of organizing a large administrative machinery. It is a guarantee for the individual member of staff that everything has been checked; "we could by accident insult another country". Hierarchy, formal lines of reporting, control, surveillance and predictability are important work organization principles. From the point of view of the subordinates it can be unsatisfactory to lose the sense of what is being thought at the top of the hierarchy.

The price one has to pay for it is, of course, that one need not go very far down in the hierarchy before the sense of what the minister thinks in the fields for which one is responsible at that level of the hierarchy starts disappearing. And it is a balancing act that is very difficult (male manager).

On the other hand, I feel that as compared to other ministries we are extremely well-organized administratively because we have so many fixed procedures. There is no doubt that on the technical, administrative front we are quite well-developed in this ministry. Sometimes, you may call this heavy (same manager).

Many describe it as "heavy", particularly in relationship to when things have to be taken care of quickly. This heavy aspect concerns also the fact that even high up in the hierarchy it is difficult to get access to the minister. Notes and messages passed down through the hierarchy are not the same as listening to the minister's own statements, therefore it is a question of becoming good at communicating things in the correct way so that flow of stream of information becomes 'even'. Some of those interviewed feel that they have become relatively good at this, although they do not always succeed, however.

Many think that there is a general interest in reducing the hierarchy, achieving a structure that is more 'flat' and which is divided into smaller units. Because of the "authoritarian" hierarchy (as it is called by some) and the bureaucracy, the ministry is regarded as a little more old-fashioned than other ministries also in terms of the style and appearance of the personnel. The ministry appears more conservative than many other parts of Danish public administration, and traditions for clothing are, for example, somewhat old-fashioned.

You will not find any women wearing blue jeans. Nor will you ... or only very, very rarely will you find men wearing blue jeans. There are a few who have come from other agencies where it has been natural. And these have not really adapted to the organization. But you will see it only very rarely for everybody knows that we get all sorts of visitors (female graduate).

All the men interviewed wore a jacket and tie and all the women wore skirts with the exception of one graduate in trousers. As is pointed out in the interview, people from other ministries and workplaces joining the ministry need a certain period of adaptation as regards clothing. They must get used to the style first.

Yes, we are more formal in the Ministry of Foreign Affairs. But this is also related to the fact that so many people from abroad come visiting. They would find it strange if we were wearing roll-neck sweaters and no tie. For when I was working in the commission (in Brussels), you did not see a man without a tie. I should think that if somebody came to work without a tie, attention would be called to it. At least I remember once at a meeting ... (male manager).

And the ministry has, in fact, always been known to be the most conservative in its dress code. The question is, then, whether this more formal attire affects or reflects more general attitudes, an unpersonal and conservative workclimate.

I don't think so, but I am not quite sure that this is quite correct for, as already mentioned, I don't know how things work at other places, but one could perhaps say that the clothes we wear alone shows that we are a little more conservative in our attitude in general (male graduate).

Even though the organization is in parts, almost 150 years old, it is difficult to describe it as old-fashioned given that the architecture counteracts this impression. It is designed like a fashionable-looking 'warehouse' and with modern furniture, and among the staff one sees many fashion-conscious, elegantly dressed clerks and graduates. Those higher up in the hierarchy are more traditional. Their style corresponds to the image of the Ministry of Foreign Affairs, viz. that it is a ministry with high prestige that can 'pick and choose' among applicants for jobs there.

Not everybody, though, acknowledges that the ministry has a high status. They question how much prestige is actually connected to the ministry at the present day.

In the old days it probably had prestige. At that time it was believed that polished floors and that kind of thing was something special and something very distinguished. Once one is inside one may question how much prestige there is related to it all (female graduate).

The fact that it was regarded as something distinguished, something posh is probably a misunderstanding for, in fact, it is hard work like everything else, but people believe that it is something which is very, very distinguished, where one goes around to cocktail-parties all day (male graduate).

Internally the different departments and sub-departments differ in status with the political sub-department at the top. This may be related to the fact that this sub-department was the original Ministry of Foreign Affairs which existed as a department before 1848. One graduate expresses it as follows, "Everything else is just mushrooming, something new that has been added".

For this reason the political sub-department feels somewhat superior to the other sub-departments. One of the male managers interviewed believes that the more down-to-earth the work, the lower is the status and prestige of the sub-department.

At one time there was a tendency that those with the thickest carpets and the closed doors and corridors felt they were somewhat above those who like us got a little dirt on our hands because we came too close to the market place. We were not sitting there issuing decrees on the way of the world and things like that (male manager).

Being responsible for the connections to other nations is something special – this is so also in other countries, it is being somewhat closer to God than to what the rest of us are doing (another male manager).

On the basis of this notion of the nature of the work, the Department of International Development is regarded as having the lowest status. In this department there are relatively more female graduates, presumably on account of the nature of the work. Apparently women are attracted more by work concerned with aid and personnel questions. Alternatively, superiors believe that they should work there. Interviewees say that the Department of International Development has lower status because "the work is more down-to-earth, more specific, more tangible." It could, however, also be related to the fact that the composition of the staff is different in this department. Those who are employed as specialists have a longer professional experience behind them and are therefore on average some-what older than those who are employed in the ordinary service. Their educa-tional background is also more varied, from teachers, social workers to engi-neers, social anthropologists, etc.. It should be noted that the style when it comes to clothing is more relaxed in this department than in the rest of the organization. In general, however, the Ministry of Foreign Affairs has a high status.

9.2.2 The working environment

In the ministry, people talk with each other and about each other, they have friends across the departments and sub-departments, and many see each other privately. This is seen by one interviewee as a consequence of their being in the same 'boat' as regards being transferred backwards and forwards.

Even though many also build up friendships with foreigners when stationed abroad, the experience is that these are more difficult to maintain, which means that the circle of friends established at home is cared for. Yet people often be-come rootless when they continually alternate between being abroad and at home (and alternating between a high standard of living and a more average standard). It is difficult for others to understand this peculiar life style. When people are working in the Ministry of Foreign Affairs they easily isolate them-selves from the rest of society. They easily feel they are something "special", according to many of the interviewees (women and men).

It is generally believed that special characteristics are required to be in the ministry.

It requires that one is open-minded ... that one is flexible. It requires that one is very extrovert. That is almost the most important, for the work consists in having contact with other people and getting other people to provide one with a lot of information, and it requires negotiating and convincing them that the view held by Denmark is the only right view.

There is some (but relatively limited) social life in the Ministry of Foreign Af-fairs outside the normal work context. There is the usual Christmas lunch party at work – and a tradition has been established with a little wine on Friday after-noons, an idea that many enjoy for it gives them the possibility of talking about things not related to work. And finally, there may be farewell parties for those who are to be stationed abroad. Outside the organization it is more difficult for people to get together, especially when those high up in the hierarchy do not attend. One of those interviewed said that some had attempted to arrange an evening out, but when the heads sent an excuse none of those lower down in the hierarchy wanted to "waste time" on it.

The workplace is described as being characterized by "esprit de corps" though this can perhaps seem a little paradoxical in consideration of the keen competi-tion for the managerial positions.

On the one hand people have sharp elbows, on the other hand people really stick together. There is an esprit de corps here which you do not find at very many other place in the central administration. However, I do think it would be wrong completely to ignore the fact that there is also a battle for the managerial positions.

Those interviewed state that the Ministry of Foreign Affairs is probably one of the ministries with the strongest interest in careers, or, as the people within the ministry describe it, the greatest fixation on numbers. The designation is explained as follows:

Well, yes we call it 'fixation on numbers' for when a person is appointed manager he enters what is called the 37th grade, as a civil servant, and that is getting a number. And we are very fixated on everything related to our career. Among other things because one must be in the 37th grade or over in order to become an ambassador and therefore we talk about it a lot. The Ministry of Foreign Affairs is also famous for talking much about itself when people from the Ministry of Foreign Affairs visit other ministries. I know that many people are tired of listening to us and our career prospects and our looking up in the little grey book where all members of staff are listed with date of birth and date of when they first came to the ministry, where they have been, so there is a lot of talk (female graduate).

The fact that it may cost something in relation to family and friends is a problem, but the problem can be overcome.

If you are career-minded, and I think I can say that in general you are when you get into this system, well, then I don't think that it is a problem, for you will willingly sacrifice it. I don't think you look at the problem that way, for you willingly do this. And in general people are interested in their career.

All are career-minded. They'll do anything for their career. And the system is arranged so that you feel all the time that you are on your way up.

The interviewees state that climate or the environment is not to a great extent affected by the fact that a number of the university graduates employed do not obtain the popular 37th grade, and this they believe has to do with the fact that hope never disappears. Even though everybody knows that not all can reach the high positions, every individual believes that he/she will be among those that get such a position. "Everybody believes they will reach a high position and probably we all believe that" (male graduate).

I think that people will always have this hope, I have myself wondered about it a lot for in my opinion the administrative office would have to back out at some point in time if they really felt that there was no possibility for people of getting managerial posts and then a niche would have to be found for them. ... I have myself worked with a colleague who has for the past 5-6 years felt that now it would be his turn to be promoted and when I discussed these thoughts with him on a theoretical level he said that hope should never be taken away from people for that would destroy their ability to work and their joy in working.

Only a few of those interviewed have complained that the career orientation has had a disadvantageous influence on the working climate. Some describe the tone of voice people use at the place of work to be 'barren'- there is no climate. Others feel that the climate is affected by the fact that some staff groups do not have access to the top positions and still others feel that they are often ignored. Many interviewees believe that it is a general (or political) wish that more women obtain managerial positions. Some think that it is also related to considerations as regards the working climate, that in consideration of the climate it would be better if more women obtain these posts.

9.3 Recruitment for and career tracks within the Ministry of Foreign Affairs

9.3.1 Start of the career

There are many applicants for positions in the Ministry of Foreign Affairs. Most often university graduates in political science or economics, law graduates and science graduates are in demand but some humanities graduates have also been employed.

Formerly considerably more men than women were recruited but now it is different. The administration office has provided the information that women now constitute approximately 25% of the applicants, 33% of those that are interviewed and 50% of those that are employed (1988-89). This seems to be a rough classification. Statistics have not been available and unfortunately it has not been possible to obtain information on the share of women in various recruitment rounds and in relation to the number of applicants for promotions to managerial positions.

When new staff are recruited, the Office of Administration cooperates with the sub-department that needs the new staff, "However, it is rather difficult to state any rules, most of what takes place is under the table rather than over" (male graduate).

A basic principle is that the person in question must be one who can be deployed anywhere. The reason for this is that a job in an embassy demands that the employee must be capable of coping with everything, it is no use being capable of doing some specific work only. Those employed thus must have a feeling of what is going on in the other sections as well. Therefore, the candidate in question is interviewed in various sub-departments (an interview lasting 30 minutes at 5 or 6 different places) and it is tried to get an impression of the ability of the person in question to fit into the system in Denmark, but also of his/her ability to fit into the system at the embassies, etc.. The candidate will be asked to give an account of, for instance, the conflict in the Lebanon, to interpret a section of the constitution and to say where Kuala Lumpur is and in the Office of Administration the candidate is also asked about family status and other matters that may be of importance for being stationed abroad. There have been discussions as to whether other 'objective' criteria should be used, but such criteria have not yet been introduced.

The other sorting out process takes place during the first two years' trial period where people are employed at two different places. The managers observe the new members of staff and prepare bi-annual reports on them. New members of staff who are regarded as being unsuitable for the job however will get a report after six months (if possible) which says that they are not suitable.

These reports concern the personality of the members of staff, their way of coping with various matters, their abilities, including their ability to make contacts, and their relationship with colleagues, internally and externally, and their ability to distinguish between important and unimportant aspects when dealing with matters, and whether they are generally suited for foreign service. All of this will cover one A4 page. The report will be filed together with the personnel notes in the Office of Administration and the members of staff receive a copy. People who are not found suited are asked to apply for a job outside the ministry. Only in extreme situations are people sacked. "It is attempted as discreetly as possible to make people understand that the best is for them to disappear of their own free will. But I think that they rarely say, now it is over" (male graduate).

During the first 15 years of employment a report will be prepared every time a member of staff changes from one sub-department to another. The reports are not detailed. For those who have become permanently employed they are in general more positive. Many people think that they are not of very great importance seen in relation to qualifying for higher grades. In this connection altogether different matters are of importance, as discussed below.

9.3.2 Stationing abroad

After the two-year trial period comes the first overseas posting. It lasts for three years. It is decided at top level where the member of staff is to go, according to agreed guidelines. The members of staff apply for posts themselves and get them according to seniority. After the first posting, lasting for three years, the person in question returns and is then stationed abroad for four years. In this instance the member of staff applies for a post but seniority is no longer the decisive factor.

The compulsory overseas posting makes some people leave the Ministry of Foreign Affairs. All along, more women than men leave the service. Most of them have left the ministry for family reasons. They did not want to be stationed abroad after having had children. "We should have known this. I thought that I would be able to manage at some point in time or other" (female manager).

The problem of working abroad has also become relevant for men who have married career women. These women will not any longer automatically join their husbands when the men are stationed abroad.

Competition is keen for the attractive jobs in for example Rome, London and Washington. Advance notice is published of the posts that will be vacant during the year to come. The guidelines for deciding who will get the post are complex and hard to grasp.

Applicants talk with various people and try to find backing for being chosen according to rather complex rules that are not to be found in print anywhere. This is just as suspect as the rest of the system. The Office of Administration will claim that the procedure is according to fixed rules, but it is not (male graduate).

Typically, the applicant will try to get the support of his/her sub-department. "You will not necessarily get those with the best qualifications for the best posts in this way. But there is nothing you can do to change it."

Once it is known who is the next candidate for a position as manager, many do not consider applying for the position at all, for it has already been 'filled'. Everybody knows that it is not just a question of formal merits as such, it is more a question of one department's battle against the other. Everything is decided in the corridors. If one department has managed to secure the position of manager for a member of staff, a different department will demand to acquire the next, since getting one's candidates through involves prestige.

Some believe that this way of fighting over the posts does not serve the interest of the organization. Stationing abroad for the first time is much less complex as the rules are more straight-forward. After that it is more up to those at top level to decide – and here the sub-departments support their own candidates.

9.4   The job as a lifestyle

There is something attractive about the Ministry of Foreign Affairs because the work is interesting and it is regarded as a place with very great possibilities for varied, challenging and exciting work. For many it is a fascinating thought to have the possibility of becoming an ambassador. "Everybody believes when joining the ministry that they will end up as ambassadors."

Many of those interviewed state that at an early age they have taken an interest in foreign policy. Most of these have been conscious from an early age that they wanted to work in the Ministry of Foreign Affairs. Some of them explain that their interest is related to somebody in their family having been concerned with something similar in foreign affairs.

Most of the members of staff have reached the decision to find a job in the Ministry of Foreign Affairs while completing upper-secondary education or early on during their subsequent course of studies. Several of them, both women and men, have a past in the ministry in that they held student-jobs there while attending upper-secondary education. Most come to the Ministry of Foreign Affairs fresh from university.

As already mentioned, the wish to work in this ministry and become ambassador plays a role, "that is indeed the aim for us all". The general opinion is that those applying for jobs in the ministry, both women and men, are career-oriented. Ambassadors are chosen among the managers (heads of division) and there are more managerial posts than in any other ministry. The problem is that there are not enough for everybody, but many interviewees believe that it is better to keep people in suspense.

This is the carrot that is held in front of people in order to make them work so much and it is the task of those high up in the hierarchy to make everybody believe that they will be promoted to a senior post at some point in time (male graduate).

Should they not get that far and if they do not reach the level of manager there are a number of posts abroad which have a compensating effect.

The members of staff regard themselves as generalists. This means that they must be prepared to work in the ministry as a whole.

We are generalists and we are expected to be operative, at least within a month's time after we have taken up a position. If you are not operative within a month, then you are no good. To put it in rather brutal terms. It is not at all as in other ministries where they say when people have been there for a year (I know this, for I have myself been in a different ministry), 'He has been here only for a year, we must be indulgent' (male graduate).

This attitude clearly contributes to provoking keen competition. So does the two-year trial period where in the opinion of most a battle is actually taking place, a battle to be noticed and to do things well. This requires people of a special calibre.

A number of those interviewed express the view that the work load is very great and some of them are able to collect one week's extra work per month. It is difficult to arrange time off in lieu of payment for overtime. An example is given by one of those interviewed. He states that he hands in overtime statements once a month and that he has between 40 and 50 hours of overtime in this period. This does not include the time he spends at home reading international journals, and during weekends he brings work with him home. Many state that they have a workday of 9 to 10 hours. This is countered by one of the other male graduates that was interviewed who thinks that it is very exaggerated. "However, it fits well into the style of the Ministry of Foreign Affairs – exaggerating one's role, importance and effort."

Even though many declare that it is very difficult to maintain one's old hobbies, to maintain one's circle of friends, get time for social life, visit family, etc. the work in itself is apparently so varied that it compensates for these costs. For instance, one of those interviewed explains his absence from his family in the following way,

I am not sure that my absence differs in any major respects from what may be experienced elsewhere. It need not be the ministry's fault, to put it that way. It might well be my own fault. It may be my attitude to my work. I do not think one could say – at least I would not claim that it is the ministry's fault (male manager).

It is not work suitable for people who are fond of repetitive work. According to several of those interviewed there is a richly varied offer of opportunities in the Ministry of Foreign Affairs, it is not a place where one strikes root in individual fields or becomes over-specialized. One relates that when he has been concerned with the same fields for 18 months he feels that it is becoming too much of a routine.

If one has the attitude of a nomad to one's work and physically – if one likes travelling around, well, then it is not possible to find anything better. And we are really imbued with it from the very beginning.

Spouses must be prepared for a changeable life (as members of staff are stationed at a new place every third or fourth year). But many of them are not and cannot take it in the long run and husband and wife separate.

What was earlier no problem when there was only one who had a career in the family has become a problem now as most of the graduates employed have partners with a higher education. We then experience the phenomenon which is today entitled the 'double career family'. Formerly one spouse (usually the wife) joined the other as a matter of course when the latter was stationed abroad. This is no longer self-evident, partly because the spouse may also have a job or a career to look after, partly because it may be difficult to obtain leave of absence from this job. If the spouse in question must give up the work during the period of the stay abroad it is impossible for him/her to receive unemployment benefit if the stay lasts more than two years. The spouse will be in a bad situation when they return unless he/she can find a job.

Here is one example of one who had difficulties in getting leave of absence during the stay abroad:

During the first stationing abroad my wife got leave of absence for three years, during the second stationing abroad she could not get leave of absence but she was told that she could apply for a job again, such an application would be favourably received. During this stay abroad she received a message from her workplace that if she wanted a job again she would have to come home at once and then she had to go back to Denmark one year before me – to ensure that she would get a job.

Several of the interviewees conclude that there are many costs related to being employed in the Ministry of Foreign Affairs – among other things, as far as marriage is concerned. A small number of spouses have been so lucky as to get a job in the country where the other spouse was stationed. But this is not the ordinary state of affairs. Some have chosen to live off one salary (the spouse has simply had to give up working completely). Others have chosen a weekend marriage and others, in turn, have 'chosen' to get a divorce. "It is no coincidence that the percentage of divorces is relatively high. Many have been married. Diffi-

culties arise much more easily in the marriage on account of these career problems."

Many agree that they are a high risk group. It was attempted through an association of spouses to put pressure to bear on ministers and public organizations
with a view to getting through reasonable arrangements for leave of absence. In
some parts of the municipal administration, for instance, leave of absence is not
granted for long periods of time. Then we have the problem of marriages being
split up owing to rigid statutory provisions. The Office of Administration tries to
facilitate for married couples to stay together in connection with one of them
being stationed abroad. The association of spouses does not, however, have any
investigations to show the actual number of divorces. (Therefore, we cannot
confirm the suggested high frequency of divorces.) At the same time the attribution of marriage problems to the career pattern of the Ministry of Foreign Affairs
cannot be taken at face value. The divorce rate is high in general among Danish
middle class, perceiving stationing abroad as the cause of divorce may be a gross
(and psychologically comfortable) over-simplification.

For many of the employees, their job is their life style. Friberg (1984) points
to the ego needs of a small minority, the so-called workaholics who are characterized by living for their work. These are to be found, first and foremost, in the
higher social strata, often they are well educated, they talk about work with their
friends and they tend to allow work to invade all spheres of life, including their
spare time. The 'typical' workaholic is a man and if he experiences progress, he
is married to a loyal wife who adapts to the conditions called for by the working
life of her husband. The 'typical' workaholic is interested in making a career
individually and is willing to sacrifice a lot to make progress in his career and it
does not involve major costs moving to a different city and to a new position.
This description fits well with the graduates employed in the ministry.

The problems that have appeared during the past years are related to the fact
that women are no longer as 'loyal' as they used to be. The family pattern has
changed, the typical situation is no longer a husband who is the breadwinner and
a wife who is a full-time housewife, instead both husband and wife earn money.
Often women have received a higher education themselves and they would not
like to waste it because the husband is transferred.

It seems to be a transitional problem, however, for there is a risk that people
will object and do not want to be transferred to posts where there is no meaningful job for the spouse or that they will accept stationing abroad only if their
spouses do at least have a guarantee that they will get their jobs back (or can
receive unemployment benefit) when they come back from abroad. If these problems are not solved there is a risk that members of staff will not function as well
or that the ministry develops into a workplace for bachelors only.

9.5   The gender composition within the organization – and at top level

As mentioned above, in the Ministry of Foreign Affairs approximately 14% of the university graduates in the ordinary service are females. Women hold 3% of the top positions (4 out of 136). Women's share out of the total staff is, however, as mentioned by way of introduction, considerably higher as the female share of clerical staff is 75%. The clerical staff constitutes approximately half of the total staff; the ratio between women and men within the organization as a whole is 49:51 (1988).

The vertical segregation of the sexes was earlier even stronger. One of the female managers interviewed recalls,

In the old days, when I was a student, it was really grotesque, at that time all the clerical staff, all those that were able to type were women and all those with manager duties were men, or all graduates were men, and therefore when you spoke of 'the ladies' you meant, of course, the typists … .

In 1950 five of the university graduates were women. This figure has now increased to 47 (approximately 20% of the university graduates, exclusive the managers). The share of women of the university graduates (inclusive managers at all levels) in the ministry (14%) is below the average share of female university graduates in other ministries where the percentage is 23.6%. Only a few other ministries have a share of women of university graduates that is equally low; the Ministry of Energy, 13% (0% of top positions); the Ministry of Defence, 5.5% (0.9% of the top positions); the Ministry of Public Works, 10% (7% of top positions) (The Politic/Economical Committee of the Danish Parliament, March 1988).

A number of those interviewed, women and men, express the view that they would like to have a more equal balance between the sexes, also at the graduate level, partly to provide women with the possibility of having influence, partly with a view to the office climate. A manager states that he has made an effort to get more women into the office.

For I find it is detrimental that matters such as these are male products only. It is mostly for reasons of principle that I feel this is wrong. Not because I believe that there is any difference. I think that the idea that there is a difference is greater than the differences actually existing. I could imagine that it will affect the atmosphere at the office, but it will not affect the work as such. It is a human factor – it is a question of social conventions and that kind of thing.

I think the tone and the atmosphere will change, social conventions among men and women differ from those among men and men or among women and women. It is simply healthier to have people of both sexes at the office, also as far as the work is concerned.

He believes it is an instinctive feeling but that it for him has something to do with obtaining a different kind of enjoyment in his work. And as he thinks that it is a natural part of human existence that the other sex participates it is also essential that both sexes are present in the Ministry of Foreign Affairs.

In fact any agency is sorry to be described as a place without any female managers, a place where no women get to the top of the system. ... However, there are a number of barriers – one is that there are not so many women to choose from simply because they somehow disappear before the top of the pyramid is ever reached.

There is not agreement as regards this statement. It is true that the female share of (non-managerial) graduates is only approximately 20%, however, quite a number of these have reached an age at which they could become managers.

Another manager is of the opinion that although it is good to have women represented, he himself will not at any cost employ a woman. It depends on whether she fits into the set-up. The majority, however, state that they are interested in a better balance between the sexes.

I think that it is healthy for any workplace to have both sexes represented and that both sexes have different functions. I do not think that it is healthy for a place of work that all graduates or superiors are men and that all women carry out the service functions.

There is disagreement as to whether a reasonable distribution of the sexes is of importance for the environment, the climate, etc..

Some male interviewees do not think that the atmosphere can be explained on the basis of the ratio between men and women even though there are, for instance, differences in the work method and the atmosphere in the Ministry of the Environment, where there are more women, and the Ministry of Foreign Affairs. It cannot be concluded that this is an outcome of differences in gender ratio. One of them suggests that he does not think that the distribution of the sexes is of very great importance.

On the face of it I don't think so, well, possibly it is of some importance, but it is not the only factor. It is simply different people who feel at home in the Ministry of the Environment from those who feel at home in the Ministry of Foreign Affairs and I can mention many of our female members of staff who use exactly the same tactics as men do. Who are just as...negative...how shall I put it. As you know, I participate in it myself, well, the game of attracting attention and getting the most of it and staking on a career. Women do the same. So I don't think that the Ministry of the Environment is necessarily run in a different way because there are more women in this ministry.

He makes a decisive point to the effect that if women were so much against the rules of the game they would not have applied for jobs in the Ministry of Foreign Affairs. Another possibility would be that they would leave the ministry and there are examples of people doing this if they do not feel at home.

As has appeared from the above, the gender composition in the Ministry of Foreign Affairs is unequal at the level of graduates and very unequal higher up in the hierarchy. Only few other ministries have a percentage of women that is so low both in relation to the number of graduates and in relation to the number of people higher up in the hierarchy. Several of those interviewed have expressed the view that they would like a more equal balance between the sexes, mostly because they think that it would provide slightly different social conventions if the majority of the women were not in the service function and almost all managerial positions were held by men. The general opinion, however, seems to be that the gender ratio is not of great significance for the operation of the workplace.

9.6   Recruitment for managerial positions

Some of the interviewees say that the system exploits people's own wishes of advancing. It may be more difficult not to take part in the competition as in comparison to many other ministries, there are relatively many senior or managerial positions in Denmark and abroad. Approximately 1 out of 3 graduates holds a managerial position whereas, for instance in the National Board of Social Welfare it is 1 out of 10. As we have mentioned before, we reserve the category of managers for senior positions with several subordinates, excluding jobs with some supervisory functions and without work tasks that primarily concerns management.

The first promotion takes place when a member of staff becomes a manager. These positions cannot be applied for by members of staff until they are "mature"; that is, they are rarely appointed as managers until they have a seniority of 15 years (only 3-5% are appointed before they are 40, most between the ages of 40 and 50).

Managerial positions are advertised in the Danish Official Gazette and then applications are submitted. A meeting is held in a special personnel committe in which the senior officials of the hierarchy are represented. The permanent secretary chairs the meeting together with the undersecretaries of state and all deputy secretaries of state of the Ministry of Foreign Affairs plus staff representatives for those that have already been appointed and those of the ordinary service below the managerial level, commercial attachés and aid attachés, etc.. During the meeting the recommendations of the senior official of the ministry are presented and possibly taken up for discussion. Not until this procedure has been finished does the permanent secretary of the Ministry of Foreign Affairs present them to the Minister who will then approve or reject them.

This formal procedure obviously does not prevent the permanent secretary and the Minister from speaking with each other in advance so that allowance can be made for the views, if any, of the minister. Everything that takes place during the personnel meeting is strictly confidential. University graduates are represented only when somebody is promoted to manager, etc. (union rules). It is difficult for the staff representative to point to one applicant rather than another, when he is the representative of both applicants, interviewees said.

In connection with promotions at senior level, importance is attached to the course of the career of the person concerned and the reports that have been prepared. As said above, reports are prepared all the way through, during the first years every six months and then it is decided whether the member of staff in question should be permanently engaged. After that, a report is prepared every time the member of staff is transferred during the first 15 years in the ministry. That is to say when a member of staff is transferred from one division to another or when he/she returns home after having been stationed abroad. Gradually a file is established and a picture is formed of weaknesses and strengths, etc..

There are no clearly defined, objective criteria in relation to promotion to managerial positions. Importance is attached to an overall evaluation of the conduct of the person concerned during the years that have passed. It is well-known that it is a question of 'using one's elbows' to get through. You must have shown that you are good at your work and that you have a sufficiently comprehensive view of things to be concerned with a broad field of subjects.

How to get a manager position is described by a female manager as being at the right place, at the right time, with the right persons.

At any rate I feel that as far as I myself am concerned it has to a great extent been a question of mere coincidence. For if I had not been transferred I would have had no real possibility of getting the job six months later and really I did not want to be transferred.

Some people have criticized the fact that on the appointment of a manager the general qualifications of people are not taken sufficiently into consideration; what is considered is the post they are to hold for the next three years and not the fact that they should be qualified for various posts.

… and the person in question will be there for the rest of his/her life, changing from one post to another, either out in the world or alternating between foreign countries and Denmark. Therefore it is, as far as I see it, very important that people are really capable of cooperating with others when they are appointed to managerial posts, in particular if they go out to a small embassy or a relatively small embassy, then it is hell, if the person in charge is not qualified in a country … where you are truly a long way from home.

Opinions differ as to how to become recognized in the ministry, one thinks the decisive factor is being willing to take up new and untried matters – that this is more important here than elsewhere. That is a male graduate's experience from this organization. At the same time it is important to be noticed.

One needs to be noticed here. The best is if one has presented new ideas – this is probably necessary in most systems, but my impression is that here it is more essential than at most places. My experience is that one does not get very far here through ordinary solid routine. I think that one can get ahead if one dares to jump into the deep water and try things that have not earlier been tried. This probably applies here more than at many other places. And this is probably related to the fact that international cooperation differs from national cooperation – it is a question of building on well-reputed systems. In particular for a small country that participates in international cooperation, this is probably the only way to get ahead, if one has some good ideas that others would also like to try out, this is a way to get ahead, it is not enough to be receptive to the suggestions of others, one must also oneself show some initiative.

After the position of manager, one is 'ripe' for the post of ambassador and one can go on in the system to deputy secretary of state and secretary of state.

When people do not get the position of manager that they have wished for they do not in general leave the ministry but apply perhaps for a 'quasi-managerial position' abroad, as chargé-d'affaires, at a place where there is no ambassador. The number of chargés d'affaires is limited, however. Formerly some went over to private trade and industry, but competition has grown there.

9.7 Women and career

The female university graduates appear, on the whole, as very work and career-oriented. The combination of an interesting work content and the symbolic and material rewards associated with higher positions in the hierarchy are attractive to many women.

I want to show that I am capable of holding a responsible position, in addition to this, the work is more fun. The higher one gets in the system, the more interesting is the work, the interesting work is often to be found high up in the hierarchy (female graduate).

Confronted with the claim that is often made, viz. that many women prefer to be at the centre or in the middle of a network rather than at the top, the woman interviewed says that she believes this claim is correct, only it does not apply to herself and her colleagues in the Ministry of Foreign Affairs.

I do not think that any of my female colleagues, apart from those working part-time, well, there will be a few who feel that way, but apart from these I think that most of my female colleagues would like to be at the top.

Women are regarded as being just as concerned about their career prospects as men. According to one of the interviewees, it is obvious that if one applies for a job with the Ministry of Foreign Affairs where in the nature of things the job is not a 9-5 job, then those who stay want to advance within the system. This claim concerns those who actually stay after the two-year trial period and the first stationing abroad. It is generally believed that some people apply for a job with the ministry without fully realizing what the obligation to be transferred actually involves and therefore they disappear again after a couple of years. Some women (and men) have also left because they did not like having to be general-ists, not being able to go into detail within specific fields.

We shall not dwell too much here on the fact that the career involves certain costs, but it is a fact that a large number of the women within the organization are not married and do not have children.

I have never discussed it with them, but it may very well be that they have staked more on their career than on having children. Many of them are not married, but I don't think too much importance should be attached to this, they have just arranged their lives differently (female graduate).

It appears to be difficult to combine a career with the more traditional 'life of a woman'. Therefore, it must also be emphasized that three of the four female managers are consultants, which does not involve an obligation to be transferred. In order to become a manager which is the first hurdle on the way, one must typically have been stationed abroad once or twice. So if somebody objects to the ordinary obligation to be transferred, it may have consequences. It may, for instance, mean that the person in question has opted out of the race to obtain senior positions. The exception is the small number of consultancies but here there are in general no further steps on the way from the manager position, while potentially others can go on to higher senior positions (deputy secretary of state, secretary of state).

Some women choose to leave the ministry because they cannot get their family to go abroad or they choose to give higher priority to the career of their husbands. Others (though only a few) stay in a job where they are not obliged to be stationed abroad. The disadvantage of this is that they get into a routine, they do not get the exciting tasks. Those who run into problems on account of their obligation to be stationed abroad more often leave the ministry. As mentioned earlier, many are of the opinion that the men working in the Ministry of Foreign Affairs are also experiencing problems because their wives have careers, but in general they experience the problems later on and to a smaller extent.

The general opinion among those interviewed who still work in the ministry seems to be that there is nothing in the system that has a limiting effect on the possibilities of women of getting ahead, but that it is rather factors outside the system that make it more difficult for women.

Indeed, it is more difficult to make a man accept the role of housewife than to make a woman accept it, even though it may become increasingly difficult. In that respect our male colleagues do have an advantage, but there is nothing as such in the system to prevent or limit the career possibilities of women.

With one or two exceptions, the interviewees (in the ministry) do not think that there is anything favouring either men or women. One of the members of staff expresses the view that women must do more in order to advance in the system. Even though most of the interviewees do not feel that there is any kind of sex discrimination in the ministry, one could, based on the statement below, get the impression that such discrimination has existed earlier.

My feeling is that there has not, at any rate during recent years, been any form of discrimination to the effect that a man has been preferred to a woman if they had equal qualifications (female graduate).

One or two of the interviewed employees point at minor gender bias in evaluation and treatment. What is regarded as equality of status by women is understood by some men as the opposite, viz. that women have lately been given
preferential treatment.

What one is thinking about is that sometimes one feels that some females are appointed to
managers who may not seem qualified to be appointed as compared to the males. In these
instances it has, then, actually been an advantage being a woman on the grounds that the
ministry is not known to have very many women (in managerial positions) and then those
in charge have felt that it was simply necessary to avoid having the percentage of women
fall to zero so they appoint some women and one can say that this is really unfair, this is
discrimination against men, purely and simply (one of the male interviewees).

Actually, according to several of those interviewed, it is greatly desired to get
women for the higher posts, "because in these times of equality between the
sexes, they feel that it is a little embarrassing that Denmark does not have a
female ambassador".[2]
As there are only very few women in managerial positions in the Ministry of
Foreign Affairs, the statement that being a woman is an advantage appears somewhat exaggerated. It is a fact, however, that no women had been appointed for
managerial positions for a period of approximately 15 years, and that staff representatives have pointed to the fact that this seems strange. Shortly before the
time of the investigation, however, two young women obtained managerial positions. This may seem overwhelming. And it may be that there have been men
with better qualifications for these jobs. On the other hand, the interviewees who
have left the ministry point to the fact that among those holding managerial
positions there are many "mediocre men" whereas "mediocre women" do not
have a chance of obtaining managerial positions.
In general it is not felt by the men interviewed that being a man in the system
has been any particular advantage.

Not really, on the contrary. If one is a woman and good, one must have every chance of
making a career for oneself in this system as a political demand has been expressed to the
effect that more women should hold managerial positions. The general demand in society
is that women should be better represented.

If there is any truth in this statement – why, then, are there so few women in
managerial positions in the Ministry of Foreign Affairs?
One explanation that is given is that many women have not reached the age
for getting managerial positions. When one is to consider why there are so few
women in managerial positions, it is essential to look at the age pyramid. If there
are many women at the bottom of this pyramid one cannot expect very many at
the top. It is a fact that the share of females among graduates is not high (20% in
the ordinary service) and the average age of women in the organization is lower
than that of men. There are simply fewer women of the age required for the
managerial positions. Still, it may seem strange that none of the women who

were employed during the 1950's and 1960's have been appointed for managerial positions. The four women currently (the beginning of 1988) holding managerial positions were recruited in 1947, 1949, 1973 and 1975. In connection with the appointment of people for managerial positions as at January 1981, the staff representatives have calculated that approximately 90% of the women have been overlooked while the percentage of men was only 40, which means that less than 10% of the women had been appointed as compared to approximately 60% of the men.

Another reason that is generally given officially is that it is a problem that women cannot be sent out to a large number of countries. This argument is not valid, however, firstly, only very few countries would not accept a woman, secondly, Denmark actually has female foreign ambassadors from seven different countries (1989). (Which of course tells us something about the opinions of the countries in question of Denmark.) So this is hardly a good reason for not appointing women. So perhaps it is rather a question of avoiding being confronted with the question of why women are so rarely to be found in managerial positions than actually an explanation of the phenomenon.

The women interviewed who are employed in the MFA show a certain ambivalence as regards the question why there are so few women in managerial positions, most of them defend the organization and mention that a number of appointments are on their way, more women have been recruited than ever before. On the other hand it is perhaps a fact that it has been more difficult for women to make a name for themselves in a male-dominated ministry.

As a woman one can always assume that it is more difficult to obtain a managerial position in this ministry for women than for men, but whether it is true, I don't know. But one could imagine that many women in here would think that it is perhaps in reality a little easier for men than for women. I do not know whether it is correct, but it could be a typical view among the female members of staff (female graduate).

She imagines it is possible that there are more women than men who are frustrated, and there have been some visible expressions of this frustration. Some years ago a number of women started a petition to protest against the fact that so few women held leading positions. Two thirds of the women supported the petition, however, as the promoters wanted 100% backing, the protest was not delivered.

The group of women is still in existence, it meets once a month for lunch, it consists mostly of young women, however, it does not function as planned. Mostly because opinions differ as to what should take place during meetings.

An equal status committee has been established which is to keep an eye on the distribution of the sexes in the ministry. As far as we know, no initiatives have been taken, however.

9.8   Women in the minority

Obviously, a small proportion of anyone category, whether it be women or men will attract attention, everybody knows who the women holding managerial positions are, their names and when they got their present job. In other words, they are visible. When there are so few, discussions may arise as regards the circumstances relating to the appointment, for instance, whether the person in question has been appointed because she is a woman when it is at present expedient to have a number of representatives of the category. The minister must make allowance for the fact that half of the voters are women. Discussions may also arise as to the qualifications of the person in question, whether she actually has better qualifications than a man with more seniority.

One consequence of the visibility is that one is noticed more, for better or for worse."If women make mistakes and do a bad job, then it is of course discovered more easily than if men do the same" (female manager).

Another aspect of the visibility, which is more positive, is that one quickly becomes known, and this has the effect that it is perhaps easier to be heard in contexts where people actually remember one's name. It may, however, be a balancing act, as described earlier, if one is to be accepted both as a woman and as an individual with qualifications. One woman has had the experience of being gradually regarded as qualified and competent in the context of OECD, then when she returned to the same committee seven years later, most of the participants were new and she felt that she had once again to prove her qualifications (which was not demanded to the same extent of men).

Then I come back and it is quite obvious that the older men were thinking, what is that young woman doing here, she does not know anything about this (female manager).

This she felt among other things because they did not discuss various matters very much with her in the corridors at the beginning and this, she says, lasts until they find out whether the person in question is qualified or not.

I am absolutely convinced that when I go down for a meeting in the OECD again then they all know me, now they have placed me wherever that may be. Then the uncertainty, and it is to a great extent uncertainty as to whether they should take her seriously, flirt with her, what are they going to do, has disappeared. Therefore, I think it is just a question of time until people get to know each other.

If it were really a question of time, one could imagine that men are not included straightaway in the large community either, but in this instance it is generally taken for granted that those who attend such a representation are, by definition, qualified. The production of evidence is the opposite for men. They do not need to prove first that they are qualified, it is rather the opposite, unless they prove otherwise, they *are* qualified. All of this is according to the experience of those interviewed.

Another one of the interviewees mentions the possibility that new men are treated in a similar way, but can hear herself that it does not sound convincing.

They may treat new men in that way, I don't know. But they do not start flirting with them, do they? But I also think that many men wonder whether the woman in question is there just because she is a woman or because she is qualified (female graduate).

Although the interviewed women (still working in the MFA) have not themselves felt any differential treatment in Denmark, they have experienced this elsewhere, while having been stationed abroad, for instance. It is a general experience that abroad they are stereotyped as representatives of the social category of women and not primarily as a person with a specific function or status.

Internationally I have had a feeling that some have thought, well, what is that little girl doing here. But it has never been a problem and it has only been a temporary very brief phenomenon. And of course I have experienced all the classical situations. 'Women are their worst enemies.' I remember clearly when I called somebody at Brussels in particular, in the commission and wanted to speak to somebody and the secretary kept on asking me who wanted to speak with him and could not understand that I was the one who wanted to speak with him (female manager).

The person interviewed believes that these situations which she calls classic cannot be avoided and that nobody can be blamed for it is a question of custom. They are used to a secretary calling, and one cannot expect them to understand that suddenly it is not the secretary, but the charge d'affaire or whatever the title is. The fact that female managers are often their own secretaries is a different matter that will not be discussed here.

A few women can be included in the male tribe without it being necessary to change the rituals of the tribe, for instance, the concept of a "men's lunch" does not lose its touch of masculinity and any rituals connected with it, if only one woman joins the men.

My ambassador used a concept, an old-fashioned expression, viz. 'men's dinner' and 'men's lunch'. I tried to teach him to call it work lunch or work dinner, and there was I as the only woman. And therefore I kept telling him that now he must learn to call it a work lunch, because it was so ridiculous writing 'You are invited to a men's dinner or a men's lunch', and then I came along (female graduate).

This situation took place at the beginning of the 1980's. Of course we cannot immediately say for sure that this is a sign of (significant) sex discrimination. As we mentioned earlier much discrimination is not intentional and conscious but has more to do with tradition or custom. Still the woman in question tries to change the habit but does not succeed. In this instance, when the discrimination is highlighted and there is no change in the ambassador's behaviour, we deal with sex discrimination.

Other problems that are mentioned relate more to what is a question of tradition than to discrimination as such. For instance, one of the women interviewed had a special experience in Rome where a meeting had been agreed by telephone with a number of managers in the Italian Ministry of Foreign Affairs.

I was sitting in the receptionist's office waiting, because he was engaged and then the manager came out and I said 'hello' and stood up because I thought he was coming to meet me. He said, 'Hello, I should very much like to talk with you, but unfortunately I have not got time now for I am expecting a visit from the first secretary of the Danish embassy' (she was the embassay secretary, but he expected to meet a man). I could get a lot out of him for he was so embarrased (that he had made a mistake).

In Italy women are more rarely found in senior positions in the Ministry of Foreign Affairs than in Denmark and the event mentioned is more a sign of thoughtlessness than of sex discrimination, a situation which will perhaps be different if and when a larger number of women are recruited to the Italian Ministry of Foreign Affairs.

A female manager mentions that she has not felt herself that it has played any role that women have been in a minority (in the group of university graduates) in the MFA. This she attributes to the fact that she is not herself oversensitive and therefore it is most likely important who one is talking to. But perhaps it is not a question of how sensitive one is to discrimination but rather how one reacts when exposed to sex discrimination.

Something that also plays a role is that I can always answer back and am not easy to fool, this is what my male colleagues of my age would probably say, so if somebody has attempted to talk down to me because I am a girl then I think I have been able to stop them relatively quickly and then it does not really matter. I am not oversensitive myself in that respect and therefore I have not really experienced discrimination.

It should be pointed out there is nothing in the previous part of the interview that can give an association to possible discrimination, it is the woman interviewed herself mentioning that perhaps some will talk down to "girls", (the expression "girl" is used only in this interview in the MFA). It is indicated here that she has experienced these situations and felt that she has coped well with them and therefore she does not consciously regard them as a problem. She also touches on the fact that she has received both positive and negative attention on account of her being a woman, for instance, she is of the opinion that it can often be an advantage when there are few women. In an international context, in the UN, where there were less than 10% women in a committee of approximately 150 she has experienced becoming known quickly and this she regarded as being important. At the same time, she points out that it was very difficult to balance on the very sharp edge.

For if you were too business-like and not feminine you were uninteresting, but if you were too feminine and not sufficiently business-like, well, then you were just a woman and were not respected as far as work was concerned. Clearly, it was a balancing act, and I think the same applies here in the ministry.

The balancing act is also made visible by the clothes people wear. Normally this woman, who holds a managerial position, wears a skirt and blouse, but she also has a pin-striped dress. This is the outfit which her male colleagues have commented on most. She takes this as an expression that they think she is making fun of them, as this outfit is the female counterpart of their pin-striped suits. With this dress she is on her way to crossing the border, she has reached a point where they do not know whether she belongs on one side or the other. This is the way it could be interpreted as she does not otherwise hear any comments on her clothes. Her pin-striped dress is regarded as a provocation. Perhaps she is too much 'one of the guys'? It seems that clothes are an important means of empowerment, as also suggested by Pringle (1989:197):

In wearing suits women are not transgressing gender, becoming 'men', but expressing a more masculine, instrumental relation to the body. To dress in this way is to *feel* like a man does, sexually empowered, an actor rather than an object to be looked at.

No wonder that this act causes confusion.

Another woman in a managerial position feels that people have indeed noticed her but that she has been regarded as and accepted as the representative from Denmark. The discrimination she has noticed and which she regards as positive is that when she formerly held speeches outside the ministry men would say, "it was fantastic that a woman could give such a speech". The men regarded her as the "big girl" who managed well. Nor did she resent it, if anything, she was proud of the attention.

I think it was wonderful. I have never resented that kind of thing. I found it was great fun. But I have never forgotten it for I find it was really amusing. And it is a good story to tell today with the equality of status of the sexes.

The compliment does not concern the quality of the contents of the speech but instead the unexpected behaviour of a woman giving a speech. Thus the praise is also a reminder that this kind of behaviour is expected to be rare. It should be noted, however, that this event, like the one regarding the "men's lunch", took place a number of years ago.

One of the men holding a managerial position says that he has not wondered about meeting female civil servants,

One has of course thought about it, I mean, been aware that it was a woman. ... if you understand what I mean, but it has not been ... it has been an absolutely normal conversation as it would otherwise have been. One is perhaps a little more gentlemanly when leaving and when saying hello. I mean, one is courteous to women, but that, in my opinion, is the only thing.

As appears from other literature on female managers, women in managerial positions become 'public figures' if there are not very many of them. As mentioned in Chapter 5 they are called tokens by Kanter (1977) among others. Visibility tends to lead to an increased pressure on women to perform and this is also the case in the Ministry of Foreign Affairs. The problem for 'tokens' is that they will appear as representatives for the rest of the category of women, especially when they 'make mistakes' – and as unusual as compared to the rest of women when they manage well, which appears also from what has been stated previously. The special irony of the token situation is therefore that women may be treated both as representatives of their type/category and as exceptions from this type, even by the same people.

One way of incorporating tokens is to give them a stereotypical role whereby the ordinary social conventions between tokens and the dominant group can be preserved. Such roles have not been observed in the Ministry of Foreign Affairs. Perhaps 'giving' people roles is not such a necessity in a classical bureaucracy, the social conventions are defined already and the hierarchic system will not change just because a few women obtain managerial positions.

A weak tendency to use stereotyped roles in the Ministry of Foreign Affairs is experienced in two different ways: 1. when it is attempted to place female delegates in a traditional sexual role; 2. the women of the MFA are expected to have the main responsibility for the family and are therefore not expected to be as 'eager' to be stationed abroad as men.

In general, one cannot claim, however, that there are large problems for women holding managerial positions in the ministry in Denmark. The interviewees employed have not felt that there is any significant differential treatment of the graduates/managers. At the same time they refer to the fact that there may be others in the organization who hold a different opinion. And this is true of those women interviewed who have left the ministry. If one compares with the difficulties that are reported in much of the literature on the subject (see e.g. Symons, 1986; Walters, 1987), both the Ministry of Foreign Affairs and SAS and the National Board of Social Welfare appear by and large to be unproblematic workplaces when it comes to women functioning as managerial members of staff.

9.9   Women in managerial positions

As mentioned earlier, female university graduates are regarded as being just as concerned with their careers as men, the exceptions may be women who have had children. Many of the women do not have children.

I don't know whether they actually live together with somebody, I don't know that much about my colleagues, I just know that they do not have children for we who have children quickly discover that this can give rise to problems and we talk about this. So, actually, quite a number of them do not have children (female civil servant).

Of the four women holding managerial positions (out of 136) only one is obliged to be transferred, i.e. follow the normal career track. Out of six managerial positions in the MFA to which no obligation to be transferred is attached (consultant positions), the women form half. Of 130 managerial positions with an obligation to be transferred (and the possibilities inhererent in these positions as regards being appointed ambassador or any other promotion) only one is held by a woman. The consultant positions are described by some as "a glorified side-track"; the designation refers to the fact that these positions do not lead any further but as far as salary and superiority are concerned, they are at the managerial level.

One of the women holding one of these positions thinks that she has been favoured as a woman because she did not take part in the men's 'race' for making a career. She has not, however, obtained her position without any effort of her own.

It is correct that I have worked hard for it and it is correct that it has been stated now and again that probably more is demanded of a woman than of a man. I have never felt any discrimination or any animosity against me because I was a woman and not a man. I have always been accepted on equal terms.

Another woman holding a managerial position says that she likes being a woman in the system, but she does not think she would have liked working in the MFA so much if she had been a man. She has never herself experienced any differential treatment and she has felt that people have listened to her points of view and attitudes all the way up through the hierarchy. Some of it she attributes to the fact that the manager where she worked formerly was atypical and perhaps atypical for the system. She indicates that competition has been keener among the men, that this battle for reaching a specific grade has not to such a great extent affected her.

The above-mentioned statements to the effect that there is no differential treatment are not accepted by those who have left the MFA. The latter indicate that the last two appointments of women for managerial positions would probably not have taken place without the social (and political) pressure that is being exercised as a general principle to get more women in managerial positions. This does not mean that the women in managerial positions have not been qualified, but makes it understandable that they have not experienced any negative differential treatment.

Nevertheless, a female formerly employed graduate states that it has been a handicap being a woman because they are not taken seriously by the men holding managerial positions, as they expect the women to leave the ministry.

Applying the same yardstick to all women, and expect them to leave the ministry upon marriage and childbirth, this attitude is degrading and may have the effect that women's chances to 'rise a little above the crowd' are reduced. It is difficult to find out how widespread this attitude is, but given the fact that hardly any of the women interviewed still working in the MFA could point at discrimination in the organization, it does not appear to be salient. The problem for women is described by some of those who have left the ministry to be that women rarely obtain the key positions that lead to managerial posts. And some of those interviewed regard this as being of decisive importance if one is to become known. A key position will also more often mean that one has an errand on the sixth floor where managerial managers sit – and it is regarded as being a clear advantage that one is known by these when a decision is to be reached as to who should next come into a higher grade.

Another great advantage for a candidate for a managerial position is to have been noticed within the sub-department as the distribution of managerial positions is also to a great extent a question of a battle among the sub-departments. It is regarded as prestigious to have a large number of employees appointed to managerial positions. In this respect, some women feel that it is much more difficult for them to attract attention to themselves and be appointed. Part of the problem is, according to one of those interviewed, that often women think it is enough to sit for years and do a good job, then they should be safe.

One must have the chance of travelling with one of those holding a senior position and join him in the bar. The problem is that women often go to bed instead and do not consider where decisions are being reached.

In addition to this one must apparently (as was pointed out also by a female manager in SAS) choose the 'right' superior. One of those interviewed says that she has received much support, but not from the right managers. What is most important is of course to receive support from the most senior managers.

This expectation that women will probably stop working in the MFA when (if) they are having children is related to what we described earlier, viz. that it is difficult to combine both a family and a career, especially when the husband also has a job in the ministry. Some of the female graduates (and managers) do in fact doubt whether it is possible to manage the job if one has a family with young children.

One of the women holding a managerial position thinks that women themselves must take a large part of the blame for the fact that in general, there are so few female managers in society.

I think that perhaps women are very often more critical of themselves than are men and perhaps a little more uncertain as to whether they will be able to cope. And not until they are absolutely convinced that they can manage just as well as he can then they have a go at it. Men have ensured that they were more up to date, that is one thing one has to do.

The cultural gender expectations naturally also affect women. Another woman in a managerial position states openly that unfortunately she has not contributed with any "female norms".

To my shame I must confess that sometimes I have checked myself saying when I was to have a new correspondent and I heard about somebody with very young children, 'Then she will very often have to stay at home if the child is ill', etc.. As I do not have these problem myself I must check myself so that I do not use the norms that we refer to as being male, to my shame I must confess this.

It is difficult to maintain that there is any significant difference between female and male members of staff/managers in the MFA in the context of work. Some have claimed that men have a different way of attracting attention, many of them working overtime but also pretending to be very busy while women tend more to sort out or give priority to some matters because they have to, in particular if they also have obligations towards a family. It is to a great extent regarded as a question of being good at organizing.

When you are in the situation you don't think about it for then it just has to work. And then you must organize things one way or another to get everything to function, for you don't feel at ease at your workplace if things at home do not work or vice versa if your work is not OK. So this is something which is very closely related.

It cannot be excluded that the ability or need to organize/make priorities is related to less time being reserved for the work perhaps on account of restrictions caused by the family. A difference that has been noted in research, between women and men holding managerial positions is the classical, viz. the orientation towards relations (cf. Chapter 3). Women in managerial positions are somewhat more concerned with the social, personal relations. One of the interviewed female managers in the MFA said that she would be willing to go downwards in the hierarchy again because she wanted to spend more time with her family. Another said that she would do the same if the work of her partner should necessitate this. None of the men in managerial positions have touched on this question. The parallel to the SAS-case is striking. In addition to this all the women holding managerial positions in MFA have said that members of staff come to them with their personal problems. Men in managerial positions may have had the same experience, however, it has not been mentioned during the interviews.

It is difficult to judge whether women and men actually have different leadership styles. Below, two examples are provided of how a woman and a man in managerial positions in MFA describe their leadership style.

The woman mentions that characteristics she would attach importance to with a manager is that the manager should be able to have a current dialogue with his/her subordinates, that the manager can leave matters to the imagination and initiative of subordinates so that both parties feel they can influence on what is being done. This she regards as a very difficult task.

The man describes his management style as being able to define the tasks, whether they come from outside, from higher up in the hierarchy or from himself, clearly to his subordinates so that they become capable of performing the task in question. According to him, "The worst managers are those who follow, the best are those who lead".

How is this difference to be evaluated? Broadly, one may describe the woman's management style as more process-oriented, relation-oriented, while the man's management style can be characterized as more goal-oriented. In order to analyse the difference in more detail it would be necessary also to describe the fields of work of the two which may necessitate different management styles.

A more general and clear difference concerns the fact that female managers do not attach quite as much importance to status, something we have also mentioned in the case-study of SAS. Two of the women in managerial positions (of the three women managers interviewed) would actually, as mentioned earlier, give up their managerial position if this was necessitated by personal circumstances. Another example is that when they mention differences between the three departments they talk about differences in the work functions, not differences in status, as some of the interviewed men did. In addition to this, they mention that they carry out secretarial functions themselves, for instance they call others themselves, they answer the telephone themselves. When the interviews were agreed it was also a characteristic that if the male managers were to change the appointment, then it was done through a (female) secretary and appointments were arranged via the secretary. The female managers, on the other hand, made the appointments themselves.

A kaleidoscopic description has been given of a number of differences between women and men and a number of differences in the experiences of those employed in the ministry and those who have left the ministry, respectively. We have been cautious in reaching specific conclusions on the basis of the interviews, among other things, because the material is so limited, regarding the female managers (which is related to the fact that in the entire organization there were only three women in managerial positions that could be interviewed). A considerable difference is that there is only one woman holding a managerial position who is under an obligation to be transferred. The other women in managerial positions are consultants and perhaps it is easier to be relaxed about this position and be ready to go downwards in the hierarchy if circumstances so require. Nevertheless, there are good reasons to believe that even though the women in the Ministry of Foreign Affairs are in general career- and promotion-oriented they are more relaxed about hierarchy, status and have a different opinion as to what a managerial position will involve than many of the men. A complementary interpretation could be that they are more ready to give their work lower priority if personal limitation and demands on the part of family/spouse would so require.

9.10 Discussion

There is not accordance between the descriptions of those interviewed who are still employed in the ministry and the description of those who have left the ministry. The game relating to the appointment of managerial positions is interpreted very differently by those who are former members of staff. Thus their comments will also be weighted below where we deal with the question of which conditions are of importance for women's possibilities of obtaining managerial positions. Obviously it is not unproblematic to rely more on these than on the other statements, but they are in better accordance with the phenomenon that is intended to be illustrated, the very low percentage of women in managerial positions.

Obviously, there are conditions which have the effect that the likelihood that a female university graduate obtains a managerial position is considerably less than is the likelihood that an equally qualified man will obtain a managerial position (10%, respectively 60%). We shall attempt to explain this. First, we shall point out, however, that there are also a number of circumstances which should make it easier for women to obtain managerial positions. In the group of university graduates there is no direct gender division of labour, at least not during the first years of employment, and the female and male university graduates are equally qualified when they start working in the Ministry of Foreign Affairs. This should constitute a good basis for equal treatment and equal possibilities within the organization. Even though the result, by way of the career prospects of women, indicates that this basis for equality has not had any significant impact, it should have some impact (though weak) in improving women's possibilities. And it probably contributes to explain why most of those interviewed did not feel that they or others were exposed to discrimination or differential treatment in the Ministry of Foreign Affairs.

Another circumstance which has obviously increased the number of women in managerial positions, or rather meant that the number was not reduced to zero, is the general political pressure to ensure that in particular public organizations have at least some female managers. It simply looks bad if there are very few women in managerial positions. It is important for organizations, and in particular those that exist in a political environment, to signal accordance with the values of society at the formal, i.e. visible level (Meyer & Rowan, 1977). Otherwise there will be a problem of legitimacy. According to the information available, such considerations have been behind the appointment of one or two women for managerial positions in the Ministry of Foreign Affairs.

Below, we describe the conditions that make it more difficult for women to obtain managerial positions:

– In certain respects it is an old-fashioned ministry with fixed limits to the surrounding world/society with strong traditions as regards civil servants and consequent expectations as regards sexual roles.
– Women get to a lesser degree than men 'a position by chance'. One must rise above the grey mass in order to assert oneself.
– Mechanisms/games that women do not master/understand.
– Inscrutable promotion system which opens the possibility of 'chance' and arbitrariness in evaluations and decisions.

– The obligation to be transferred which means that some women leave the service and the understanding that in some countries female graduates cannot be employed.

On the basis of the interviews, the Ministry of Foreign Affairs may be described as a somewhat old-fashioned bureaucracy, with in certain respects, somewhat traditional gender expectations. According to several investigations, this is a precise description of a place where women have only little chance of asserting themselves (Martin, 1985). What contributes to reproducing the hierarchy and the system is the fact that socialization is so effective, it leaves a profound trace so that the members of staff all the time act as if they are in a situation of competition. "Everybody is bound to adopt the idea of reaching grade 37". One does not contradict one's superior, if one is opposed to something, one does not show it – if one's superior criticizes a subordinate, one should not discuss whether this is reasonable or not. The disciplining or the indirect socialization takes place through a veritable flow of signs and clues on what one should think and what opinions one should hold in relation to the outside world – and through the fact that everything is to be approved. A number of introductory courses which new members of staff are to attend in addition to the compulsory French and English courses are being incorporated at the moment. What one must otherwise learn in order to cope, one must find out for oneself. The socialization is reinforced by the fact that candidates are employed fresh from university so that they do not have behind them any experience from a different kind of system.

It should be mentioned that the three departments differ. The difference is related, among other things, to how long the departments have existed but also to their functions. Therefore the principles of leadership also differ, with the oldest department which is concerned with foreign policy by some described as the most rigid and the management style there described as being "out-of-date".

The fact that there are many of the same age group competing for fewer posts and that there are less managerial positions than formerly has had the effect that competition has intensified even further. This means that there are many capable men in the queue for any managerial position and according to some, that as a woman, one must rise considerably above the grey mass to have a chance. The problem is also that the number of managerial positions has not increased to the same extent as the number of members of staff in the remaining service. In addition to this, increased competition has been brought to bear by other personnel groups. The suggestion made by the groups of personnel to those in charge in the ministry has been that independent fields of work should be created for the many who cannot obtain a managerial position. And this is actually the problem, everybody 'worships the golden calf' and nobody sees any alternative to the position as manager (apart from approximately 15 chargé d'affaire posts) – and on the other hand, one cannot manage being for the rest of one's life at the level of graduate when one knows that there is a possibilty of getting more independent work and more status, prestige, influence and pay. Everybody wants to become ambassador, not until then does one enter "the eternal orbit" as it is called by some, and relax about the future.

A significant element of the route to promotion is a number of key positions which lead on to a grade 37 job – and the important thing is to get such a job. And in this field differential treatment takes place according to some, for women are said not to get such a post as frequently as men. If and when one gets such a post it is easier to go to the sixth floor (where the top executives have their offices), the more one has to do there the greater is the chance of establishing contacts with deputy undersecretaries of state and undersecretaries of state. One must simply have a chance of becoming noticed. The problem is that women often think that it is enough to do a good job for a number of years and that at some point in time they will be rewarded. Many women do not think in terms of strategy and do not know where and when decisions are reached, therefore they are not at the right place at the right time, female interviewees told us. A different matter is that it may be more difficult for women to get such a 'glorified position' that will lead to a position in the 37th grade. One of the reasons why women do not as easily get the glorified key positions is perhaps related to the fact that they are expected to stop at some point in time. Therefore, they are more often than men not regarded as sufficiently serious candidates. Instead they are, according to one of the women interviewed kept in a kind of incubator.

Another problem for women is that not only the reports prepared throughout the years count in connection with an application for a job. When one applies for a job in the 37th grade, the manager prepares an additional report on the qualities of 'leadership' of the person in question. Women often act differently from men in this respect, according to some research. A number of investigations of women with higher education show that they will not 'naturally' or spontaneously assume the function of leader (see e.g. Carbonell, 1984) so when, in connection with the appointment of somebody for a managerial position, importance is attached to qualities of leadership (in addition to what has been mentioned above) the problem is that women have not had much chance or have not done much to prove that they may be able to act as superiors, according to conventional standards regarding this issue. The kind of leadership style reported by a female manager (in section 9.9) is less salient than the more masculine leadership style excercised by her male colleague, especially when exercised from a non-managerial position.[3] What is easily recognized as 'leadership qualities' may thus not reflect 'true' such capacities, but rather institutionalized, masculine values on what is to be counted as 'leadership'. This point does not, however, fully account for women's passiveness (in relationship to a male norm) when it comes to taking initiative and exercising influence from a formal position.

In order to understand this, all the factors outside the organization must be taken into consideration: factors relating to gender production, general male domination, sexual roles, socialization (cf. Chapter 3). The fact that some women have not demonstrated what are perceived as potential qualities of leadership need not mean that they do not possess such qualities when they do become responsible for management. On the other hand, this absence of any visible qualities of leadership – socially recognized – may intensify the uncertainty as to how women are to be judged in this respect. It is, of course, worse if gender stereotypes play a part so that women are not expected to have any qualities of leadership. This will obviously limit their possibilities of getting on in the hierarchy of an organization. Leadership qualities are not easy to define – and perhaps they are more related to specific situations than actually qualities that can be defined in constant terms and which work in all respects. Some writers even think that it is a question of the attribution by the surroundings of characteristics to a specific person (Calder, 1977).

When women cannot as easily as men act informally in a way which can with a little ingenuity be interpreted as leadership qualities they are in a position that is inferior to that of men. It could also be noted that the general idea that leadership is more in accordance with male than with female characteristics, will not contribute to making it easier for women to be judged as suitable managers (cf. the examination of literature in Chapters 4 and 5). The leadership profile is thus important – and presumably it is expected that it can more easily be filled by a man in a traditional, hierarchic bureaucracy. For this reason it may be very difficult for women to 'profile' themselves as potential managers.

As already mentioned an active process is carried on during the first fifteen years of the life of the members of staff within the organization of sorting out, judging and evaluating them and the results of these evaluations are entered in their files (reports). As this evaluation is carried out by the managers, it is mainly men who evaluate the employees. And those at the top who are responsible for appointments and promotions are only men.

The same is true in Great Britain where at the end of the 1960's a representative selection of reports on female and male civil servants were compared (Walters, 1987). Their immediate superiors were asked to evaluate their performance by way of a list of specific characteristics. Only minor differences between women and men were reported with the exception of two fields in which women and men were evaluated significantly differently.

Firstly, women were much more often than men evaluated as being *less stable*, that is to say, it was less likely that they would be 'highly dependable', and they were not as good at adapting to new situations, they were more often nervous, more easily brought off balance, and so forth.

Secondly, they were evaluated significantly differently from men when it concerned *an evaluation of the position* that they were expected to cope with. 50% of all men were regarded as capable of functioning at a level above the level of manager, whereas only 33% of the women were regarded as capable of this. The conclusion was that it seemed that when women and men were compared in specific fields as regards the performance of their work, those making the evaluations (mainly men) reported only minor differences between the sexes. However, when evaluations were made as regards the general style and as regards the candidates' potential as managers then the evaluation was that women lacked something as compared to men. And Walters (1987:23) concludes,

Certainly in the higher civil service ... the designation of individuals as 'outstanding' is unhesitatingly made and committed to record. There is a lot of evidence from the past twenty years which shows that women practitioners are, as a group, always judged as providing a smaller proportion of 'outstanding' practitioners than men.

Something similar seems to apply for the MFA. The effect of a candidate's sex seems to be stronger in general evaluations (for instance the ability to function in a job at higher levels) than in a more specific evaluation of a concrete and limited performance. And as already mentioned the reports on staff in the MFA during their first 15 years are rarely very concrete.

Officially the obligation to be transferred is always mentioned as the important factor when the MFA is to explain why so few women hold managerial positions in the ministry. And indeed a number of women resign before being stationed abroad or after having been stationed abroad once or twice because their families cannot join them. In addition to this, a few women obtain leave of absence because they are married to men employed in the MFA and then they join their husbands when they are stationed abroad. As mentioned earlier there is seldom 'space' for two graduates in an embassy. However, there is still a large number of women left, who are not married or have children, and who have nothing against being transferred. Some of them have actually applied for jobs in the MFA for this very reason. So the small number of women in managerial positions cannot more than partly be explained by the obligation to be transferred, it is still only just under 10% of the women who have obtained managerial positions as compared to approximately 40% of the men. When people point to the system of overseas postings as one of the reasons why the female employees seldom are promoted to managerial ranks, they are not aware of the gender substructue of this system, the fact that the system is not neutral to gender, but favours male colleagues. Gender bias becomes a part of the picture in that those in charge have established a system (structures) where the precondition for making a career (at higher levels) is stationing abroad, and in that there are also preconceived expectations that women will be more reluctant to accept stationing abroad. The gender bias of the career system is, of course, not primarily a matter of arbitrary male dominance over women, but tightly coupled to a rational way of operating. Without employees being stationed abroad, the ministry could not function. One could, however, imagine a more flexible system, where greater variation in career patterns could be allowed.

One may wonder to what extent the relatively greater 'breaks' of women in the ordinary career pattern reinforce the notions (stereotypes) within the organization as regards women being to a a greater extent oriented towards the family and less likely to stake everything on a career. In an organization in which career-orientation is a very central factor, it may be that in the event of a few more departures from the norm within a group, this will be communicated to how this group is 'perceived' by others. The large number of women in the MFA who are obviously career-oriented will, however, most likely counteract this tendency of a 'distorted perception' becoming too strong. It is possible, however, that in ambiguous situations women will more often than men be judged as less 'reliable' when it comes to their career.

To conclude this chapter regarding the very low degree of female managers at the ministry, we would like to point at the significance of nuances and details for how the two sexes are distributed along the career hierarchy. We have found no clear signs on discrimination against women. All the women still employed and working in the ministry feel that they have been treated fairly and also those interviewed that have left the organization and express themselves more critically do not present indications on crude discrimination.[4] The examples of stereotypical gender thinking quoted basically refers to female employees encounters with foreigners in international contexts or to events which happened a number of years ago. In a few cases, the political pressure for appointing female managers and showing consistency between organizational policy and general societal values regarding gender equality seems to have facilitated the promotion of females to managerial posts.

Nevertheless, the career prospects of women are, or at least have been, considerably worse than those of men, despite strong interests in career and promotion among the female employees (i.e. those with a university degree and on the career track). We will not here repeat our interpretations of what processes and mechanisms which account for this outcome. Of particular relevance appears to be how family conditions affect men and women in different ways, how the interests of the women are poorly reflected in a somewhat rigid career system and how evaluations and expectations of people's potentiality, including their leadership ability in a managerial job, may handicap women.

An important insight is the possibility of considerable variation in the career outcomes of men and women, being a matter not primarily of discrimination, prejudices, stereotypes, women being different than men in terms of style, ability or motivation as much as more subtle conditions, in which rational and reasonable arrangements and processes involve minor elements which affect career routes in a gendered way.

Notes

1 Within two years some become eventually head of section. Then they will compete for a managerial post (= head of division), later on maybe deputy secretary of state (= head of sub-department), and finally secretary of state (= head of department).

2   One week after the publication of the Danish edition of this book a female ambassador
    was appointed.
3   The possibility that men and women may differ in their exercise of 'informal leader-
    ship' does not, of course, contradict claims that male and female managers do not
    exhibit significant variation in their styles of leadership (as reported in chapter 4).
4   Of course, one can not rule out the chance that more sensitive observers could have
    perceived signs on subtle discrimination or that those employed at the ministry would
    be inclined to express themselves in a 'diplomatic' way about their workplace. Their
    strong interest in careers may have encouraged such an attitude. By interviewing peo-
    ple who have left the ministry we have tried to counteract this problem. A difficulty
    with this move is that some of these may have been frustrated with their careers at
    MFA and somewhat antagonistic to its promotion policy, so their statements can not
    be taken at face value either. The solution we have chosen is to try to balance the
    various opinions, experiences and evaluations and also to rely on deductions, partly
    based on other investigations, when identifying and explaining significant practices
    and processes in the organization.

Part Three: Discussions and reflections

10 Reflections on the case-studies

In this chapter we will compare and discuss some of the results from the three case-studies. As mentioned earlier we do not intend to generate the central results from the case-studies through careful comparisons of specific variables of the three organizations investigated. Many of the interesting conclusions and results are based on the interpretations of each individual case-study. It is to a great extent through a more detailed study of the unique combination of circumstances and conditions that are characteristic of a specific organization that important dimensions and mechanisms can be brought into focus. We are aware that such an approach does not permit us to 'prove' or strictly test interpretations and theses, however, on the basis of our present knowledge within the field of research, we find an approach generating ideas and theses more important. Therefore, the comparisons that follow will first and foremost be of a descriptive and discursive nature. An important aim of the chapter is to sum up and complete some of the conclusions that are to be found in the previous chapters and to develop some ideas further on the basis of an overall discussion of the three case-studies at a wider level.

The chapter starts with a brief summary of a number of important aspects of the three organizations investigated. Then follows some discussion of the existence of various barriers to women's career, promotion and functioning in management positions and after that, the question of inequality between the sexes at various types of places of work. After these discussions, which provide descriptions and interpretations of the ways in which organizations function from the perspective of gender, we attempt to demonstrate central factors behind the organizational conditions in question, in part based on how social developments are reflected on the organizational level, in part based on the composition of the sexes within the organizations. Finally, we discuss briefly the possibilities of generalizing on the basis of our studies and on the basis of this we provide an answer to the question, 'Why are there so few female managers?'.

10.1 Summary of the three case-studies

An important motive for concentrating this investigation on the organizational level was, as pointed out in the introduction to this book, an impression that at this level the variations are considerable as regards women's possibilities of obtaining and functioning in management positions. In the majority of research into women and management the implicit assumption seems to be that the organi-

zational level need not be taken seriously. At any rate it is common for researchers to send out questionnaires to or interview people from various organizations without investigating these organizations in depth or give an account of
the local social context that creates the specific difficulties that are often reported to apply to female managers. It is true that this procedure provides a
number of valuable results and it would be adequate if there were no major
variations at the organizational level. However, if such variations can be ascertained, it becomes important also to take the organizational level seriously and to
completement overall and general studies with case-studies that are specific to
certain organizations.

Our three investigations do indeed confirm our initial impressions and provide
strong arguments for investigating the problems of gender not just at a societal
level or within broad categories such as the private versus the public sector, but
also at the level of a specific organization. Later on, we will discuss the problem
of how case-studies of this type within this area can be used as inspiration for
more general reasoning and interpretation.

As has appeared clearly, the three case-studies show very large differences as
regards the way in which different organizations (social areas) function from the
perspective of gender. In the National Board of Social Welfare it is hardly possible to find any sign of a significant inequality between the sexes or barriers that
prevent women from obtaining or functioning in senior positions. In the Ministry of Foreign Affairs the picture is somewhat diffuse and difficult to grasp, but
it seems clear that the organizational and working conditions make it considerably more difficult for women than for men to make a career and obtain senior
positions. Roughly, one could say that while women's prospects of obtaining a
senior position in the National Board of Social Welfare equal those of a man
with the same qualifications, the likelihood that a woman will obtain a senior
position in the Ministry of Foreign Affairs is considerably less than for a man
with the same qualifications.

From a gender perspective, the National Board of Social Welfare shows an
almost 'idyllic' picture. The share of women in senior positions almost corre-
sponded to the share of women in the group of university graduates. None of
those interviewed referred to experiences or observations that pointed to women
being exposed to any kind of discrimination or in any other way being exposed
in the local context (the place of work) to influences that made the preconditions
for wanting or being able to obtain senior positions more difficult as compared
to male colleagues. This does not exclude the possibility that such a social and
cultural influence may in a very subtle way characterize the organization in question. Reproduction of gender patterns is indeed to a great extent exercised at a
concealed and non-conscious level, and this can hardly be fully illuminated completely in interviews, however well these are arranged and however open the
persons interviewed are and however much they have reflected on the issues at
hand. On the basis of general analyses of the gendered nature of society, it

would be unlikely if a certain production and reproduction of the 'general' societal perceptions and gender patterns did not in fact take place, even in an organization such as the National Board of Social Welfare. With this reservation it must be noted, however, that by and large the National Board of Social Welfare effectively questions those common theories and reasonings which claim that patriarchal circumstances and mechanisms at the social level will *in general* create a vertical division of labour with women at the bottom and men at higher levels in organizations (cf. Chapter 3). A generalization as regards this type of theories and the force and unambiguousness of the general reproduction of patriarchal conditions must be questioned.

The question is then, how (a-)typical is the National Board of Social Welfare? A rough comparison with Danish ministries – which are the organizations that can best be compared with the National Board of Social Welfare as regards the nature of work, the educational level of the staff, etc. – indicates that the National Board of Social Welfare is not a typical organization, but on the other hand it is not an extreme exception. In four other departments there is more or less accordance between the share of female university graduate (non-managerial) personnel and the share of women in senior positions (The Ministry of Housing, the Ministry of Ecclesiastical Affairs, the Ministry of Social Affairs, and the Ministry of Education), but apart from this, women's share of senior positions in the departments of the ministries (12%) does not as a whole correspond to their share of the positions of graduates (32%). Half of the ministries had only one or no women in senior positions. At the level of secretary of state and permanent secretary (senior positions) there were two women out of 29 (7%).

From a gender perspective if we look at the circumstances that seem to contribute to how the National Board of Social Welfare has developed, it should be noted that the field with which the organization is concerned – social questions at an overall, administrative level – can be seen as a synthesis of a 'male' and a 'female' field of work. Thus, there are good preconditions for gender neutrality. The characteristics, values, attitudes, etc. of those who are recruited for and remain in the organization will to a certain extent overlap this. Nobody in the organization is extremely 'masculine'. An additional factor that affects the progressive appearance of the National Board of Social Welfare in the respects relevant here is related to the political and social progressiveness that to some extent characterizes the social welfare sector as such (in Western societies during the past decades) and more specifically many of the members of staff working in the National Board of Social Welfare.

The picture that emerges of SAS on the basis of our investigation is of an organization which is by tradition characterized very strongly by a very far reaching gendered division of labour, both horizontally and vertically. The groups that have traditionally dominated in the organization, engineers and pilots, have almost exclusively consisted of men. At the same time, major parts of the field of work of SAS throughout the past decades has been typical women's work, for instance check-in and cabin crew. Traditionally, and to a very great extent also today, SAS reflects the general gender pattern and gender division of labour, vertically and horizontally that characterizes the western societies. As was mentioned in Chapter 8 only 6 of 156 senior positions at a high level were held by women, i.e. 4% (in 1985). In the entire company more than 40% of the employees are females. (These figures apply to SAS as a whole, i.e. not only to SAS Denmark.)

Our field investigation of SAS has to a great extent focused on the changes that have characterized the organization in the 1980's.[1] This focus seems reasonable in the case of SAS as it is not possible to deal with our issue without making allowance for the changes of the experiences, frames of reference and evaluations of those interviewed. In SAS the assumptions and understandings of female employees has to some extent been coloured by the changes that have characterized the organization in recent years. It may be added that the fact that so much attention is focused on the change is both good and bad for our analysis. The positive aspect is that the change means that various matters are exposed more clearly – the fact that something is changed means that the phenomenon in question can be looked at in a new way as well as the old. It is not taken for granted in the same way as was formerly the case. It also becomes easier to describe. Qualitative phenomena are often difficult to describe, as they are not absolute, but relative. The problem of quantifying hierarchy is obvious if one wants to capture something in addition to the number of formal levels of the hierarchy, for instance, the qualitative relation and the dynamics between various levels. On the other hand, one can say that it is more or less hierarchic than any other organization or more or less hierarchic than it used to be. Focusing on change can also be problematic, however, in that too much attention is centered on the direction of developments. The fact that an organization, such as SAS, is experienced as 'less hierarchic' than formerly can easily be understood as the organization appearing and being described as 'less hierarchic' than other organizations in general. The figure appears all too clearly whereas one is not conscious of the ground, the frame of reference for what one is seeing.

From a gender perspective, SAS appears basically as a traditional and old-fashioned organization, but it has also changed in recent years in a way which means that there are also some new thoughts as regards the gender division of labour and the earlier priority given to men when it came to promotion to the middle management level and to higher positions. These new thoughts are not voiced very strongly in the organization as a whole, however. Women have a clear interest, expressed in the network called Scanweb, and a certain, less pronounced interest exists at management level in improving the conditions for women so that they can be candidates for management positions on equal terms with men. Progress is not on a major scale or very clear. The number of women who apply for management positions and are promoted to managers seems to have increased somewhat, but it does not seem to be a marked increase. The attempt at promoting the careers of women through Scanweb has not been carried on with much vigour.

Even though neither the present situation of SAS nor the changes experienced in the organization during the 1980's make it appear very modern or 'progressive' as regards our issue, it seems that the organization is to a great extent characterized by an interest for (certain types of) aspects relating to gender and an awareness that there is a clear discrepancy between the potentials of female employees and the 'utilization' of these in management positions. Thus, it should be possible to describe SAS as an organization which is on its way to changing some elements of its earlier way of functioning and the traditional gender division of labour in relation to the utilization of qualified female employees. In other words, the organization (i.e. parts of the staff) attempts to make itself more up-to-date with regard to gender equality. The great concern with the fact that women do not apply for management jobs is a manifestation of this.

While the study of SAS shows a clear interest in and awareness of the difficulties that exist for women in applying for management positions, the investigation of the Ministry of Foreign Affairs gives an altogether different impression. The most striking point here is that whereas the members of staff – women as well as men – almost in unison claim that female members of staff (university graduates, i.e. those formally qualified for promotion) have the same possibilities of being promoted, the present gender division of labour shows a very widespread vertical division of labour in which women are extremely underrepresented at the senior level. Some of those interviewed who have left the ministry are of the opinion that discrimination exists in various ways while those interviewed who are still employed in the ministry do not think so even though some of them are open to the possibility that discrimination might have existed formerly.

The low figures are usually explained by spokesmen of the organization in terms of women not being interested in foreign service (transfers) to the same extent as men, have not reached the age when they could obtain senior positions to the same extent as their male colleagues and cannot be chosen for positions in certain countries with a conservative view of women. These explanations contribute only slightly to an understanding as to why so few women hold senior positions. Only a few of the senior positions are to be found in countries which exclude women. Women who have reached the age when they could hold senior positions are promoted much more rarely than men of the same age and the number of women who renounce the foreign service for family reasons (and thus reduce their possibility of being promoted) is, it is true, percentually larger than the number of men, but not so large that this could explain the low number of women in senior positions. As, in general, the women just like the men in the Ministry of Foreign Affairs take a strong interest in their career, want to hold senior positions and have the same qualifications and have worked within the same fields as their male colleagues (there is no strong gender division of labour within the group in question), the low number of women in senior positions is an enigma to put it mildly and something which spokesmen of the ministry cannot explain more than partially.

One gets a strong impression that in the Ministry of Foreign Affairs there seems to be no interest in reflecting on the importance of the gender dimension for senior positions. The discrepancy between the opinion that on the one hand women have the same opportunities as men and are not discriminated against and on the other hand the extremely low number of women in senior positions is striking to an outside observer, but it seems that there are no serious efforts at exploring the question in the organization. Perhaps it may be expressed as a lack of awareness in the organization of the importance of the gender dimension for the career. The difference between the ministry and SAS is striking. In the latter organization there is much more openness when it comes to talking about the situation of women and factors that result in women being discriminated against as far as career is concerned. It is true that the problems in SAS are in part more obvious – or have become more obvious – whereas the differences between the sexes as regards attaining senior positions are more difficult to grasp in the Ministry of Foreign Affairs. Women and men are obviously more similar in the ministry than in SAS when it comes to background, education, jobs and values (for instance the interest they take in their career) and perhaps personality.

However, there are clear differences as regards the *interest* taken in the question in SAS and the Ministry of Foreign Affairs respectively, not only as regards the ability to illustrate the question. Perhaps it is to a great extent related to the fact that whereas the question of female managers is supported in SAS by top management – with the CEO as a symbol of the importance of 'female' characteristics in the context of management – those at the top of the ministry do not take an interest in the subject, at least not one that is visible.

The picture that emerges of the Ministry of Foreign Affairs from a gender perspective on the basis of the interviews is strikingly full of contrasts as opposed to the more concordant pattern that emerged from the interviews in the National Board of Social Welfare and SAS, respectively. This applies, in part, to the discrepancy between the statements of those interviewed who are in the service and the actual distribution of the sexes in senior positions, in part, between the accounts of those employed in the ministry and the accounts of former members of staff. Those currently employed felt that women were not treated unfairly, neither in formal situations nor in everyday work life in the ministry, but that they had precisely the same opportunities as men. Those earlier employed claimed that in practice women were discriminated against in that promotions took place according to tacit premises, social relations and contacts and through persons who were wished/expected to be promoted being assigned tasks that meant that they became visible and could thereby more easily be selected for a senior position. In terms of 'rational' human resource management, it makes some sense to assign important and developing tasks to people expected to perform well and be suitable for promotion. 'Rational' intentions are, of course, no guarantee against discrimination.

On the basis of the above, it is difficult to express an opinion with certainty as to whether the procedure used by the ministry in connection with promotions discriminates against women. Presumably, however, the likelihood of subjective and random considerations and taken-for-granted assumptions influence the process of promotion. As research has demonstrated, the existence of an effect relating to the sexes in evaluations and assessments is common (see Chapter 5), and it is hardly likely that the Ministry of Foreign Affairs would be an exception to this. Presumably such a gender effect – which will generally discriminate against women – will be more pronounced when using a procedure like the one in the ministry than in connection with decisions where 'objective' criteria weigh more heavily and the process is more formalized.

There is no basis for claiming that the Ministry of Foreign Affairs is strongly characterized by sex discrimination. Some women formerly employed experience it this way, but this is not sufficient for being able to claim that discrimination does take place, particularly not when a number of those interviewed claim the opposite. It may be assumed, however, that the 'depth structure' of the organization – i.e. the not 'fully' conscious values, patterns of interpretation, etc. – support the career prospects of men more than those of women. Here we refer to dimensions that are specific for the organization and not, for instance, to family matters, etc. which in the Ministry of Foreign Affairs constitutes an external limitation which often makes it more difficult for women than for men. In an organization where reliability and control are important values that are given high priority – which follows from the nature of the activities – and where important parts of the work is carried out at foreign locations (embassies, etc.) it may be obvious, first and foremost, to promote those who are 'safe' – perceived as reliable and predictable. The uncertainty is always experienced as greater when it comes to those who differ from oneself. As all those holding senior positions, from the level of the deputy secretaries of state and upwards, are men, and women have still by and large not tried holding positions at the higher levels there is most likely a tendency that men are regarded as more suitable. Marginally, sex may affect various decisions. This does not mean that a less qualified man will be preferred to a visibly more qualified woman, but it may mean that of two more or less equally competent candidates of opposite sex, the man may have a minor advantage.

Here it may be added that the research into perceptions has shown that different people evaluate candidates rather differently before their employment as well as in later assessments of their performance (Johns, 1983). There is every reason to believe that in a situation of choice, it is only possible occasionally to choose 'the best' candidate for the job. A similarity with the one assessing the candidates on the basis of the former's experience, will for instance increase the

likelihood of the candidate of being regarded as the one with the best qualifications (the 'similar to me' effect). In an organization with a very large qualified
staff this may have a more drastic impact on the share of women promoted than
in organizations where the number of people competent to become managers is
smaller. In the latter case the differences with regard to competence may be
greater and then it is more likely that the most competent will be chosen. Owing
to the nature of the Ministry of Foreign Affairs – where a predictable behaviour
and reliability are important ingredients – the tendency towards homosocial reproduction is probably stronger than in many other organizations, which may
lead to men somewhat more easily being promoted to the senior positions. This
is also related to what we described earlier (in Chapter 5) as lack of congruity of
sexual roles, the fact that there is a stronger tendency that women are discriminated against in areas that are traditionally 'masculine' (and the job of diplomat
is regarded as such) because in such areas there is a stronger influence from
social cultural notions of the sexes. The picture of the diplomat is – as is the case
for people in senior positions – that of a man. The gender effect related to the
evaluations is stronger here.

In the National Board of Social Welfare the field of work is by tradition not
'masculine' but rather gender neutral, which can be assumed to mean that evaluations of people will not to any great extent discriminate against one or the other
of the sexes.

10.2 Barriers

The *external, structural barriers* are of a certain importance in SAS for the
career prospects of women. The gendered division of labour means that women
and men are unevenly distributed in the divisions. Vertically, men dominate at
the higher levels while women are strongly over-represented at lower levels and,
as mentioned earlier, the possibility of making a career is related to the gendered
division of labour. In other words, if people are not in a career track but have
routine work, they tend to become uninterested in/indifferent as regards a possible career. Generally speaking, higher education has not previously been a precondition for being employed in SAS in general where in-service training is
offered. This means that many of those who start working in SAS do not have a
particular career direction based on earlier education or training and that therefore they can end up in various tracks in SAS.

There is no corresponding gender division of labour in the other two organizations as far as the group of university graduates is concerned (and as already
mentioned we concentrate on this group in the National Board of Social Welfare
and the Ministry of Foreign Affairs). There is no reason to go into detail about
the National Board of Social Welfare as it has been found that there are no
barriers in this organization. Women have just as many opportunities as men of

obtaining senior positions. As regards the Ministry of Foreign Affairs, it was earlier typically university graduates with a law degree or an economics degree who were recruited but today recruitment is more general.

Educational requirements do not, in themselves, explain the unevenness in the distribution of senior positions in the Ministry of Foreign Affairs. It may explain why the share of women is still rather small in this organization where women hold approximately 20% of the posts of non-managerial university graduate personnel. Women have not completed university courses on a major scale until the 1970's. In other words, they have joined the organization at a later point in time.

What role does it play that women constitute a minority (one third in SAS of the total and one fifth of graduates in the Ministry of Foreign Affairs) in the two organizations where the number of women in senior positions does not correspond to the percentage of women employed in the organization as a whole? A number of researchers have pointed out that *the composition of the sexes* is highly significant for the career prospects of women (see Chapter 5). Investigations have shown that different psychological mechanisms work depending on whether the group in question is balanced, whether the group is uneven or whether there is a majority of one sex. It is often claimed, as appeared from Chapter 5, that a reasonably large share of women at the workplace is more or less a precondition for women's possibility of advancing. This statement is in part supported by our investigation, but it is difficult to say what factor has played the greatest role, whether it is the composition of the sexes or a number of 'qualitative' organizational conditions, for instance the culture of the organization, the management style or the contents of the work. The problem here is, among other things, that the composition of the sexes may be assumed to affect culture, management, etc. and at the same time this will affect the ratio of men/-women who are recruited for the organization. As the composition of the sexes is so intertwined with other variables, it is not easy to ascertain the specific effect of this factor.

The theory of critical mass, which says, among other things, that women do not have a chance of asserting themselves (and obtaining senior positions to an extent corresponding to their relative share of the organization) until they constitute approximately 30% cannot, however, be confirmed by our investigations of SAS and the Ministry of Foreign Affairs which show that the number of women in the organization as a whole is no guarantee. It may become important when obviously two candidates are equally qualified, which of course is seen most clearly in the case of members of staff with a long prior higher education. In that case, it will presumably seem more obviously unreasonable that there is a difference between the percentage of total personnel and the percentage of senior positions than if there is, for instance, a marked division of labour between the sexes – and candidates for senior positions are recruited exclusively from certain fields, where men dominate. In the National Board of Social Welfare women have, as already mentioned, the same chances as men of obtaining senior positions. This could be due to the fact that there is an equal number of female and male university graduates but it could also be due to the nature of the work attracting people who are not in general quite as career-oriented but have a more progressive view of things, also as regards the composition of the sexes, so that there is also room for women to advance? The problem of evaluating the importance of the composition of the sexes is, of course, related to the fact that this variable does not exist isolated from a number of other circumstances.

Our studies point clearly to the fact that it is not possible to just look at the share of women in organizations as a whole. It must also be seen in relation to various groups, subdivisions, etc.. The distribution of the sexes in SAS differs very much in the various divisions. In the National Board of Social Welfare and the Ministry of Foreign Affairs 'caste-like' conditions exist in that the senior positions are reserved for university graduates while in SAS all (suitable) candidates can in principle become managers. This has the effect that the distribution of the sexes within the group of university graduates becomes central in the Ministry of Foreign Affairs and the National Board of Social Welfare while at lower levels – and in the organization as a whole – it is of less importance for the issue under discussion.

The barriers to women most often mentioned in literature are related to the *cultural expectations* of the sexes and the role expectations of the sexes. These may be structurally conditioned – a low share of women gives rise to/reinforces certain perceptions and expectations – but more important, are value and interpretation patterns determined by cultural tradition. In an earlier chapter (3) we gave an account of various approaches as to how social and psychological inequality between the sexes is reproduced. The ideological consequences of the division of labour between the sexes which 'gave' women a special role in relation to reproduction are very difficult to combat. What we have in mind here is the ideology that most women should have the main responsibility for the home. These cultural expectations exist as a restriction and factor of influence from the surroundings, but are also 'internalized' by many women in such a way that an actual 'inner' barrier[2] arises against making a career for oneself or even wishing to do so. We have earlier touched upon the question of how the original expectations are reproduced in the system of rewards so that there are different attitudes to the two sexes where for instance evaluations relating to work tend to be to the advantage of men. These expectations, obviously, have a limiting effect on women.

Our overall material from the three organizations can hardly with certainty prove any clear and widespread differential treatment by way of discrimination as a result of sex stereotypes, etc., which obviously does not exclude the possibility that such sex stereotypes exist and do, at least to some extent, influence decisions relating to, for instance, questions of promotion. Slight indications that this is so were found, first and foremost, in the Ministry of Foreign Affairs and to some extent in SAS.

In the National Board of Social Welfare these differences of expectation were not found. Of course the expectations differ from person to person, but these are not dependent on sex. At a meeting of managers that we observed it was not possible either to find any differences in the time allotted for speaking, initiative, etc.. Men were interrupted just as much as women, they were made fun of just as much, etc..

In SAS, on the other hand, the culturally determined expectations are experienced clearly, especially in the context of meetings where women have often felt that the best strategy for getting things through would be to play the game of men. Here, also an internalized lower self-confidence was experienced among women which was formulated as women's 'fear' of applying for management positions. In addition to this, these expectations were manifested when people from outside have difficulties in understanding that the manager is a woman. Why these expectations are expressed in this way can to a certain extent be interpreted in terms of what we referred to earlier as a discourse on power theory. The implicit conditioning – which is communicated to the sexes and which maintains a belief that the order of things is natural and that one must adapt to this order of things – is a necessity and a precondition for the maintenance of the traditional, perhaps soon obsolete, societal form of organization (of the sexes). At the same time this organization is continuously changing and it may well be that the implicit conditioning has the effect that the mental functioning of some human beings is behind current developments and supports the form of society of yesterday rather than the form that is currently the most functional.

As opposed to the difficulties reported by female managers of SAS where they adapted to a number of male strategies it was interesting to note that the women holding senior positions in the Ministry of Foreign Affairs did not experience such difficulties or pressure indicating that they should change their style. In the Ministry of Foreign Affairs it is difficult for women to obtain senior positions but those who succeed are, according to themselves, encountered with no clear negative expectations or male or female-linked games.

The boundary between cultural expectations and *internalized barriers* is very often vague. An example of internalized barriers which are reinforced by the socialization at the place of work is that one makes much of routine work, lacks ambitions (because one does not think one can), has been trained to function as a secretary and has difficulties in giving up that role. The fact that SAS has also traditionally hired women on the basis of their sex appeal (stewardesses) reinforces the differences between women and men and means that it is perhaps also more difficult for women to be regarded as and to regard themselves as potential managers. However, the increased attention to the service-side of the company in the beginning of the 1980s gave rise to higher status to this part of the SAS and had the effect that more men were hired as stewards. An interesting question raised by Mills (1992) is why the job of flight attendant became a largely female occupation, equally interesting however is what makes a job change status from male to female, and vice versa, or what could make it gender neutral. We shall deal more with this aspect in Chapter 11.

On the basis of the interviews with people below management level, it seemed that in SAS the internalized barriers are important. As mentioned earlier, these barriers may be seen as a result both of the early socialization (influences during the early years) and of the socialization at the place of work that has taken place throughout a number of years where the gendered division of labour has been even more marked than it is at present and where managers were recruited from among specialists and where women, generally speaking, were marked by their absence. Finally, it is of great importance that women do not have any cultural capital, by way of higher education, which could have provided them with a certain basis so that they could assert themselves and move more freely in career tracks.

In the National Board of Social Welfare we found no particular, formal or informal barriers to women, neither external or internal.

In many instances the external barriers are of importance only when they are to be found together with internal barriers. The obligation to be transferred in the Ministry of Foreign Affairs is a structural restriction which will have far-reaching consequences for many women as long as women are expected to assume the main responsibility for the family and as long as they themselves are psychologically prepared to do so. The external, objective restriction becomes problematic in that it is related to expectations and patterns for the gender relations within the framework of the family that are disadvantageous to women. It is obvious that women feel that they are not given the same opportunities and conditions of employment as their male counterparts, when employers relate their working capacities to domestic work and the care of children, regardless of whether or not the women concerned have or want to have children (Billing, 1991:63-64). Discrimination is often associated with cultural expectations regarding what women are like and what gender roles women and men should fit into. The implicit basis for negotiations in a partnership is based on what first and foremost men, but also women have by way of more or less unconscious notions as to what priority should be given to various wishes and demands. As a rule, the career of women is not given first priority.

Another barrier which we mentioned earlier concerns the sensitive nature of the work of the Ministry (diplomatic work), the fact that the organization is ostensibly interested in sending leading representatives to foreign countries who are more 'reliable' and as long as women are comparatively new in the organization and thus an unknown category, it is perhaps safer to send off a man for key posts. This is not necessarily very rational nor conscious, but choosing people comparable to those who have traditionally held senior positions and posts as ambassadors, i.e. men, is presumably in accordance with the theory of homosocial reproduction. So the barriers here are a combination of notions about the nature of the work and structural conditions within the organization – and finally, it is a cultural question. The latter point refers to the gender assumptions and expectations that exist within the family and in society as a whole, but also of cultural ideas suggesting that women may not be regarded as suitable as managers. The problem here is that it may be more 'natural' for a man to demonstrate 'leadership qualities' (cf. Chapter 3 on socialization and sexual roles). This kind of evaluation will obviously not be to the advantage of women, they may be suitable as managers but they do not demonstrate this until they actually obtain a managerial position. Therefore, it is natural to assume that socialization, gender roles, general notions as regards management, etc. make it somewhat easier for men to be accepted as managers.

10.3 Differences/similarities between women and men in management

Several investigations have shown that there are no major noticable differences in the behaviour of women and men when it comes to leadership style (see Chapter 4). A few investigations had reached the conclusion that female managers were more supportive and more concerned with social relations. Managers were described in general terms, no allowance was made for the fact that they might be working in different organizations with varying fields of work. The differences regarding managerial style found in our investigation concern rather organizations than gender.

Our point here is that the culture at the workplace will affect the attitudes of managers (and vice versa). When the culture in the National Board of Social Welfare is described as very caring, then it is to a certain extent the same qualities that are characteristic of managers, independently of their sex. The cultural understanding of the nature of social work may put limits to the differences between managers and the rest of the staff. In the National Board of Social Welfare everybody should preferably be equal, the collective spirit dominates, "nobody should venture to show their face". Obviously such an attitude sets limits to how much impetus senior employees can have and how authoritarian status-minded they can be. Nor does it seem that there is any major change in status for those who obtain a senior position. And those in senior positions are not interested in creating a distance from the rest of the staff. Values in support of the community were supported at this place of work. In the National Board of Social Welfare most members of staff, women as well as men, give a high priority to the family, which is to be taken to mean that they are very conscious of their family, overtime is not regarded as a virtue, and they prefer not to bring their work home with them. The family became involved in the work, for instance, members of staff took their children for a visit at their place of work and employees would talk about their families. It seemed that the work pressure was also weaker than in, for instance, the Ministry of Foreign Affairs.

In contrast to the National Board of Social Welfare, there are clear differences between male and female managers in SAS. This is illustrated by the espoused opinion that meetings gave rise to other problems for female managers owing to their different style (see Chapter 8). Any differences that might exist between female and male managers were, however, removed over time because women adapted their style to that of male managers. That is to say, they consciously chose not to use their original way of handling matters because they felt that it would not be effective/good/acceptable. So we may conclude that in SAS, only minor differences in management style, patterns of communication and interaction can be found. There was a more distinct difference, however, in *relation to status*. Almost all the female managers interviewed expressed the possibility that at some point in time they would do something else, they would like to stay in SAS, but at a lower level as they would not necessarily continue as managers. Salary and status were not so important to them. It may be that men have similar interests but these have not been expressed spontaneously during the interviews. The female managers saw their role as a kind of mission, when this or that task had been solved they would go on to the next task. One man, holding a management position, expressed a similar view.

In the Ministry of Foreign Affairs it is not possible to say anything about differences in leadership style of men and women holding senior positions on account of the very few women in senior positions. The women have not, as in SAS, stated anything about a changed style, only that they have been met with reactions that differ from those with which men are encountered, in particular on travels abroad. Nor are there any histories about 'lopsided' communication during meetings, etc.. The fact that such matters are not emphasized either in the National Board of Social Welfare or the Ministry of Foreign Affairs may be related to the fact that both women and men have the ballast of a university background. With such a background, the sexes will have experienced a more similar socialization which has probably contributed to more similar conventions as regards work, communication, etc.. Here we see no differences as regards concern with status either. According to the information obtained, many women as well as men pay attention to obtaining senior positions. This need not be related to status even though it is the way to the desirable post of ambassador where one has reached the top, but it may be related to the fact that such a post means a more interesting job. People are in general career-minded and there is a high consciousness of status in that everybody knows who hold which positions, who are on their way to the 37th grade, etc.. In the Ministry of Foreign Affairs more of the female members of staff than male follow their partners when these are stationed abroad and, relatively speaking, more women than men leave the ministry. This may have an effect for the 'reputation' (the evaluation) of the other women irrespective of whether these have families or not. Two women holding senior positions have also mentioned that they would give priority to their families if they had to choose. The problem is that in this organization it is actually very difficult for women to combine family and career and for many men it is not possible either.

Our general impression is that many women (in the three organizations) take a relatively great interest in a senior position. Or perhaps a better way of phrasing it would be to say that they are both interested and ambivalent. Potential candidates for senior positions among women still differ from men in that men to a greater extent take a great interest and are less ambivalent. The impetus to get upwards in the hierarchy and stay at the highest level possible is more marked.

A question that has often been raised as regards women and senior positions is whether women are actually just as motivated to apply for and function in a senior position, this question was touched upon in Chapter 6 and we shall discuss it in more detail below.

Family matters – and in particular children – seem still, in general, to reduce women's interest (and possibilities of choice) when it comes to aiming at a career in a senior position. Relatively few women holding senior positions have children living at home. It is a matter of debate whether women's motivation to have a career in a senior position is reduced for this reason. Many women voluntarily abstain from giving priority to work/career and where this is the case they are less motivated to work than men. Others change their motivation once their children have reached school age.

This was true for a few of the women holding senior positions. However, it is one thing voluntarily to give priority to husband and children, quite a different matter if the factors behind the lacking motivation are restrictions and necessities and the woman's experience is that actually she has no choice. In that case, the central question is how the children are cared for and how the relationship between the sexes develops in the family. Here it is presumably often a question of subtleties in the interaction between the parties and implicit negotiations. The husband can often make use of 'resources' by way of internalized notions and expectations as regards sexual roles with the effect that his career will be given first priority. However, among parents it may be that many more women than men experience the greatest satisfaction in having a normal working week. Formulating this exclusively in terms of one kind of unitary and consistent motivation will imply that the social factors are underestimated. Alternatively, one could say that to many women the sum of all kinds of motivations – of which some are diverse and contradictory – will be less in the direction of giving priority to career and senior positions. Children, less need for status, etc. play a role. The differences between the sexes seem, however, to be in the process of being reduced.

It may be worth pointing to the discrepancy between a strong interest in senior positions and the personal preconditions for functioning well in such positions. Presumably the differences between women and men are considerably greater as regards the *motivation* to become a manager than as regards the *ability* to function well in the job. Even though the willingness to stake much on a career

probably makes it easier to do well in a management job, and in certain jobs may
be a precondition, the correlation between careerism and leadership ability is far
from obvious. In our case-studies we found that there is a very marked tendency
for women to consider going downwards in the hierarchy. This flexibility might
be seen as an excellent 'quality' from an organizational perspective in connection with the recruitment of managers, compared with the situation where traditions and the psychological attitudes of managers make downward mobility impossible.

10.4 Social change and organizational change

One way of understanding the different patterns that characterize the three organizations is to take the societal context as a basis. It may be fruitful to look at the
relation between society and organization in dialectic terms as is for instance
mentioned by Mills (1988). He believes life at the organizational level exists in a
dialectic relationship with the broader social system of values and the two are
shaped and reshaped by each other.

We see Scandinavian and other Western countries going through a change
which leads to a certain weakening of the division of labour between the sexes in
general and the vertical division of labour in particular. A change[3] is in general
taking place, even if organizational exclusion may hinder women's progress and
the relative gains made by well-qualified women may be considerably less than
those of men at the same level of qualification (Crompton & Sanderson, 1990).
The scope, unambiguousness and rate of speed of this change is open to discussion, but it seems that the number of women obtaining management positions
has increased during the past decades and is on its way to being increased further
at least up to the middle management level (see Chapter 2). The fact that there
are more women than formerly in the labour market, that more women attend
higher education and that more women see wage labour as a central (necessary)
part of their existence can be seen as an expression of a general change. (The
fact that many women are unemployed does not mean that they are uninterested
in wage labour.)

Organizations and workplaces are no doubt strongly affected by this trend
which is to a great extent experienced in sectors of society outside the actual
labour market, for instance, changed gender ideologies, conventions relating to
care and the family and new educational patterns. At the same time the work
organizations (and here we disregard institutions of education, etc.) are a very
central part of society and changes in these determine to a great extent changes
in the gender pattern. The most important consequences of, for instance,
changed educational patterns or ideologies relating to the paid work of women
are not felt until these changes outside the work organizations are communicated
to the organizational level and the workplace by way of employment and careers

within trade and industry, etc.. Most vocational training or plans for paid work do not lead anywhere until employment has been achieved within an organization. The number of self-employed is, after all, limited. Thus, social changes outside the organizations and those taking place inside organizations are mutually interactive. A dialectic view of the relationship between society and the organizations is thus justified for neither the overall pattern of society nor variations within various trades, types of organization or individual places of work should be treated lightly.

One way of illustrating the problems taken up here, i.e. the low representation of women in management positions is to assume a general trend in the direction of more female managers and then discuss how this is more specifically brought about in various contexts. The general though weak trend, i.e. the aggregate of changes at various places of work, is the sum of quite different patterns at the concrete level, i.e. the organizational level. The latter can correspond fully to the trends of society, i.e. a moderate improvement in women's possibilities and in the number of female managers, first and foremost at lower levels and at middle management level. Organizations can, however, be ahead of or accelerate this trend by being particularly 'affirmative to women' or they can have a preservative effect through maintenance of male dominance at management level or even have a 'reactionary' effect by being contrary to the general trend and reinforce male dominance at management level. The latter should be less general, however, and does not appear in our investigation but was, for instance, found at top management level within BBC between 1969 and 1979 (Fogarty et al, 1981) where the percentage of women decreased from 3% to 1.5%.

It is easy to rank the three organizations studied as regards their position in relation to the trend mentioned. The National Board of Social Welfare comes first, followed by SAS and the Ministry of Foreign Affairs, respectively. It almost seems as if gender differences have been abolished in the National Board of Social Welfare when it comes to the functioning of the organization and the handling of questions relating to the recruitment of people for senior positions. Thus, the National Board of Social Welfare is ahead of social developments in general. SAS seems to be more or less in parity with this trend. The nature of the organization involves both preserving elements and elements of change. The combination of a technically advanced and heavy enterprise on the one hand and service-orientation on the other has, as already mentioned, the effect that the gender division of labour is pronounced. This has a conserving effect. It appears as natural for women and men to be concerned with different fields and as men are strongly overrepresented in the areas which have traditionally been regarded as being the most central and prestigious it is 'natural' that they also hold the majority of the senior positions. In addition to this the relatively low formal educational level of the employees on average, (at least compared to our two other case-studies) also plays a role when it comes to counteracting the traditional vertical division of labour. The uncertainty and ambivalence of the female

employees as regards application for management positions is to some extent
related to this. As said before, the general rule is that higher vocational training
arouses an interest in and perhaps even provides, a sense of security for persons
in management positions. The importance of education as a symbolic support is
presumably greater for women than for men in that women are at a disadvantage
on account of their lack of role models, the expectations of their surroundings
which are often negative, internalized sexual roles, etc.. Education can counteract the uncertainty as regards career and management jobs which women experience as a problem to a greater extent than men.

While the circumstances mentioned thus point in the direction of preservation,
market forces indirectly represent an influence that is to a greater extent oriented
towards change in the case of SAS. The management of the organization also
played a role here in relation to the restructuring of the organization ("the cultural revolution"). SAS' situation of competition at the beginning of the 1980's
led to strategic changes which also influenced the functioning of the organization from a gender perspective. The parts of the organization where women constituted a majority, i.e. the service activities, were given a higher priority. 'Typical' female qualities and the style of management were regarded as being in
harmony with the new structure of the organization. Using abstract terms, one
could perhaps talk of a kind of 'demasculinization' of the organization – in that
the male-dominated field of work became less trend-setting than formerly. The
description given by the CEO of the new style of management in terms of gender (a synthesis of female and male qualities) was not without importance either.
All this led to a tendency for female employees to have a greater self-esteem and
more self-confidence. The general tendency in the direction of change also involved a kind of general base for the unfreezing of various notions and patterns,
including gender patterns. The result was a general 'modernization' of the way
in which the organization functioned and, at any rate, of parts of the self-under-
standing of the staff from a gender perspective. As far as can be judged, developments within SAS have been more rapid in the course of the 1980's than for
society as a whole. It does not follow, however, that as regards women's possibilities of making a career for themselves and functioning in management positions, SAS is today ahead of average developments in society in general. We
find it hard to judge this. But one thing is certain, developments during the past
years have been dynamic compared to what is usual in that type of organization.

The same can hardly be claimed for the Ministry of Foreign Affairs which in
the respects relevant here is in sharp contrast to the National Board of Social
Welfare. If one looks at the Ministry as a whole, i.e. not just the groups of
university graduates on which we have concentrated our investigation, but also
other parts of the organization, there is a large majority of women at the lower
levels while men dominate strongly at middle management and higher levels.
Thus the ministry has a traditional and old-fashioned gender pattern. This pattern is reinforced and maintained by the way in which the service obligation and

careers are organized, general demands being made on service abroad as an important premise for promotion. In addition to this making it to a greater extent difficult for women than for men to live up to the demands of the organization, it leads to the ministry in practice having an influence in the direction of a traditional family pattern in which the husband's career is the most important and the wife adapts to this. Traditionally, the Ministry of Foreign Affairs has thus to a greater extent than other organizations promoted an old fashioned family pattern and a traditional gender pattern. For the majority of the old and even to a great extent the young (male) members of the organization the rule has been that their wives have not been able to stake very much on a career. This means, therefore, that in the 'world-view' of those employed in the Ministry of Foreign Affairs (male university graduates) the historical notion of women being normally full-time housewives or at least not giving priority to job and career can live on longer and more stubbornly than in many other sectors of society.

A structurally (organizationally) maintained traditional family pattern thus characterizes the Ministry's male university graduates in general and in particular those holding leading positions so that the general changes in family pattern and gender relations are not communicated very rapidly or to any great extent. In a 'modern' middle class family the professional differences between husbands and wives are very small. However, in general men have a certain lead. Typically the husband's education is somewhat longer, his formal position somewhat higher and/or his field of work is a half or one step higher up the ladder of status. If the wife is a junior teacher the husband may for instance be a senior master. If both of them are medical doctors, he may for instance be a surgeon while she 'typically' is a specialist in psychiatry or gerontology, e.g. a less prestigous speciality (Bengtsson, 1983; Wahl, 1992). In the Ministry of Foreign Affairs a more old-fashioned, conservative family pattern is still common, however, where the role of the wife is to follow and support the career of the husband, which means that she will not herself be employed on the labour market or at least she will not see her job as the most important. This will probably influence men's way of thinking as to what is women's 'role' in life. It is true that this way of thinking is disappearing (or taking a different shape), but as already mentioned the process is presumably slower in the Ministry of Foreign Affairs than in many other parts of society.

Also in other respects the Ministry of Foreign Affairs is characterized by circumstances which counteract full communication of the general trend in the direction of new gender relations. It is a world with more well-defined boundaries towards the surrounding society than those applying to other places of work. Stays abroad, difficulties of maintaining old relations in Denmark, long working hours, giving priority to work and career, the existence of a specific esprit de corps, the survival of an old civil service tradition, and so forth, all of these factors contribute to this. The nature of the work where reliability, security, the ability to handle matters in a diplomatic way, the importance of the ability to observe formalities, etc. presumably also contribute to the Ministry of Foreign Affairs not being a place where radically new measures are taken, where experiments are made or anything else which could promote the tendency of change. A certain conservatism and relatively well-defined boundaries against the surrounding world can thus be presumed to contribute to changes to a deep-seated gender pattern being slower in the Ministry of Foreign Affairs than in many other sectors of society and other organizations. It should also be remembered that the picture of the Ministry of Foreign Affairs as somewhat conservative when it comes to gender roles is far from unambiguous. The (few) female managers in the ministry reported no problems and did not share the experience of the women employed in SAS of sexually related role-playing and subsequent collisions.

This section may be summarized as follows: the general, slow and far from unambiguous trend in the direction of an improvement of the position of women on the labour market, including an increase in the number of women holding senior positions, makes itself felt very differently in various organizations. Various circumstances can reinforce or counteract this trend. Typical factors that can reinforce the trend are to be found abundantly in the National Board of Social Welfare (see Chapter 7 for an examination of these). In SAS we find a mixture of circumstances reinforcing change and preserving factors. In the Ministry of Foreign Affairs the preserving forces are obviously strong even though the existence of a number of highly qualified women, who are not clearly treated unfairly in the gender division of labour during at least the initial years of their career, should increase women's possibilities of being promoted to senior positions. Also the political pressure that is brought to bear to satisfy public opinioin, including female voters, in the direction of a reasonable number of women in senior positions should point in this direction, but obviously the forces that are opposed to change are stronger in the Ministry of Foreign Affairs. These forces are to be found partly within the organization partly in family life which makes less women than men prepared to realize their career ambitions.

10.5 Can we make generalizations on the basis of our results?

To what extent is it possible to make generalizations on the basis of our empirical study and our general argument? Whether the National Board of Social Welfare, SAS and the Ministry of Foreign Affairs are representative can be judged only if knowledge is available of a large number of organizations. Such knowledge is not available to us. It may be assumed, however, that taken as a whole our investigations provide a relatively good picture of important aspects of the situation in Denmark and Scandinavia as far as the question of women and senior positions is concerned. This is because the three organizations differ as regards the gender composition, the gender division of labour, the nature of the work and as regards the sex which de facto works within the field of work in question and the sex which is commonly associated with that or the corresponding field of work.

On the other hand, large parts of the labour market are not represented in our choice of three organizations. In particular industrial workplaces and workplaces outside Copenhagen are not included.[4] It may be that women have more difficulty in reaching higher positions in enterprises in rural areas and within industry as a whole than in our three cases. It is possible that the circumstances and mechanisms which result in women being strongly under-represented at all levels except the lower levels at most places of work are underestimated if the results presented here are taken to be general and if allowance is not made for the fact that the results apply first and foremost to organizations offering advanced services on a large scale and to central administration in the Copenhagen area. At the same time the difficulties experienced by women with ambitions for a career may be underestimated.

Our main objective with the study has not been, however, to provide an extensive empirical description of the average situation of women and management. Instead our intention has been to illustrate the circumstances, processes and mechanisms within various organizations which support or make it more difficult for women to obtain and function in senior positions. We have found no serious problems for women of functioning in these positions, but we have indicated some difficulties which women face in obtaining positions at the higher middle management level. Our (general) conclusion is that it is not possible to arrive at general conclusions. Obviously organizations exist in which there are no major problems for women to attain and function in managerial jobs.

The nature of the difficulties may differ in those (normal) cases where the situation is not unproblematic. External, organizational barriers and internal barriers deeply rooted in the personality may be more or less central. Less motivation (a lower degree of interest in making a career) and a greater ambivalence as regards staking on management positions are important barriers. Both psychological factors, created via socialization both early in life (before entering the labour market) but also at work, as well as organizational circumstances (equality/inequality between the sexes, etc.) and family conditions (children, equality/inequality between husband and wife) may be presumed to play a role. Complex and dynamic circumstances are important. Simple statements to the effect that women are discriminated against or do not want to (dare) apply for management positions will not provide a good picture of the problems.

We shall now attempt to summarize our view of what should be taken into consideration in order to provide an answer to the question as to why there are so few female managers. This answer is to a great extent based on the overall research, in a broad sense, carried on within the field and not just in our own empirical study.

In order to understand the likelihood of a female employee obtaining a senior position, three factors can be identified: individual (psychological), organizational and family conditions. The former include qualifications, abilities, but also a capacity to handle the cultural context of work and career, etc., i.e. the capacity to act tactically correct (to play the cards in the right way, etc.). One can also talk about having the right tactical/cultural competence. In addition to this, it is important to make allowance for self-confidence and motivation. Obviously an interest in making a career and obtaining a senior position are basic factors. Many, both women and men, choose to give priority to other aspects of life. Our argument concerns only those who are (or may become) interested in becoming managers/executives. The reason why, in addition to this, we emphasize the importance of factors of motivation is, among other things, that motivation may differ and there may even be some ambivalence. If those in question have a high score as regards these four variables, qualifications, abilities (including 'ability to play the cards'), self-confidence and motivation, our claim is that it would probably be possible for them to obtain senior positions within many organizations. (We refrain from a discussion of the socially constructed nature of what are considered as 'qualifications'[5], etc. but concentrate on a more superficial, broader level.)

Women are often at a disadvantage as regards the latter three of these factors, their ability to 'play their cards' is not as good as that of men, they are sometimes less self-confident (in relation to management positions) and often less motivated to make a career. Education and earlier experience in the labour market differ between the two sexes and are not always as useful for the career of women as for that of men. However, we shall not go into detail here about this obvious partial explanation as to why women are under-represented in managerial positions.

It is more important to illustrate the other three factors (tactical/cultural competence, self-confidence and motivation). How can we understand gender differences in these respects? Researchers who regard the structure of organizations as the central factor (Kanter, 1977) have a number of suggestions and so do researchers concerned with socialization emphasizing childhood and/or learning of notions about the sexes, etc. (see Chapter 3). A third aspect which is of importance concerns family conditions. Obviously family conditions may influence the motivation to apply for and function in a senior position.

It may be tempting, on the basis of gender political considerations or more short-term ambitions of achieving change, to disregard the importance of socialization and its deeper consequences for the personality in favour of the more superficial aspects such as how sexual roles limit the scope of action of the individual. Nevertheless, socialization should be taken seriously. The gender dimension of socialization seldom supports women's preconditions for or interest in obtaining a senior position. Socialization is, of course, not just gender socialization and one must be aware of the determinism involved in pointing solely at this aspect. As a minimum it may be assumed, however, that the gender aspect of socialization will often create a certain sensitivity to social conditions which signals ambivalence in relation to women in managerial positions, which can have the effect that an endeavour to utilize management qualifications and an interest in a career is not always given first priority amongst women. It is obvious that socialization does not end on entry into the labour market. On the contrary, the various organizations will influence their staff strongly. This influence can reinforce or counteract a traditional gender socialization. An organization with a strong, traditional gender division of labour can reinforce perceptions of the sexes and gender identities established earlier and may therefore have difficulties in both stimulating and assessing potential female managers 'correctly'. The National Board of Social Welfare is an example of the opposite, here we did not find any gender bias.

When one is to judge the importance of socialization it is important to realize the depth of its consequences – to go further than, for instance, the notions as regards gender roles and sex stereotypes – without holding a deterministic view of the influence of social and cultural factors on the personality and gender identity.

Our empirical studies have not directly investigated aspects of socialization apart from those that are directly related to the organization in question – and in this connection we are thinking, first and foremost, of SAS – however, this does not provide a cause for not including this dimension in a broad discussion of the problems taken up. Internal barriers against utilizing one's potential in working life are no doubt an important limitation to many women and the interrelation with external conditions and the area in between internal and external factors, i.e. cultural factors, is an important focus for studies of gender and organizations. The patterns of the organizations cannot be understood if the life history of the groups working within the organizations are not taken into consideration. This is why we emphasize the pre-organizational socialization first and foremost of women.

So much for the internal barriers to women's possibilities of obtaining senior positions. The external barriers concern in part organizational conditions, in part the life situation as a whole of an individual, first and foremost family conditions. The first can be understood on the basis of three 'structural aspects' (stable factors) and four 'aspects of process' (the course of events). The former consist of (a) structural aspects specific to the organization, such as type of organization, the gender composition, the gender division of labour, etc.; (b) the nature of the field of work; and (c) significant organizational actors (their perception of basic ideas, values and leadership style). Points (a) and in part (b) are 'objective' in nature in that they refer to an external 'reality' which is relatively easy to describe while (c) refers to mental structures of those in charge.

The reason why it may be fruitful to distinguish between structural conditions within the organizations and the nature of the field of work is related to the fact that the former refer to the specific nature of an organization while the field of work concerns rather the activities of a certain group and is also related to the latter having also a symbolic dimension: the majority of fields of work must be regarded as having a 'masculine' image (e.g. diplomacy, aviation, top management) or 'feminine' traits (e.g. many service jobs, welfare work). We will develop this idea in the final chapter. Often there are several fields of work within an organization, for example associated with different professions. In our three cases we have dealt with both the structural, organizational aspects and the fields of work in question and we do not define this dimension more specifically here.

The third point, i.e. significant organizational actors, refers to the concrete basis for making evaluations and reaching decisions as regards the career of women. This point thus concerns the ideas, possible stereotypes, of those holding senior positions, those recruiting staff and other decision makers which can give rise to perceptual bias, etc. that are important at the micro level. The way in which significant actors behave is in part shaped by the other two more structural dimensions. However, there may still be considerable variations as to how those holding senior positions reach their decisions, etc.. The structure thus affects but does not determine the way of action of the actors. Even though selection for senior positions and the influence brought to bear on senior managers (socialization) within the organization lead to a certain homogenization of the group, actors in one and the same organization may show great differences as to prejudices, values, aims, unconscious assumptions, etc.. Not least the extensive research into the gender effect in connection with evaluations (Chapter 5) shows that aspects of perception, which are sometimes understood better at the level of the actors than at a sociological/structural level, should be taken into consideration in context. Another reason why we have included organizational actors as an important part of our model is that the actions of leading actors can have an impact throughout the whole of the organization when it comes to the possibilities of women. The top manager Jan Carlzon's view and formulation of leadership in SAS illustrates this.

The connection between the three factors mentioned (which form part of working and organizational conditions) are of importance. These are external factors existing, de facto, independently of the consciousness of the individual whose situation and prospect we try to understand (in this context the female candidate for a top position). In the interaction between this and the organization there are four mechanisms and processes which we want to emphasize. Thus we are focusing on the border area between the external and the internal, even though in a number of instances more focus is brought to bear on the external/'objective' aspect. We have the following four process-related phenomena: (a) (selective) perception, including bias ('sex effects') as regards evaluations and prognostication; (b) homo-social reproduction which contains a number of aspects from bias in perception to a wish of promoting one's own category; (c) social games and bias as a result of different rules of interpretation for men and women; and (d) the phenomenon of tokenism.

There is a certain overlapping between the four aspects, however, the most complete picture is given by including them all. There is also a certain overlapping in relation to the structural factors mentioned above. The latter concerned characteristics of 'the system' and prominent actors, however. These characteristics do not determine specific courses of events, for instance, the perception in a given situation. We take it that the reader will now have an idea as to the meaning of the four aspects of process. Our own empirical studies have to a greater extent centered on games specific to the sexes and to forms of understanding related to such games (e.g. how the game is played in SAS) and homo-social reproduction than on the other two aspects, but as mentioned above this does not prevent us from providing a more complete picture than what can be based on an empirical study of a research project such as the present one.

Often literature on the topic emphasizes that the four aspects mentioned are a consequence of external conditions, for instance the gender composition, and are not directly related to women themselves and their consciousness or their actions. For instance, it appears that Kanter (1977:219-222) is of the opinion that tokenism is a (mechanical) function of a low percentage of women in a social group, which has the effect that these are perceived as representatives of their sex and are (stereotypically) regarded as having certain specific traits. A clear exception, such as for instance Margaret Thatcher, indicates that it may be wise also to allow room for the impact of individual characteristics. Our point is thus that the four mechanisms/tendencies mentioned will not automatically and deterministically make themselves felt. The internal characteristics of women and the degree to which they consciously or through their actions correspond to or differ from stereotypical notions of the sexes mean quite a lot for the extent to which a selective, biased perception of women's way of functioning and qualifications, homo-social reproduction, 'erroneous' plays and tokenism arise and affect women's (limited) possibilities of having the same chances as men. Even though the ratio between the sexes or the perceptions of senior managers should in themselves point in the direction of tokenism/homo-social reproduction and a biased perception, respectively, such trends can be counteracted by individual actions (cf. quotations from interviews in Chapter 8). This is not a variant of the 'blame-the-victim' theme. Avoiding looking at the problems and obstacles that may be experienced by women with ambitions of making a career solely in structural, mechanical terms opens up the possibility, however, of getting a more varied understanding of the whole issue and points towards the possibility of handling, within a certain context, the 'external' obstacles. The latter are, as will be known, not made of cast-iron but, first and foremost, consist of cultural constructions and social interaction patterns in which male as well as females are involved.

By way of conclusion, the family sphere should be mentioned – the third factor in our model of circumstances which reduce women's possibilities of making a career or obtaining senior positions. We have not systematically studied the importance of this factor, however, it is expressed clearly in the interviews with most of the female managers. The fact that women are expected – and even tend to – take more responsibility for children and housekeeping than do men no doubt provides in some measure an explanation as to why the number of female managers and executives is so low. What is just as interesting as the actual restrictions brought about by children, etc. is perhaps the *notions* in this respect. These are to be found in partnerships, but also at the place of work. If – which is not unlikely – senior managers and others within the organization assume that the career of women is to a greater extent encumbered by children than the career of men, this may have the effect that women are discriminated against, not only as regards special decisions concerning promotion but also as regards subtle communcation which may even affect self-perception and notions as regards motivation, interest, priorities, etc.. As stated by Salancik & Pfeffer (1978) the individual is sensitive to the presentation of information by its social surroundings on important 'needs' and the satisfaction of needs. If a certain mild pressure exists in a partnership in the sense that the ambitions for a career of the woman are somewhat reduced (and reduced more than the ambitions of the husband) in connection with the couple having children and a corresponding expectation exists at the place of work, this can in many instances have the effect that the woman's interest in a career and her wish to obtain a senior position is reduced, at least for a while.

In the following chapter we want to argue for a more differentiated approach to the issue of gender and organization. This approach concerns 'physical' groups of women and men (including the outcomes of socio-cultural influence following from the socialization they are carrying, i.e. personalities), the abstract categories of the 'male' and the 'female' as well as organizations and similar institutional arrangements (places of work, professions, strata, etc.). We suggest an approach according to which neither women, images of maleness (masculinity) nor organizations are seen as homogeneous and unitary. Given the difficulty in taking all our suggestions into account, especially when it comes to differentiation in all these three regards, we shall just suggest a possible outline of a more sophisticated framework for dealing with variations of gender/organization patterns.

Notes

1   A similar development perspective has not characterized the study of the other two
    organizations where there have been no similar major changes during the 1980's of
    relevance for our issue.

2   The metaphor 'barrier' – whether external or internalized – must be used with caution
    in this context. It points to restrictions in relationship to the goal of climbing upwards
    (to continue the use of physical metaphors). It is, of course, important to critically
    reflect on how careers, hierarchies, ideas of human worth and inequality are socially

formed and reproduced. It should not be taken for granted that the natural or normal way for people – once all restrictions have been removed – is to fairly compete for higher positions in bureaucracies. Wishes to do so must be respected, and in this context it is important to indicate the barriers that prevent people who belong to the disfavoured groups making careers and being represented in for example managerial jobs. For many women as well as men barriers to the good life are less a matter of gender equality in relationship to career competition, but involve broader polical and social issues. Our focus in this book is mainly on gender in relation to managerial jobs, but we discuss broader issues on gender, work and organization in the last chapter.

3   Of course, social change regarding gender has and will always take place. In relationship to gender and management, however, men have almost always occupied the higher positions in bureaucracies. Current changes involve a significant expansion of the number of females on at least the lower and middle managerial levels and the reduction of formal as well as informal obstacles for women to attain and function in such positions strongly differ from past decades for example the first three quarters of the twentieth century. In this respect it makes sense to emphasize the changes taking place at present in many Western countries on this particular issue.

4   It is true that SAS has considerable technical activities which in their nature may have clear similarities with many industrial places of work when it comes to the questions taken up here. However, our study concerns primarily the administrative sectors of SAS and therefore we must acknowledge that we cannot say anything about industrial enterprises and organizations that are characterized by technical work.

5   How qualifications are perceived and recognized must be seen as socially constructed. Gender relations are important here. We have earlier reviewed studies indicating social biases in evaluation processes (Chapter 5). It would, however, be reductionistic to claim that gender bias account for all evaluations of women. Given a certain socio-cultural context, it still is likely that women have a fair chance of getting recognition for their skills and achievements. The majority of our interviewees seemed to perceive their workplaces as far from strongly biased in how women were evaluated. It should be recognized that the yardsticks employed may reflect norms affected by male domination. So was especially the case in MFA. On the whole, it appears misleading to see the norms and evaluation processes as being totally arbitrary or being fully understandable in terms of power. What women actually are capable of and do is far from insignificant in their careers.

11 Gender and organization – a differentiated understanding

The absence of women at higher levels in organizations can be seen as a product of earlier, historical patterns involving the division of labour between men and women in a public and a private sphere, stereotypes, prejudices, etc.. These patterns also characterize contemporary social practices. Changes are, however, taking place as the modernization process, involving a 'rationalization' of the gender issue, continues. From a human resource management point of view such a rationalization reduces, at least to some extent, the importance of 'irrelevant' factors when it comes to utilizing the workforce. At the same time, it is clear that such a process does not take a linear course. Its development differs drastically between nations and different time periods. In the USA and in Scandinavia it has slowly, but steadily, increased (at least to the middle management level). As our empirical studies showed the development also differs between different organizations. The understanding of counterforces to a development which otherwise is reducing inequality is important. Many of these forces can, as we saw, be found on the organizational level.

The topic of gender has during recent years attained increasing interest in organization studies after having been neglected previously in organization and management theory. Historical examples of gender-blind approaches are well illustrated by Mills (1988). The gender and organization orientation is broader than the women in management (WIM) perspective which focuses mainly on female managers, whereas the majority of all women are not treated or are seen as a group of secondary interest and importance. While most of the earlier writings on the topic of women in management emphasized equality in the sense of equal access to and equal chances of functioning in higher-level jobs, some recent scholars have started to question the 'gender neutrality' of managerial jobs, workplaces and organizations in themselves (Balsamo, 1985; Calás & Smircich, 1992b; Ferguson, 1984; Hearn & Parkin, 1987; Mills, 1988; Mills & Tancred, 1992). This is a discourse with which we symphatize, even though our focus in major parts of this book has been on gender (with a certain emphasis on women) and managerial jobs. In this final chapter, we broaden our approach and contribute to a general understanding of gender and organization.

As we remarked in the introduction to this book, we see the study of female managers and the relative absence of women at higher levels in organization partly as an entrance to a more general theory about gender and organization. Women and management is one issue, but far from the only significant issue regarding gender and organization. We do not have empirical material on other groups than those belonging to the middle and upper middle echelons of organizations, but this material can be interpreted in ways which also illuminate broader organizational conditions and processes. In the present chapter, we draw to some extent upon our three case studies, but we also go beyond these, rely on other studies and theoretical sources and make a number of theoretical points.

11.1 Gender bias in organizations

We accept the argument that the historical dominance of men within the public sphere and, in particular, when it comes to the field of management and domination of organizational life, has lead to a fusion of traditional 'male' standards, assumptions and rules which makes the whole field of management in itself somewhat alien to many women (and some men too). This would suggest that the basic problem has less to do with the barriers and obstacles for women to get managerial jobs than with the prestructuring of management and organization, and with the way these organizations function. The former are only expressions of the latter, existing institutional arrangements are "themselves fundamentally flawed" (Ferguson, 1984:4).

If we use an analogy with sport, we can say that according to a narrow view on gender/organization (i.e. the focus on women/managerial jobs) the problems have to do with foul play by male players, and that referees are not making fair judgements, either because of their incompetence (inability to perceive and evaluate situations correctly) or because of their bias to the male players. The real problem, according to the broader, more basic orientation, is that it is the male players that made the game, the rules, and manufactured the arena, in accordance with their specialities, skills, and interests. Instead of studying foul play, the effects of some players having a longer training and more helpful coaches, that referees un- or consciously are in favour of certain players, and so on, the interesting question is to look at the game itself, and whose interests and preoccupations it expresses and preserves. In addition to that, it is of interest to study if the game could look otherwise, and to investigate the pros and cons of other designs. One could also go further and question not only the structure and rules of the game, but also the very idea of a game (instead of, for example, another form of social activity) and ask whether this is not biased in favour of male participants.[1]

In the MFA we questioned the career structure and whether this favours men as long as their wives are more willing to accompany them when stationed abroad than the husbands of the female employees are. As long as it is a precondition regularly to be stationed abroad, more men than women will be favoured by these rules in becoming a manager. Not until men find difficulties as well in playing by the established rules will they be changed. In the MFA the 'game' is constructed based on the gender-biased assumption that the employees give the job their highest priority, and that they are not severely restricted by their families. It is hardly a coincidence that out of eight interviewed women, seven were single.[2] This issue is perhaps a somewhat superficial aspect of the gendered nature of organizations and it is still more related to career issues than a broader questioning of organizational patterns, but it indicates the gendered nature of some of the ground rules. A perhaps better, although a bit more uncertain example of women advocating other principles than those dominating organizations, is the preparedness of female managers in SAS to step down from managerial jobs. Perhaps flexibility in relationship to organizational hierarchies and mobility could be seen as a significant element in organizational forms favoured by (many) women.

Even if some women should 'manage' to get through the obstacles created by unwritten rules of the game and incompetent/unfair referees and attain managerial jobs in larger numbers this would not automatically produce harmony between most contemporary women's subjective orientations and the (average) management field. If there exist basic tensions between most women's interests and values and the functioning of most organizations in present society, they will not necessarily be reduced even if the number of women managers increases, and an increase does not necessarily correspond to the interest of many women. If managerial jobs normally demand attributes that are not in line with many women's 'traditional' socialization patterns, then this discontinuous relationship between social demands and interests, values, symbolic skills – even personality – creates frustration and stress. Such a misfit might explain why female managers report such symptoms to a greater extent than males (see Chapter 4; Cooper & Davidson, 1982; Davidson & Cooper, 1984; Weinstein & Zappert, 1980). This might also explain why female managers to a large extent have difficulties in coping with a career and a family (Finkelstein, 1981; Rix & Stone, 1984; Nicholson & West, 1988). The investigations we have come across show the same picture, female managers are more often single or divorced than male managers, on average half of the female managers are single and do not have children, almost all male managers are married and have children (Harlan & Weiss, 1980; Finkelstein, 1981; Cahoon & Rowney, 1987; Case et al, 1987; Nicholson & West, 1988).

Even when a successful adaptation is reached, this might be the result of a resocialization process involving ethical, psychological or social costs. Socialization and resocialization processes are inevitable in a nonstatic society, but the following question arises: *To what extent should people adapt to organizations and to what extent should the opposite be the case?* If a particular group is consistently forced to adapt/resocialize to a much higher degree than another group, in order to attain the better life chances accompanying career and promotion in bureaucracies, then issues of political interests, fairness, domination and equality enter the picture. This is hardly addressed by traditional organization theory and only to a limited extent by the WIM literature. Another type of 'loss', although one in which no consensus can be expected concerning its negative

features, regards the possibility that for women "conformity and the abandon-
ment of critical consciousness are the prices of successful performance in the
bureaucratic world" (Ferguson, 1984:29). It can also be stressed that more
women adapting to male norms and becoming managers is hardly in itself contributing to gender equality, unless it is complemented by more men obtaining
positions requiring 'female' socialization. Equality is hardly achieved by a one-
sided adaptation of the one sex to the standards of the other.

However, the assumption that an increase in the number of female managers
might involve serious costs in terms of frustrating resocialization processes or
conflicts between the women concerned and the external demands has not been
investigated thoroughly. Neither have the effects of a contradictory relationship
between the demands and most women's (stable or temporary) attributes been
investigated, much less have they been proven to be 'correct'. Proofs of that kind
cannot be expected. We cannot more than marginally get support for this idea in
our empirical material. In our study of BSW we saw that men had to adapt to the
organizational 'rules', they (as well as the women) had to remain 'soft' when
they were promoted to managers. There were no signs at all that women had to
adapt to job requirements in a way that involved frustrations when they were
promoted. In MFA there were some statements that more women than men were
frustrated but this was attributed to the fact that they had not become managers.
Another source of frustration was that many (women and men) had difficulties
in combining work with family and this problem could account for less women
wanting to be recruited to or continued in this organization. In SAS one could
talk about a resocialization of women who were appointed managers, they complained that they had to adapt to the male style, in meetings etc. in order to be
heard. On the whole, however, we found very little indication that women's
functioning in managerial jobs involved significant reorientations of a negative
kind, and we are left with the impression that being managers on the whole was
a positive experience. We have, however, not studied this issue in depth. The
results of studies of stress and managers, indicating that for women having to
adapt to the world of management often involve substantial psychic costs, are
worth further investigations.

Clearcut answers to complicated questions are not possible, unless at the expense of oversimplifications. In addition to that, we must remember that we
move on a territory which is very mobile. Gender and gender relations con-
stantly change character. Men and women in Western society are hardly the
same today as they were 20 years ago. Gender is socially constructed and reconstructed. No final answers, except possibly when it comes to some biological
differences and perhaps some minor psychological differences can be expected
in this area. We do not want to suggest postulates neither of the harmonic nor of
the conflictual kind between women's 'nature' (at a particular historical moment) and managerial jobs. (For an overview of and a discussion of some common postulates, see Billing & Alvesson, 1989.) The point is to suggest that we

must carefully reflect upon the matter and consider the possible validity claims – if only temporal ones – of various types of proposed relationships on the matter of whether managerial careers for women on traditional ('male') premisses often create substantial frustrations. In this area, empirical studies are, of course, also necessary, less in order to produce the final words on the matter, than in order to provide better material for 'advanced reflections' and, perhaps, to counteract ideas that are 'too wild'. We have tried to interpret our case studies not as a matter of the processing of objective 'data' leading to firm 'truths', but more as interpretations and ideas which give insights regarding how one can understand conditions and processes regarding women and managers in a particular historical and cultural setting.

11.2 Women – alike and unalike in an organizational context

In the present book we have focused on managers, which gives an appropriate focus for an empirical study involving three cases. The issue of 'women's interests' in relationship to management and organization is partly illustrated from the 'above' perspective focusing on managerial jobs and the route to these. The normal situation of women in (most) organizations is however, not at the middle level, e.g. as a professional worker striving upwards, but as a low-level participant. The position as a subordinate, where sex reinforces this subordinate position in a number of respects from status and influence on wages, is a typical female one (Ferguson, 1984). A 'bottom-up' perspective is therefore called for in order to illuminate organizations in terms of gender. Understanding the gender/organization area demands that we study both the processes preventing women from climbing upwards and the ones keeping them at the bottom of the career structure. These processes are not necessarily the same, as they may concern different groups of women. Subordination is a crucial experience for working class women, while obstacles to attaining privileged positions may be a more central feature for the situation and prospect of female professionals (middle class women).

In the Marxist feminist literature, debate has been going on concerning the relationship between class and gender. Which matters most in determinating the social situation and life chances? Here we will not engage in this debate as we are focusing on the gender issue, without wanting to neglect the fact that class and other social differences certainly intersect with sex (see e.g Crompton & Mann, 1986). In the literature on gender/organization there is, however, a tendency to focus on the similarities between women. It is normally recognized that there are some differences between women, but these tend to be seen as less important. As Ferguson (1984:158-159) puts it:

Divided by lines of class, race, ethnicity, and so on, most of us nonetheless encounter a characteristic set of linguistic and institutional practices constitutive of the life experiences of the second sex. The world of women, thus qualified, is distinguished from the world of men by different notions of individual identity, by different standards of morality, and ultimately by different approaches to the problems of politics.

This idea of a uniform world of women, different from the one of men, can be questioned. A number of psychological studies found no consistent, important psychological differences between men and women (e.g. Maccoby & Jacklin, 1975) (see Chapter 3). Besides our own study also a rather large body of literature on male and female managers have shown a lot of similarities and very little differences in terms of style, values, and so on (e.g. Bartol, 1978; Ferber et al, 1979; Bayes, 1987; Kovolainen, 1990). Such consistency is rare in social science. These results do not, however, rule out the possibility of the existence of the type of similarities indicated by Ferguson. The issues addressed by Ferguson (1984), Maccoby & Jacklin (1975), and the leadership literature are not exactly the same. In Gilligan's (1982) research, for example, there is some evidence of different moral codes for women and men. Therefore it seems reasonable to assume that similarities, shared by the majority of women, exist up to a certain point in the present historical and cultural situation. Empirical studies of the quantitative type preferred by people interested in comparisons may not be sensitive enough to grasp these differences, but they raise doubts about the homogeneity of the world of women.

The assumption that women differ substantially provides another point of departure than the one favoured by most writers on gender and organization. For instance like men, they differ in terms of the class to which they belong. Instead of trying to capture all people in a fine net of stratification concepts (from upper to lower strata, social groups or whatever) it is, enough, in the present context, to operate with two social groups: people in low-level positions, with little prospect for a substantial improvement of life chances in work, and (modern) middle-class people (professional women) in positions where there are chances of climbing up the career ladder (e.g. to managerial jobs). It could be assumed that the gender/organization dynamics are not the same for working class and middle class women and men. According to Burris (1989:175), the transformation of organizational forms into more technocratic ones – characterized by polarization into expert and non-expert sectors, flexible configurations of centralization/decentralization, skill restructuring etc. – implies that "'expert' and 'non-expert' women face fundamentally different types of discrimination".

More generally, it can be argued from a meritocratic point of view that while employers in the longer time spectrum have incentives for utilizing well-educated and ambitious women in professional and managerial jobs, they would be interested in counteracting discrimination against parts of this group. Large parts of the women in management literature underscore the rationality of this (Adler, 1986/87; Grant, 1988). At a seminar with some top executives from Swedish business and public administration (1990), many stressed that they were interested in promoting female managers. Some gave the reason that with a large proportion of female employees, they just could not afford not to utilize the qualified female managerial candidates. The top bureaucrats from public organizations acknowledged, that apart from everything else legitimacy concerns forced them to attend to the matter and led to an interest in having a fair amount of women managers. Even though we doubt that this issue is of primary concern for many top managers and that lip service certainly often characterizes expressed concerns, it is quite likely that a number of capitalists and executives have some 'objective' as well as recognized interest in counteracting discrimination against female professionals and managers (managerial candidates). The executives had themselves chosen the topic of female managers as one of ten topics for a seminar series. The rate of attendance at our seminar was high. This indicates a concern for the issue.

When it comes to working class and other lower hierarchy positions, the situation appears to be quite different. The major interest of employers appears to be to utilize the gendered division of labour in order to attain cheap labour from women (Baude, 1989; Clegg & Dunkerley, 1980; Thompson, 1983). A contemporary study (Baude, 1989:74-75) shows that it is not an "invisible hand" that segregates the sexes but that the segregation rather functions as "a means for the employer to staff the key areas at the lowest possible average cost". Baude points out that her studies indicate

how segregation is utilized in order to expand the employer's options in achieving a stable male labor force, especially in the case of key jobs higher up in the organization. Since men so clearly indicate that they do not want to have monotonous and unskilled jobs, the employer is dependent on the willingness of women to perform such tasks and to accept the conditions which the employer is prepared to offer. Excluding women from other types of work increases the company's opportunities to fill these least attractive positions. (p 74-75)

This leads us to the following reflections: there are clear social class differences between women in terms of orientations to work and in the way they are treated by employers. These differences may be greater than gender differences. Kanter (1977) found that the characteristics of the job meant more for attitudes to work than gender (see Chapter 3). One's occupation is a core aspect of the social class to which one belongs. Heterogeneity, not only on a social level, but also on a psychological one, must likewise be considered. Emphasis on the psychological level might lead to the misunderstanding that social dynamics is a secondary phenomena which triggers off critique for reductionism or essentialism. Differences on the individual level can, however, be seen as a reflection of variations in socialization patterns and internalization of gender characteristics of societal culture and subcultures. It may sound trivial to emphasize that women too are individuals, but this fact has not been taken seriously in many gender and organization studies. It can also be argued that it is difficult to take psychological variations into account in developing social theories on gender and organization because the situation becomes too complex. However, we suggest the following two general statements as a way of capturing these individual variations, without getting lost in exercises on the individual psychological level.

Women vary in terms of class background history, psychology, values, interests and social resources and – as a result of this – in terms of the degree of congruence/incongruence with social patterns of typical 'male-dominated' organizations (and other institutions). This indicates that there are variations among women in terms of preconditions for adaptation to various social situations, including different workplaces and organizational positions. In the study of the 25 female top managers, Hennig & Jardim (1977) found that all of them had fathers in higher positions with whom they identified. Also in our study we found that more women than men in high status career jobs (professionals in the Foreign Service) came from upper class backgrounds. Burton (1985:XIII) argues that the differences between women of different classes are more significant than their common gender identity. We do not have a firm opinion on this, but believe that sociological as well as psychological factors seriously counteract the uniformity of the world of women and that an overgeneralized view on gender must be avoided.

11.3 Gender metaphors and organizations

Our next issue concerns the character and importance of gender images. These are ideas of masculinity/femininity used in a distinct metaphorical way. Although we believe that they can hardly be used in another way, given the nature of language and reasoning about complex phenomena, we see them used in contexts where the metaphorical meaning is not clear. Much of the literature on women/men and femininity/masculinity appears to use these concepts as if they have literal meaning. Our way of perceiving and thinking about the world is structured by metaphors and images (Brown, 1976; Langer, 1957; Morgan, 1980, 1986). Objective reality does not speak to us directly, nor can we talk about complex phenomena in a literal way. We create gestalts which guide us. This goes for both the layman and the scholar. The difference is that the latter, hopefully, is more careful, reflective and has more and/or better metaphors at his or her disposal.

The increased interest and the documented importance of gender issues makes it reasonable to add the male/female dichotomy to earlier metaphors for organizational analysis. If this is the case, then organizations could be understood not only in terms of machines, tools, systems, organisms, brains, theatres, political arenas, psychic prisons, texts, cultures, symbolic fields, 'containers' of false consciousness, means for disciplining, and instruments for domination. They could also be understood in terms of bastions of male-domination or, which might be less common, expressions of feminine principles (such as care, relatedness, community or what might be covered by the term 'the feminine'). Organizations could also be understood as 'anti-families'. Many of the existing metaphors in organization theory are far from being gender neutral. Organizations are infused with ideologies, cultures, social arrangements and practices as well as material that are normally dominated by 'male' interests and principles. These may include rationality, some version of instrumentality, analytic attitude, affective restraints, competetiveness, individuality, self-sufficiency and so on, leading to a desexualized, non-expressive and emotionally controlled organizational world (Burrell, 1984; cf. Calás & Smircich, 1991; and Hearn & Parkin, 1987).

The use of a gender metaphor means that the approach goes beyond gender as a variable (Balsamo, 1985) and looks at how gender is constructed and reconstructed in organizations. This indicates a dialectic between structure and practice, and that the structures are changeable. It is suggested that traditional understandings of organizations do not acknowledge the gendered aspects of a wide range of organizational phenomena.

Can the gender metaphor supply organization theory with new ideas and a richer understanding of organizational phenomena? In some cases, the understanding of male domination as a major attribute of bureaucratic organizations seems to lead to analyses that are very close to what has earlier been expressed by proponents of (other) radical and critical perspectives or even liberal-humanistic forms of critique of bureaucracy (hierarchy, extended division of labour, formalization and standardization of jobs, impersonal work conditions, etc.). Compare, for example, Ferguson (1984) and Loden (1986) with radical humanist texts such as Alvesson (1987) or Willmott & Knights (1982), and with liberal-humanist writings such as for example Argyris (1964) and Weisbord (1987). There is considerable agreement on what the 'good' organization should be like. As recognized by Hearn & Parkin (1983), many feminist writings are rather close to Burrell & Morgan's (1979) radical humanist paradigm. Ferguson (1984:27) acknowledges this resemblance, but argues that

the feminist case against bureaucracy goes beyond the other critiques in that it constructs its alternative out of concrete and shared experiences of women, rather than out of a romantic vision of pre-capitalist life or an abstract ideal of 'human nature'.

We do not deny that she has a point, but it could be argued that the case against bureaucracy as its point of departure can include all lower hiearchy members – women as well as men and their concrete and shared experiences, needs and wants. The case made by female professionals is quite different from the one constructed out of the concrete experiences of female blue-collar workers, for whom class and sexist structures both point to low-level positions. An interesting research task would be to investigate carefully gender-specific experiences and preferences for various forms of leadership, work organization and other job conditions and organizational arrangements and practices. Such studies would make it easier to evaluate what is specific about a feminist case, founded in the concrete and shared experiences of women. From the position suggested here, we would not anticipate the experiences of women leading to a unitary critique of the predominant, nor unitary preferences for an alternative organization.

Our impression from the case studies is that female employees, on the whole, were not critical of their workplaces and alternative ideas put forward were not the sole concern of women. In BSW, for example, there seemed to be equal distribution among the sexes in arguing against the salience of rule-governed work and in SAS, the women's network supported the ideas of the CEO. In MFA, only those females who had left the organization expressed any criticism and this concerned mostly the difficulties women experienced in achieving promotion, and hardly touched upon broader aspects of the functioning of the organization. The most significant alternative position, espoused by women in our sample, was their flexibility with regards to stepping down the career ladder. This point supports the view that some women may be less rigid and committed to hierarchical social relations – a view which negates traditional bureaucracy. It must also be emphasized that our study did not aim to illuminate women's opinions about alternative organizational forms, so the validity of our empiral material is limited on this point. Our study is also, with few exceptions, limited to a study of female and some male managers and some professionals (university graduates), which may differ from other groups of women on the issue treated here.

There are still good reasons to assume that the strong imprints on organizations made by the entrenched domination of males[3] make it appropriate to stress the possibility of contradictions between bureaucracy and the orientations of women. Perhaps we could talk about several feminist cases against bureaucracies, some of which come very close to other cases (humanist, working class), and some which are very different from these (for example the one of career-oriented female professionals and managers).

Few could deny that most contemporary organizations, and especially those which are the economically and politically most significant, historically and at present, have men as their architects and heads. This certainly expresses something which is not gender-neutral. The question is, if the 'maleness' – as a set of ideals, principles and objectives – in itself is predominant also in the backbone of organizations, i.e. if organizational patterns bear significant imprints of (a certain class of) men and, in particular, of (some) men as autonomous subjects. If, however, these patterns are basically a part of industrialization, the capitalistic economy, the pressure for maximum utilization of resources, i.e. efficiency, caused by competition and/or the citizens' demands for goods and services etc, then the fact that men have held the highest positions and have held greater responsibility is a relatively superficial observation compared with more basic driving forces. In this case, accusations (and praise) would not primarily be directed against (to) men (or rather a class of men) or 'maleness', but to something overall, such as the capitalistic society or technological rationality (Alvesson, 1987; Marcuse, 1964). However, men were and are carriers of this development, acting as 'character-masks', on behalf of a capitalistic rationality. That it was men who were the actors had to do with what Hartmann (1979) refers to as the original division of labour, and with what Hartmann has described as the (former) alliance between patriarchy and capitalism (see Chapter 3). In their 'fight' for a family wage and against the cheaper women labourers, men (and their unions) historically acted as subjects.

Given the acceptance of these remarks, the male metaphor still has some illuminating power. It could certainly be used as a reminder of the resemblance of this form of rationality and typical preoccupations of a certain group of men and of the fact that "the development of the modern profession of management and its associated and legitimating theory and thinking represent a development of patriarchal authority" (Hearn & Parkin, 1987:18). That many more men than women act as carriers of this rationality would also be illuminated. It would, however, undoubtedly restrict the usefulness of some version of the masculinity metaphor, if it is mainly a 'capitalistic' or a technological rationality which is at work. A very strong usage of the masculinity metaphor might even mystify things.

The point is to resist gender reductionism, to avoid reducing present organizational arrangements to being just a function of gender relations, but at the same time to include gender into a holistic picture of organizations. This is difficult partly due to a fusion of the economic and political system and the social characteristics of its dominant group, which certainly may be described as being of a masculine type.

It is, however, important to recognize that not all forms of 'masculinity' are in line with the one that is fused with social domination in late-capitalistic society. There has been a tendency to reduce masculinity and femininity to clearcut categories and thereby obscure the possibility of different forms of masculinity and femininity. For instance it is probably primarily a (certain form of) upper class form of maleness that can be linked with instrumental rationality, emotional control, self-sufficiency, individualism, competitiveness, and so on. These upper class forms can probably be differentiated even further. Kerfoot & Knights (1993) identify two styles of managing people and organizations within the context of the financial service industry, namely "paternalistic masculinity" and "competitive masculinity" respectively. Working class conceptions of masculinity on the other hand, at least the traditional ones are quite different from upper class forms and have rather little in common with the governing principles and forms of domination in modern organizations. If gender metaphors are to be used, the relevance of a working class masculinity/upper class masculinity bipolarity, might be useful in illuminating many more manifestly opposite interests, than the male/female opposition. The tendency in gender/organization literature is to stress a particular form of masculinity as the only one. If gender metaphors are used in organizational analysis it would be interesting to use more than two of the kind (one bipolarity). There are different forms of femaleness/femininity and maleness/masculinity.

Game & Pringle (cited in Hearn & Parkin, 1987) attach gender-images to different technological processes, which gives us an idea that, in that respect, masculinity is seen as a broad concept, which even includes "soft masculinity" (equal to femaleness?).

Technology has many well-established associations, both broadly generic and specifically sexual, both within and between genders. 'Hard' masculinity is often associated with
heavy, skilled, dangerous, dirty, interesting, mobile machine processes; while 'femaleness' or 'soft' masculinity are associated with light, unskilled, less dangerous, clean, boring, immobile machinery (Game & Pringle, 1983, in Hearn & Parkin, 1987:86).

Different sorts of masculinity are well illustrated in the following study of shop-floor culture. Here the focus is not primarily on relations between the sexes, but is clearly of relevance in the present context:

The uncompromising banter of the shop-floor, which was permeated by inhibited swear-
ing, mutual ridicule, displays of sexuality and pranks, was contrasted, exaggerated and
elevated above the middle class politeness, cleanliness and more restrained demeanour of
the offices (Collinson, 1988:186).

Tolson (1977:58-59) also makes a distinction between a working-class type and a middle-class type of masculinity:

The paradox of masculinity at work is most apparent within the experience of manual
labour. For the manual worker there is an immediate alienation (his product is 'objecti-
fied' against him) and a direct, personal humiliation (constant confrontation with authority). But it is also primarily within the local traditions attached to forms of manual labour
that elements of patriarchal culture have survived. Because of the often brutal and unpre-
dictable nature of the work, the worker is directly dependent on 'masculine' compensa-
tions, and in some situations, patriarchal aspects of working-class culture may even be
potentially subversive. A male chauvinism of the shop-floor is a way of asserting collective control, and, sometimes, sabotaging the production process itself.

It would certainly be unfortunate if critical scholars unreflectively reproduced the form of masculinity that dominates in public life, and which is therefore most visible, forgetting other kinds of cultural expressions, such as those of the working class.

There seems to have been less interest in investigating various forms of fe-
maleness in organizations. Also when it comes to this theme, however, it is important to consider not only various versions of it, but also the possibilities of conflicts between these. There may, for example, be a conflict between professional women, often work and career oriented, and other women. Female man-
agers and professionals may be seen as expressing a kind of femaleness in which a balance between work and family, between being career oriented and

having/acquiring a superior position on the one hand, and being a member of a community on the other is important. Some female managers and professionals are very career oriented and give priority to work, clearly the case in MFA. In such instances, there is little point in talking about 'femaleness' in this particular regard as the concept does not contribute to an understanding of work behaviour or values. Working class women may often invest less in work, give more priority to children and family matters and view the social dimensions of work as important. To some extent the SAS case illustrates this. There is the possibility of a principal contradiction between these two orientations in society, for example regarding gender and childcare politics. The attitudes of non-career oriented women may directly harm career-interested females as the former may reinforce ideas of women in general being only modestly interested in a job and career. The normative pressure from work oriented women may also force those feeling more ambiguous about wage labour on to the labour market. Alternatively, this pressure may make them feel guilty/inadequate if they do not engage in wage labour. Occasionally these forms of femaleness may conflict in a specific way at the level of workplace, for example when women subordinates expect from their female managers, some understanding when they take care of sick children or relatives. Glimpses of such conflicts can be found in our material as well as in Martin (1987).

The 'penetrative' (!) force of the male domination metaphor(s) – and its female counterpart(s) – remains to be explored in depth. At best, they can be used to illuminate a broad area of organizational phenomena – from decision-making and strategy formulation to organization structure and various cultural phenomena (including cultural conflicts). Such a wide usage of the metaphor demands careful consideration of when it should be applied. Perhaps the gender metaphors might be useful in studies of organizational culture. The dualism between (a particular form of) the masculine and the feminine – or a playing out of a multitude of forms of masculinity and femininity – might throw light on aspects which are not otherwise well understood.

A less ambitious task for the gender metaphor would be to investigate various work areas in organizations and on the labour market in terms of their gender connotations. More specifically, the idea would be to study how the sexes 'fit' into various social positions and contexts, and especially 'misfits' between women and contexts and discrimination against women in this regard (see e.g. Cockburn, 1986). Gender is then applied in the 'neighbourhood' of where men and women are located. Jobs, positions, etc. are seen as 'gendered'. Organizations in their totalities are not 'metaphorized' (in terms of gender) in this version. Metaphorization is restricted to occupations and organizational positions and work areas. This task can be formulated in terms of symbolism, to which we now turn.

11.4 Gender and organizational symbolism

It seems as if most jobs in society and most work areas in organizations have some sort of a gendered image. We associate top executives, pilots, firemen and chief engineers with something male, while secretaries, nurses and cleaners are connected with something female. There are also internal segregations in organizations. Baude (1989) found in a study of 7 workplaces in the Swedish Food Working Industry (2,700 employees, 50% women) that most of the jobs were gender typed as either male or female, and that the male jobs were much more numerous than the female jobs, even in small companies. Also in the labour market as a whole there is a significant clustering of women's occupations (Mann, 1986). The associations of jobs with a specific sex partly have to do with the fact that one sex forms the large majority in these jobs/positions, but also, as we pointed out earlier, that men more clearly indicate that there are jobs they do not want. In the case of SAS, e.g. in the key-punch operators' department, men were employed but stayed only for a very short time, the reason being that the job was "too boring". Women as well as men tended to believe it was not men's work.[4] However, connected to work areas and professions are also images, which partly are of a gender type, which go beyond just simple facts about the proportion of different sexes in the job. We do not just expect top executives to be physically males, we also expect them to exhibit the form/style of masculinity characteristic of upper-class males, in many respects quite different from that displayed by working class men.

We suggest that *the gender symbolism of organizations* is used as a key concept for grasping this phenomena and its consequences in organizations. The point is that a particular job (function, level) signals, among other things, a certain conception of gender. The job (position, work task, etc.) stands for what are held to be the particular attributes of one sex, i.e. triggers off, or is associated with, meanings and understandings involving gendered connotations. In other words, besides the 'objective' features of a job/organizational area, it also has an 'aura' in terms of gender. This might be stronger or weaker: in some cases, perhaps, no such symbolism exists – the job is gender-neutral. In BSW we defined the work and the organization in this way. The work function can be seen as a synthesis of slightly 'male' administrative work and 'feminine' caring welfare work and thus we regarded it as neutral in terms of gender symbolism. Few people would probably associate the task of the organization to either males or females and also internally there were no indications of people associating their tasks with any strong gender characteristics.

Whether a job is associated with something masculine or feminine may vary in different cultures and different historical periods, e.g. clerks used to be men, now the majority of them are women. Recently some scholars have studied the history of the femininization of the clerical labour force (e.g. Lowe, 1987 referred to in Loft, 1992). At first firms used the supposed special feminine characteristics of women as an excuse for not employing them at all. "And then when they began to appreciate what a valuable cheap source of labour women could be, these same characteristics were referred to in justifying their employment in large numbers to do routine work" (Loft, 1992:748). In this way, it is possible for firms to benefit from – and sometimes contribute to – popular ideas and images in society of conceptions of female and male attributes, and use these ideas of 'appropriate work' for men and women to either exclude or include women. These notions of the appropriateness of the job are fundamental to reproducing the gendered division of labour. There may be some 'reactions' when changes are occuring. In the Technical University (of Copenhagen) the number of women increased to more than one third of the students in chemistry. The course was immediately renamed the "kitchen" course by students in the other more 'masculine' courses (such as mechanics and electronics) where the number of female students was low. The nickname was a way of marginalizing and degrading this specific course by positioning it in the hierarchy, with the very masculine 'hard' technology on the top and the 'soft' more feminine technology in the bottom. When the status structure is clear, the gender appropriateness is also clear.

Symbolism is closely connected to the degree to which the job (or study) is disproportionally occupied by one sex. The symbolism however goes beyond, and deeper, than pure numbers. The depth aspect means that symbolism partly exists on an unconscious level. It is not a straightforward social dynamic. The latter is suggested by Kanter (1977), who says that the quantitative factor determines the success of women in acceptance and promotion. If there are few women in an organization, i.e. less than 20 %, then they have problems, but if they move beyond this number, problems decrease. This mechanistic idea has also been critized by Calás & Smiricich (1992a) and by Gherardi (1992). Merely increasing the number of women in organization will not make much change in gender relations in the organization. We are in accordance with Gherardi that "a first level of intervention to initiate change in inter-gender relationships in organizational contexts lies in understanding how discourse on sexual differences is conducted and the practices that sustain and subvert it are mobilized" (Gherardi, 1992:29). The symbolism of various jobs/areas is only partly overlapping the quantitative factor. Gender symbolism is a cultural phenomenon and thus a deeper and more persistent phenomenon than the proportion of the sexes. Changes in proportions only slowly affect the former, which is a historical product. Given a certain sex proportion in a particular job/area, different types of symbolism are possible. An increase of the number of workers of a particular, earlier non-present sex, may not effect the gender symbolism of the work. 'Tough' women entering police work or 'soft' men working as flight attendants may not change the general view of police officers as masculine and flight attendants as feminine. In some management departments in which one of the authors has worked, the proportion of women in the faculty was rather low. Still, the workplaces were not seen as being particularly masculine, and female teachers did not, on the whole, appear to encounter any significant problems due to their minority status. A study of an advertising agency indicated that although almost all men had the creative (top) jobs and women were assistants, the organization climate and the perception of creative advertising work was far from masculine. The work was perceived as creative, intuitive, emotional, client-dependent and seductive (Alvesson & Köping, 1993). Thus in this case, a strong over-represen-tation of men as advertising professionals co-existed with a rather female work and organizational symbolism. Thus sex numbers and symbolism do not neces-sarily automatically correspond.

Symbolism implies a cultural analysis, rather than a social (structural) one. Meanings, ideas and understandings are in focus, not 'objective' social posi-tions, relations and behaviour patterns (Geertz, 1973; Smircich, 1983).

There are a large number of studies illustrating gender symbolism, even though they do not normally use this concept and rarely go into depth with the cultural analysis. In a study of lawyers in the UK, Podmore & Spencer (1986) found ideas and beliefs amongst male lawyers that women were unsuited to some aspects of legal practice. One barrister told the researchers that law

is a career based to some extent on competition and hustling and hitting people over the head and so on. Old-fashioned people like me tend to think that's more the masculine rather than the feminine role (1986:44).

Podmore & Spencer also found that the gender division of labour in legal work meant that men were more likely than women to be engaged in company and commercial work, in criminal cases and litigation, which often involves frequent court appearences, while women were more heavily involved in matrimonial cases and 'desk bound' tasks such as wills, probate and estate duty. Men's work in law was thus more prestigious, involved mainly male clientele, was often seen as requiring 'combative' qualities and implied more mobility, while women's work was characterized as low prestige, requiring 'caring' qualities, was desk bound and had a high proportion of female clients. In other words, in addition to the fact that there was a clear tendency to see legal work as 'male', different tasks were associated with what was seen as gender-specific attributes. Different areas of law symbolized different sexes.

Gender symbolism is not only an aspect of different (sub)professions or func-tional areas in organizations. It also has to do with the organizational level. It is possible, as suggested by Ferguson (1984:208-214), that the subordinate posi-tion is normally perceived as a feminine one. This is nicely illustrated by Rosen (1988) who noted that during a Christmas party in an advertment agency, men always danced with women having equal or lower positions in the hierarchy. Female managers and professionals only danced with equals and with higher level male managers.

Many male employees are, however, also subordinate, so we think that the symbolism of the subordinate position in organizations is not strongly coloured by gender. Superiority in organizations, on the other hand, is clearly associated with masculinity. The higher level in organizations, the stronger this 'aura' becomes. Positions such as president, vice president and so on are, we believe, normally associated with a certain form of (idea about) masculinity. It is possible that this – the 'genderedness' of managerial jobs – is (slowly) 'reconfiguring' as a consequence of an increase in the number of female managers and as a result of general cultural changes in society away from the old, authoritarian patriarchal bosses, but at present – and in the forseeable future – the higher managerial positions are in most organizations associated with 'masculinity'.

As mentioned by Bradford et al (1975) status, power and pay also bear an element of sexuality, and at the higher levels it is not a passive feminine sexuality.

The lumberjack and construction worker exemplify the rough masculinity of physical labor, but there is an aura of sexuality around success itself, as most clearly seen with famous individuals whose power and male sexuality are highly correlated. Not only does sexuality frequently contain elements of competition, dominance, and power, but power often takes on sexual implications. Even some of the terms used for the former are borrowed from the latter. A person's program is said to have been 'emasculated' by a certain decision, and the manager who fails is described as 'impotent' (Bradford et al, 1975:42).

As mentioned earlier, we warn against treating all organizations alike. Organizations are different in terms of gender symbolism. Heavy industry, insurance, fashion, social service agencies and technical universities are associated with different 'auras' in terms of gender. So are different functional areas, compare for example engineers and personnel. The aura of a library administrator seems to be neutral, according to Brief & Wallace (1976). Males and females were evaluated and rewarded equally by respondents when they used the position of a library administrator. The work content in different occupations may however require different 'attitudes', which can have gender connotations (in the present culture). In other words, the emotional and relational orientations perceived to be required by different occupations are different. Hochschild (1983:137) found in her research that flight attendants, who mostly were women, "were asked to feel sympathy, trust and good will", while the ticket collectors (mostly men) "were asked to feel distrust and some times positive bad will".

The stronger the influence of sex-labelling on particular occupations, the more occupational identities merge with sexual identities. Thus women in male jobs are expected to be aggressive and 'butch' and men in female jobs to be sensitive, caring and possibly gay (Scott, 1986:160).

Given a particular organizational level or function, we might expect variations between different types of organizations and even the same organization, in terms of gender symbolism.

The nature of the gender symbolism of a particular organizational area has partly to do with general societal conditions (general forms of gender symbolism, connected to patterns in the labour market, within different professions and so on), and partly with organizational-level phenomena, due to history, and gender patterns on the local level. Language, metaphors, assumptions of human nature, human relations, cultural artefacts (building, design) and dressing style all, to different degrees, carry these symbols. Morgan et al (1983) note that the language of organizational top positions (*man*ager, chair*man*) helps to sustain the gender-unequal power structure, by associating these jobs with *men*. These connotations are also well known in the organization research field ('economic man', 'organizational man') which tells us something about the strong male self-representation in science.

To summarize this section, we can conclude that different areas of organizations are seen as symbolizing gender in various ways. The organizational type, level and function/profession matter in this respect. Organizations and professions differ, on the overall level, in terms of the type and strength with which they are associated with a particular sex. So does, to some extent, the organizational level. Higher organizational levels are normally seen as 'masculine'. The higher the organizational level, the stronger the positions are associated with certain 'male characteristics', or rather, with a specific form of masculinity and its outward display.

Let us now connect this with the research on bias effects in the evaluation of candidates, and performances we referred to in Chapter 5. This research indicates that women are often evaluated less favourably than men, although their performances are objectively the same (Nieva & Gutek, 1980). Some studies do suggest, however, that this evaluation bias is connected to the area in which the performances are made (Nieva & Gutek, 1980; see Chapter 5). If it is an area which is considered to be 'typically male', then females are perceived less favourably than when the area is seen to be one in which women are presumed to be competent. Based on this, and recognizing the fact that evaluation of people is always difficult, given that experienced evaluators regularly come to different conclusions, we can suggest that women will almost always lose in sex-biased evaluations, and are especially disadvantaged in the context of organizations, professions and positions which are normally associated with some form of masculinity. The stronger the male symbolism, the stronger the disadvantage.

In other words, the stronger a position or type of work is associated with something 'typically masculine' (irrespective of the version of masculinity), the more pronounced the lack of harmony becomes between a 'typical' female employee or candidate for a position, and the organizational context. We suggest that sex bias in evaluations, discrimination in hiring, promotion and in the way particular employees (women) are treated is not a constant, organization-independent factor, but is contingent at least to some extent upon organizational and other institutional factors. From this we can expect considerable variation in sex discrimination from stronger forms in masculine gender contexts, to an absence of discrimination in gender-neutral work contexts.

The situation of professional women differed drastically among the three organizations, we studied. In the BSW the chances of attaining a managerial job are the same for both sexes, while the probability in the MFA is around one fifth to one tenth for a female professional compared to her colleagues among university graduates. In SAS, a truly established division of labour – women in service jobs, men in technical and managerial jobs and as pilots – and a traditional emphasis on those parts of the company dominated by men, has contributed to very limited numbers of women attaining management positions. Changes within the company during the 1980's brought far-reaching changes in traditional patterns, and a strong interest also among female employees in increasing the number of women managers at all levels. The study showed that women's possibilities of attaining leadership positions are related to the gender neutrality of the organization in question; the strength of the gender division of labour, vertically and horizontally; and also to the deep structure of the organization. They produced different outcomes with respect to the gendered hierarchical division of labour.

11.5 Some suggestions on how to understand gender discrimination

So far, we have argued that women are socially and psychologically heterogeneous, that the polarity masculinity/femininity might be too simple a dichotomy to cover the variations and contradictions between various forms of masculinity and femininity and that organizations and work areas differ in terms of the gender symbolism with which they are normally associated. Instead of only stressing homogeneous, strong and consistent patterns of gender inequality and discrimination, we suggest that the gender/organization field should be viewed as containing quite different and even contradictory elements. At the same time as (upper class) male dominance, a pro-male structuring of organizations, and restricted possibilities for women in attaining the same life chances as men on a general level are visible in many professions and workplaces, great variations exist.

We can capture some of these variations by indicating the forces that strengthen or weaken patterns of gender inequality and discrimination. We propose that organizations, work areas, organizational levels (positions in hierarchies), the cultural characteristics of the dominant group in the organization (work area, department, etc.) as well as the features of the female(s) concerned must be taken into consideration. The more signs of 'femininity' as perceived by superiors, colleagues and subordinates – the greater the risk that prejudice and stereotypes are invoked in the frameworks of the environment, and consequently, that discrimination enters the picture. A central aspect here is to what degree cultural definitions of 'femininity' have been internalized by the person concerned. A most significant part of male domination and gender inequality is maintained through the results of socialization processes affecting women's feelings, thoughts, identities and general functioning. Gender relations and differences thus are deeply anchored in the subjectivity of women and are not just social structures or beliefs, prejudices and norms that are easy to change. The depth aspects of socialization must be taken into account in order to understand domination and discrimination. The forces creating the latter do not just exist 'out there', in an organizational environment of men and other women, 'outside' the women concerned.

Factors that might affect the existence and degree of gender-based discrimination in organizational contexts are, as mentioned, the gender symbolism of the organization and of the work area. If the gender symbolism is strong (for example a masculine gendered environment like many technical departments) it is likely that there will be (strong) presuppositions against women as managers of the department, and therefore difficult for women to be counted as equals. The interesting thing is the tendencies in each of the factors influencing gender inequality, the strength of these, and various types of interaction effects. The latter might include how an organization as a whole and a function within it mutually effect each other. The dominant patterns in an organization might affect the gender symbolism of a particular function, so that traditional ideas, meanings, and understandings associated with that function in terms of gender are modified. In an organization, there may be tendencies that decrease or increase gender bias (discrimination against women) in terms of values, beliefs, perceptions and understandings, which diminish or increase discrimination tendencies in hiring, promotion and social interactions in and around that particular interface.

A particular function – and changes in its significance – might affect other parts of the organization. In the Scandinavian airlines company an increased strategic importance of the service functions, in which mostly females are employed, led to some changes in the understandings and beliefs in terms of gender in the company. An increased interest in recruiting and promoting women emerged and official formulations by the CEO that leadership is a matter of combined male/female traits. In this case the strategic change in what was in this instance, a traditionally strongly male-dominated company in its entirety, brought with it the reinforcement of a particular women-dominated function, which in its turn had some effect on the overall gender patterns of the company. The strengthening of the significance of service functions facilitated a 'demasculinisation' of the idea of a manager in the company. The management of the technical division also expressed an interest in recruiting more women, though with the proviso that they did not want 'traditional' women, but women with characteristics that matched the department.

A likely interaction effect on the micro level will appear when a female employee in a particular position is being affected by the socio-cultural work context. At the same time it is possible that her 'real attributes', at least if she has strong resources, will have some effect on how the social environment perceives her, and her sex. Quite often a woman is being 'defined' like other representatives for social categories when entering a workplace so that she appears consistent with the local culture's assumptions about gender. Except for very 'old-fashioned' milieus there are, however, limits to what extent biased assumptions and understandings in most modern Western organizations create strong distortions in the perception of gender.[5] Thus people in the environment might to some extent perceive a female employee's 'real' attributes in those regards where these are not ambiguous, which would counteract that discrimination tendencies, are triggered off. This situation may have some impact on the broader understanding of gender within that environment. Even if the person's virtues are not fully acknowledged and if she is seen as an 'exceptional' woman, it still might weaken the impact of stereotyped understandings. We are thus proposing a perspective in which gender bias and discrimination tendencies are built into the societal macro-culture and to a varying degree into different micro-cultures such as organizations. At the same time, we would like to allow space for the role of the subject's (the women's) capacity to either trigger off such discrimination tendencies or to weaken or even prevent them from being fully activated. After all, there are enough exceptions to 'women in general' (e.g. M. Thatcher) to realize that discrimination processes are probabilistic rather than deterministic.

11.6 Some implications of a differentiated view on gender and organization

In this section we will briefly sketch some implications of what has been suggested above in terms of how we can gain a different understanding of organizations and the organized. We structure the discussion in three parts: women/men, metaphors and organizations.

Traditionally women have mainly been at the bottom of organizations. Women employees have been seen as part of the secondary labour market, dominated by class as well as sexist structures (e.g. Clegg & Dunkerley, 1980; Crompton & Mann, 1986; Crompton, 1990). Men's domination of women has been a rather all-embracing assumption, which has provided a firm starting point for analysis, for example in conventional understandings of patriarchy. This assumption has illuminated vital aspects and to a considerable degree still appears reasonable. The present situation at least in some socially progressive Western countries indicates a much less clearcut picture. In Sweden and Denmark, for example, half of the university students are females, and even though males and females still choose (are socialized into choosing) different forms of education, and males are overrepresented in those with good employment chances, there are substantial numbers of women in education in information systems and business administration, to suggest that many women also enter the primary labour market and attain (at least) middle-level positions in organizations. There is a large and increasing proportion of middle-class women in many modern organizations and these cannot be treated only, or even mainly, as a female version of the male proletariate, nor is it appropriate only to stress their subordinate status. We also need to develop theories of women at the middle levels of organizations. Studies of female managers are relevant here, but cover only parts of this group since most female professionals are not managers.

Traditionally, female socialization has been assumed to clash strongly with male dominated organizational cultures (Mills, 1988). This still holds true, we believe, but perhaps the picture, once again, is less clearcut. The relatively high proportion of women on MBA programmes and similar, business oriented studies, reflects and creates changes in socialization patterns which have consequences for the gender issue in organizations. The fact that both men and women choose this type of education might indicate that at least this particular group (a significant one in an organizational context) does not differ very strongly in the prior socialization. We may assume some overlap in terms of earlier inspiration, values, orientations, etc. between people choosing the same education. The MBA programmes might also socialize people into a similar direction. Consequently, in important ways, the construction of these people's subjectivity reduces gender differences. Recognizing that gender socialization to a large extent takes place outside higher education, and that even the same formal education might lead to different effects on people with different sexes, it still appears reasonable to assume that a high proportion of female business students indicates that the clash between a (traditional) 'female' socialization and (many forms of) a 'male' organizational culture has been – or rather is on its way to becoming – reduced. Socialization for many women at present occupying 'middle level' positions in companies and public bureaucracies is not so different from their male colleagues. Instead of making a clearcut case of female socialization clashing with organizational worlds, we should in future talk probably about clashing as well as fitting socialization/ organization relations.

In other words, the present way in which women are socially produced differs from earlier patterns and thus, in the long term, gender differences (in terms of dispositions, values, etc.) might be weakened, at least for some groups. This might mean that gender differences when it comes to recruitment, organizational socialization, internal labour markets, leadership, interpersonal relations, etc. might become more heterogeneous and ambiguous, at least in relationship to the picture held by feminists, for example, proponents of patriarchy theory.

In terms of gender metaphors, where we now focus only on masculinity, as femininity still has less potential in illuminating contemporary dominant organizational forms, because of the domination by groups of men, we believe that operating with a single concept of masculinity obscures the multiplicity of gendered connotations of various aspects of organizational life. Similarly, a broadbrushed concept of 'male' or masculinity risks obscuring the many phenomena that are better understood in non-gendered terms. In order to develop masculinity metaphors that cover less and reveal more, means that we must distinguish between various forms of masculinity. The literature on women and leadership for example often hides the fact that we do not have only one male 'type', but many. Schein (1977) and Powell & Butterfield (1979) found in their studies of managers, both female and male, and business students respectively, that these groups more often described the successful manager in masculine terms. What we wish to question however is Schein's (1977) construction of three clear-cut categories "women in general", "men in general", "successful middle managers" which the respondents were asked to rate from 92 descriptive terms. As regards Powell & Butterfield (1979) we do not find it more helpful to rely on Bem's BSRI, which categorizes e.g. the masculine sex role stereotype as "self-reliant, defends own beliefs, ambitious", the feminine sex role stereotype as "sympathetic, yielding, shy" and the one which was undifferentiated as "helpful, conscientious, conceited". Such research designs force respondents into narrow categories and they hide the possibility of variation in terms of masculinity and femininity. Nor do they provide space for the respondents' ideas about these concepts. Variation, nuances and differentiation are important to avoid reproducing and possibly reinforcing gender stereotypes.

The gendered connotations of, for example, production, sales, personnel and accounting function probably differ in companies. Ideas about masculinity among people engaged in hard physical work, white-collar workers and top executives differ heavily. A manager might be seen as a father-figure or a technocrat – both images are very 'male', but at the same time highly different. In order to make a gender perspective sensitive for the various meanings, symbolism and understandings that structure human relations in organizational life, a one-dimensional view on masculinity and feminitity must be abandoned and the multiplicity of the forms of gender images must be explored to give sensitive readings of organizational culture, leadership and different types of gender discrimination. To distinguish between 'patriarchy' and 'technocracy' as different forms of masculinity might be one example.

A differentiated view on organizations from a gender perspective might encourage a greater sensitivity for contradictions and ambiguities, when it comes to a social (re)construction of gender relations, discrimination and equality at the level of the workplace. Within substantial parts of modern social science, a search for gender bias and discrimination has been activated on a large scale – the literature on gender and feminism has been enormous during the latest decade – and even though organization theory lags behind, the field has slowly started to follow this track. A good understanding of the complexity of social, material, structural and cultural 'rules' that discriminate against women has started to emerge (Mills, 1988). The problem is that while discrimination is highlighted, elements in organizations of the opposite type tend to be neglected. We would recommend not only the search for discriminatory practices and gender bias in organizational cultures, but also the search for gender equality-producing elements in modern organizations. At present the latter are neglected on the whole. The predominant metaphor of women is one of a 'victim' while the organization often is viewed as a 'male chauvinist' writ large. These metaphors, like all metaphors, illuminate certain things and hide others. For example they hide the fact that some organizations are less bad in these regards than others, and that some organizational structures and processes are 'gender neutral' or even 'woman-friendly'. This is clearly the case in BSW and important parts of the changes in SAS also facilitated the options of female employees.

An interesting illustration to the neglect of structures and processes that are positive for women is Mills' (1988) excellent, but somewhat one-sided overview on gender and organization. Based on Clegg's (1981) concept of "rules" (structures, not necessarily formal, underlying surface), Mills discusses gender in organizations and talks about extra-organizational rules, which "refer to social rules of behaviour which are reflected/reinforced within organizations. They take a number of overt (low pay and authority status) and covert (images of domesticity and sexuality) forms that serve to *constrain*, female opportunity, not only within, but in access and recruitment to organizations" (Mills, 1988:361, emphasis added). The formulation, typical for how the topic is treated, draws attention from the fact that some extra-organizational rules actually might *facilitate* female opportunity. Under the headline "Contradictions and resistance", Mills (1988:365) mentions the Sex Discrimination Act 1975 and female subcultures as outcomes of resistance to sexism. Some modern societies and many organizations are also characterized by social rules that do not necessarily lead to discrimination against women, but facilitate female opportunity without being directly connected to female resistance, or being of the same obvious type as legislation. These rules might be of greater benefit for middle-class than working-class women. Modern society prides itself in being meritocratic, and many people would probably confess themselves to an ideology of equal opportunity, without this only being a matter of lip service. This also applies to modern managers and other men. The need for modern corporations to produce an appealing image and score high on legitimacy might also facilitate opportunities for women to be recruited to higher positions. At the same time, efforts to rationalize personnel administration might reduce gender bias. Pfeffer (1977b) studied the effects of socio-economic background in different organizational contexts and reached the conclusion that this factor had much less influence in large than in small organizations. He attributed that to more careful and rationalized evaluation, and HRM systems of large organizations which reduced the influence of bias associated with social background. It is possible that gender prejudices also find less space in comparatively rationalized settings. Even though organizations certainly can be seen as sites of, and producers of, discrimination – and this aspect is probably the most important to draw attention to – we should not rule out the chance of them also playing a progressive and 'rational' role. Of course this role is only progressive and rational within certain limits, perhaps increasing the chances of women being employed and promoted, but not invoking larger issues of rationality, such as the structures and goals of organizations, and therefore not reflecting the needs and interest of broader social groups in society, i.e. also those of women. Sometimes one has the impression from the literature that it is gender relations in family life rather than in formal organizations, that produce gender differences and inequality in working life. Women's interest in, and attitude towards managerial jobs is influenced, in different ways, by the relationship between the workplace and the family. In particular conditions outside the organization influence the development of differing career patterns for women and men. Interactional effects between the worksphere on the one hand and the family sphere on the other seem to be important, especially for female managers who make use of different ways of coping than men because of problems combining family and career (Billing, 1991). Compared to family patterns, organizations may actually play a progressive role in relationship to equality on the labour market.

Viewing organizations as also including some 'rules' which are (formally as well as culturally) gender-neutral, or which even facilitate the opportunities for women, makes it easier to comprehend the situation. In terms of practical and normative implications, a good understanding of all types of structures that can improve women's possibilities in organizations, ought to be a valuable complement to critical studies, exclusively focusing on constraining factors (and on resistance to these).[6]

11.7 Concluding remarks

As we mentioned in the introduction to this book, we believe that it is important to study general trends and patterns in the organization/gender area. In the overall, complex social reality of patterns, unity, similarities and heterogeneity, disruptions, divergent trends, progression, conservatism and reaction, it is important to draw attention to, understand and illuminate variations. Most research in this field has tried to illuminate 'the typical' and 'the normal'. We started this project with an assumption that there are great variations in terms of the gender/organization relation and we chose empirical cases accordingly. Of course, we cannot say that our 'thesis' has been tested and turned out to have been confirmed. However, our initial assumptions have been strongly reinforced by the case studies. Our study thus departs quite radically from most of the literature in the field.

Besides – certainly not instead of – striving for a general picture, we propose a framework and a research agenda which might make researchers sensitive to discovering variations, contradictions and ambiguities in the gender/organization and sexual discrimination area. Our approach then parallels some developments in post-structuralist feminist theory and organizational culture studies, which focuses on other aspects than unified, integrated and holistic patterns (Flax, 1987; Martin & Meyersson, 1988, etc.).

We argue that organizations vary greatly in terms of their gender bias, both in terms of social practices – such as discrimination – as well as in organizational cultures and gender symbolism of various functions, professions and positions. Gender relations differed drastically in the three organizations and these patterns reflected as well as influenced the overall organizational culture and work climate. Another way of formulating this is to say that gender becomes salient as an important feature and significant as a discriminatory factor to different degrees in different organizational contexts. This has partly to do with women and men having different types of socialization backgrounds and organizations being different in terms of the gender bias/neutrality dimension. An important determinating factor here is the gender symbolism culturally associated with the organizational position. This symbolism is not, however, so stable and robust that it brings along in an automatic and deterministic way specific patterns of discrimination in hiring, promoting and interacting with female employees. Organizational (sub)communities may have stronger, weaker or perhaps no tendencies to discriminate. Irrespective of the strength and nature of the tendency, the gender bias may be 'in operation' in a differentiated way, depending on what and who is at stake. We suggest that particular subjects (females) might 'call upon' or stimulate associations to various images, stereotypes and other 'rules' (frameworks) for simplified understandings. The latter cultural phenomena are normally a part of organizational settings, but they vary. So does the degree to which particular social processes and subjects make them significant and, thus, the extent to which they contribute to discrimination. Different extra- and intra-organizational structures might point in different directions when it comes to both the socialization and construction of men and women as gender and the production of cultural associations (symbolism) of jobs, positions, and functions in the organization. Being aware of 'genderness' would reveal that reactions/discrimination and conflicts between the sexes may differ according to the degree and type of masculinity in the organization (gender-related assumptions and expectations affecting organizational culture). The patterns of interaction on the symbolic level do influence the work climate. Gender symbolism affects the organization in ways which may benefit some and may cause others to leave the organization. Gender symbolism also becomes imprinted upon other central organizational behaviour phenomena such as group relations and leadership.

As emphasized in the introduction of this book, our main interest was not to show ways in which to 'improve' women's possibilities of obtaining higher managerial positions. Hopefully we have, however, given the reader some ideas as to how to understand the hierarchical gendered division of labour, illustrated at the level of the organization by the figure shown on the front cover of this book.

Notes

1   So far, there are only loose suggestions about what kind of organizational principles
    are favoured by women. These are normally taken to be more humane and, although
    this is not explicitly said, morally superior to those favoured by men (at least those
    who have a dominating position), see e.g. Ferguson (1984); Loden (1986); Ressner
    (1986).
2   At the time of the study they had no steady relationship.
3   By domination of males we are not referring to men per se but rather models or ideals
    of masculinity.
4   Mumby & Stohl (1991) give examples on discursive processes which constitue organi-
    zational members' identities along gender lines. They also note "the length to which
    both marginalized and priviliged groups will go to preserve the given hegemonic rela-
    tions that are structured into the organization" (1991:327).
5   Minor distortions are probably common and are part of our culture. Major distortions
    are less common and are, perhaps, cases for the psychiatrist rather than for the social
    scientist.
6   Although our focus in the book has been on gender and managerial jobs we do ques-
    tion the notion of career. We agree with Benhabib & Cornell (1987:9) who also ques-
    tion the notion of success. Referring to Markus (1987) they say that it is not just a
    question of "raising" women "to a level defined by men, but through challenging the
    uniformization and prescription of aspirations and socially accepted and rewarded
    modes of life and career-pursuits. This would imply not only changing the definition
    of success but also introducing into public life patterns of behavior and emotionality
    previously confined to the domain of typically female activities: the importance of
    personal relationships for life-fulfillment, the value of work done well for its own
    sake, helpfulness to others and the like".

References

Acker, J (1992) Gendering Organizational Theory. In Mills, A J & Tancred, P (eds). *Gendering Organizational Analysis*. London: Sage.

Adler, N (1986/87) Women in Management Worldwide. *International Studies of Management & Organization*, 16, 3-4, 3-32

Agor, W H (1984) *Intuitive Management: Integrating Left and Right Brain Management Skills*. Englewood Cliffs: Prentice Hall.

Alvesson, M (1987) *Organization Theory and Technocratic Consciousness. Rationality, Ideology and Quality of Work*. Berlin/New York: de Gruyter.

Alvesson, M (1993) *Cultural Perspectives on Organizations*. Cambridge: Cambridge University Press.

Alvesson, M & Berg, P O (1992) *Corporate Culture and Organizational Symbolism*. Berlin/New York: de Gruyter.

Alvesson, M & Köping, A (1993) *Med känslan som ledstjärna. En studie av reklamarbete och reklambyråer*. Lund: Studentlitteratur.

Andriessen, E & Drenth, P (1984) Leadership: Theories and Models. In Drenth, P. et al (eds). *Handbook of Work and Organizational Psychology*. Vol. 1. Chichester: Wiley.

Antal, A B & Kresbach-Gnath, C (1986/87) Women in Management: Unused Resources in the Federal Republic of Germany. *International Studies of Management & Organization*, 16, 3-4, 133-151.

Argyris, C (1964) *Integrating the Individual and the Organization*. New York: Wiley.

Asplund, G (1988) *Women Managers. Changing Organizational Cultures*. Chichester: Wiley.

Ås, B (1982) *Kvinder i alle lande. En håndbog i frigørelse*. Copenhagen: Hans Reitzels.

Bachtold L M (1976) Personality Characteristics of Women of Distinction. *Psychology of Women Quarterly*, 1, 1.

Balsamo, A (1985) Beyond Female as a Variable. Paper presented at Conference on Critical Perspectives in Organization Analysis. Baruch College. New York.

Barrett, M (1980) *Women's Oppression Today*. London: Verso.

Bartol, K (1978) The Sex Structuring of Organizations: A Search for Possible Causes. *Academy of Management Review*, 3, 2.

Baude, A (1989) A Dialogue that Might yet Take Place: A Female Researcher Talks to Personnel Managers about Recruitment Processes. *International Studies of Management & Organization*, 19, 4.

Bayes, J (1987) Do Female Managers in Public Bureaucracies Manage with a Different Voice? Paper presented at the Third International Interdisciplinary Congress on Women. Dublin.

Bengtsson, M (1983) Identifikation, kön och klass. *Psykologi i Tillämpning*, 1, 3.

Benhabib, S (1987) The Generalized and the Concrete Other. In Benhabib, S & Cornell, D (eds). *Feminism as Critique*. Cambridge: Polity Press.

Benhabib, S & Cornell, D (1987) Introduction. Beyond the Politics of Gender. In Benhabib, S & Cornell, D (eds). *Feminism as Critique*. Cambridge: Polity Press.

Berner, B (1984) Women, Technology and the Division of Labour. What is the Role of Education? *Tidsskrift för Nordisk Förening för Pedagogisk Forskning*, 2, 5-17.

Billing, Y D (1991) *Køn, karriere, familie*. Copenhagen: Jurist- og Økonomforbundet.

Billing, Y D & Alvesson, M (1989) Four Ways of Looking at Women and Leadership. *Scandinavian Journal of Management*, 5, 2, 63-80

Billing, Y D & Bruvik-Hansen, A (1984) Women and Engineering. In *Girls and Science and Technology*. Contributions to the Third Gasat Conference. University of London.

Bilton, T et al (1982) *Introductory Sociology*. London: Macmillan.

Borgert, L (1992) *Organisation som mode*. Stockholm: Dept. of Business Administration, Stockholm University.

Bourdieu, P (1979) *Outline of a Theory of Practice*. Cambridge: Cambridge University Press.

Bradford, D L et al (1975) Executive Man and Woman: The Issue of Sexuality. In Gordon, E & Strober, M H, (eds). *Bringing Women into Management*. New York: McGraw-Hill.

Bradley, H (1989) *Men's Work, Women's Work. A Sociological History of the Sexual Division of Labour in Employment*. Cambridge: Polity Press.

Brief, A P & Wallace, M J (1976) The Impact of Employee Sex and Performance on the Allocation of Organizational Rewards. *Journal of Applied Psychology*, 92, 25-34.

Brown, R H (1976) Social Theory as Metaphor. *Theory and Society,* 3, 169-197.

Burrell, G & Hearn, J (1989) The Sexuality of Organization. In Hearn, J et al (eds). *The Sexuality of Organization*. London: Sage.

Burrell, G & Morgan, G (1979) *Sociological Paradigms and Organizational Analysis*. London: Heinemann.

Burrell, G (1984) Sex and Organizational Analysis. *Organization Studies,* 5, 97-118.

Burris, B H (1989) Technocratic Organization and Gender. *Women's Studies International Forum,* 12, 4, 447-462.

Burton, C (1985) *Subordination. Feminism and Social Theory.* Sydney: Allen & Unwin.

Butterfield, D A & Powell, G N (1981) Effect of Group Performance, Leader Sex, and Rater Sex on Ratings of Leader Behaviour. *Organizational Behaviour and Human Performance*, 28, 129-141.

Cahoon, A R & Rowney, J I A (1987) The Interaction between Worksite Variables and Personal Characteristics for Female Managers. Paper presented at the Third International Interdisciplinary Congress on Women. Dublin.

Calás, M B & Smircich, L (1988) Reading Leadership as a Form of Cultural Analysis. In Hunt, J G et al (eds). *Emerging Leadership Vistas.* Lexington: Lexington.

Calás, M B & Smircich, L (1991) Voicing Seduction to Silence Leadership. *Organization Studies*, 12, 567-601

Calás, M B & Smircich, L (1992 a) Re-writing Gender into Organizational Theorizing. Directions from Feminist Perspectives. In Reed, M I & Hughes, M D (eds). *Rethinking Organization: New Directions in Organizational Research and Analysis.* London: Sage.

Calás, M B & Smircich, L (1992 b) Using the 'F'word: Feminist Theories and the Social Consequences of Organizational Research. In Mills, A J & Tancred, P (eds). *Gendering Organizational Analysis.* London: Sage.

Calder, B J (1977) An Attribution Theory of Leadership. In Staw, B M & Salancik, G R (eds). *New Directions in Organizational Behavior.* Chicago: St. Clair Press.

Carbonell, J L (1984) Sex Roles and Leadership Revisited. *Journal of Applied Psychology*, 69, 44-49.

Carlsen, S (1987) Notat om udviklingen i antallet af kvindelige ledere indenfor det private erhvervsliv i perioden 1983-86. Copenhagen: Ligestillingsrådet.

Carlsen, A M S & Toft, L (1986) *Køn og ledelse.* Copenhagen: Forlaget Politiske Studier.

Carlsson, C (1987) Kön och klass ur ett historiskt perspektiv. In Ganetz, H et al (eds). *Feminism och Marxism. En förälskelse med förhinder.* Stockholm: Arbetarkultur.

Carlzon, J (1987) *Moments of Truth.* Cambridge: Ballinger.

Case, R et al (1987) Executives. *Management Today.* March.

Cecil, E A et al (1973) Perceived Importance of Selected Variables used to Evaluate Male and Female Job Applicants. *Personnel Psychology*, 26, 397-404.

Chodorow, N (1974) Family Structure and Feminine Personality. In Rosaldo, M Z & Lamphere, L (eds). *Women, Culture and Society.* Stanford: Stanford University Press.

Chodorow, N (1978) *The Reproduction of Mothering: Psychoanalysis and the Sociology of Gender.* Berkeley: University of California Press.

Christensen, S et al (1984) *Carlzons klister. Kultur og Forandring i SAS.* Copenhagen: Valmuen.

Clegg, S (1981) Organization and Control. *Administrative Science Quarterly,* 26, 4, 545-562.

Clegg, S (1989) *Frameworks of Power.* London: Sage.

Clegg, S & Dunkerley, D (1980) *Organization, Class and Control.* London: Routledge and Kegan Paul.

Cockburn, C (1985) *Machinery of Dominance.* London: Pluto.

Cockburn, C (1986) The Relations of Technology. In Crompton, R & Mann, M (eds). *Gender and Stratification.* Cambridge: Polity Press.

Collins, G (1982) *Unforeseen Business Barriers for Women.* New York: The N.Y. Times Company.

Collinson, D (1988) Engineering Humour: Masculinity, Joking and Conflict in Shopfloor Relations. *Organization Studies*, 9, 181-200.

Connell, R (1987) *Gender & Power.* Cambridge: Polity Press.

Cooper, C L & Davidson, M J (1982) *High Pressure: The Working Lives of Women Managers.* London: Fontana.

Crompton, R (1986) Credentials and Careers: Some Implications of the Increase in Professional Qualifications amongst Women. *Sociology*, 20, 1, 25-42.

Crompton, R (1990) The Class/Gender/Organization Nexus. In Clegg, S R (ed). *Organization Theory and Class Analysis. New Approaches and New Issues.* Berlin/New York: de Gruyter.

Crompton, R & Mann, M (eds.) (1986) *Gender and Stratification.* Cambridge: Polity Press.

Crompton, R & Sanderson, K (1990) *Gendered Jobs and Social Change.* London: Unwin Hyman.

Dalla Costa, M (1973) *The Power of Women and the Subversion of the Community.* Bristol: Falling Wall Press.

Danmarks Statistik (1990). Copenhagen: Danish Bureau of Statistics.

Davidson, M J & Cooper, C L (1984) Occupational Stress in Female Managers: A Comparative Study. *Journal of Management Studies*, 21, 2, 185-205.

Day, D R & Stogdill, R M (1972) Leader Behavior of Male and Female Supervisors: A Comparative Study. *Personnel Psychology*, 25, 353-360.

Deetz, S (1992) *Democracy in an Age of Corporate Colonization: Developments in Communication and the Politics of Everyday Life.* Albany: State University of New York Press.

Devanna, M A (1987) Women in Management: Progress and Promise. *Human Resources Management*, 26, 4.

DIOS (Dios-undersøgelsen) (1985) Copenhagen: Danish Institute for Organization Studies.

Dipboye, R (1975) Women as Managers – Stereotypes and Realities. *Survey of Business,* May-June, 22-26.

Dobbins, G & Platz, J (1986) Sex Differences in Leadership: How Real are They? *Academy of Management Review*, 11, 1, 118-127.

Edström, A (1988) Affärstänkandets metamorfos. In Beckérus, Å et al (eds). *Doktrinskiftet. Nya ideal i svenskt ledarskap*. Stockholm: Svenska Dagbladet.

Edström, A et al (1985) Leadership and Corporate Development. Paper. Stockholm: Farådet.

Edström, A et al (1989) *Förnyelsens ledarskap*. Stockholm: Norstedts.

Eisenstein, Z R (1979) *The Radical Future of Liberal Feminism*. Boston: Northeastern University.

Engels, F (1972) *The Origin of the Family, Private Property and the State*. London: Lawrence & Wishart.

Erikson, E H (1955) *Childhood and Society*. New York: Norton.

Esseveld, J (1987) Mot en kritisk feminism. In Ganetz, H et al (eds): *Feminism och marxism. En förälskelse med förhinder*. Stockholm: Arbetarkultur.

Ethelberg, E (1985) Kvinders personlighedsstrategier overfor mandlig dominans. *Psyke og Logos* 6, 173-189.

Etzion, D (1987) Career Success, Life Patterns, and Burnout in Male and Female Engineers: A Matched Pairs Comparison. Paper presented at the Third International Congress on Women. Dublin.

Fagenson, E (1986) Women's Work Orientations: Something Old, Something New. *Group & Organization Studies*, 11, 75-100.

Ferber, F, Huber, J & Spitze, G (1979) Preferences for Men as Bosses and Professionals. *Social Forces*, 58, 2, 466-476.

Ferguson, K E (1984). *The Feminist Case Against Bureaucracy*. Philadelphia: Temple University Press.

Finkelstein, C A (1981) Women Managers: Career Patterns and Changes in the United States. In Epstein, C F & Coser, R L (eds). *Access to Power. Cross-National Studies of Women and Elites*. London: George Allen & Unwin.

Firestone, S (1971) *The Dialectic of Sex*. London: Paladin.

Flax, J (1987) Postmodernism and Gender Relations in Feminist Theory. *Signs*, 12, 621-643.

Flax, J (1990) *Thinking Fragments. Psychoanalysis, Feminism, & Postmodernism in the Contemporary West*. Berkeley: University of California Press.

Fogarty, M, Allen, I & Walters, P (1981) *Women in Top Jobs*. London: Heinemann.

Forisha, B L (1981) The Inside and the Outsider: Women in Organizations. In Forisha, B L & Goldman, A (eds). *Outsiders on the Inside*. Englewood Cliffs: Prentice-Hall.

Foucault, M (1980) *Power/Knowledge*. New York: Pantheon.

French, M (1986) *Beyond Power: On Women, Men and Morals*. London: Abacus.

Friberg, M (1984) Försörjarnas protester och levnadskonstnärernas alternativ. In Friberg, M & Galtung, J (eds). *Rörelserna*. Stockholm: Akademilitteratur.

Galbraith, J K (1983) *The Anatomy of Power*. New York: Simon & Schuster.

Game, A & Pringle, R (1983) *Gender at Work*. Sydney: Allen & Unwin.

Geertz, C (1973) *The Interpretation of Cultures*. New York: Basic Books.

Gherardi, S (1992) The Symbolic Order of Gender in Organizational Cultures. Paper presented at the 10th Conference of SCOS. Lancaster.

Gilligan, C (1982) *In a Different Voice*. Cambridge: Harvard University Press.

Gilligan, C (1987) Women's Place in Man's Life Cycle. In Harding, S (ed). *Feminism & Methodology*. Milton Keynes: Open University Press.

Grant, J (1988) Women as Managers: What can They Offer to Organizations? *Organizational Dynamics*, 1, 56-63.

Gunnarsson, E & Ressner, U (1983) *Från hierarki till kvinnokollektiv?* Stockholm: Arbetslivscentrum.

Halaby, C N (1979) Job-Specific Sex Differences in Organizational Reward Attainment: Wage Discrimination Vs. Rank Segregation. *Social Forces*, 58, 1, 108-126.

Harlan, A & Weiss, C (1980) *Moving Up: Women in Managerial Careers*. Wesley: Wesley Center for Research on Women.

Harragan, B L (1977) *Games Mother Never Taught You*. New York: Rawson Associates.

Hartmann, H (1979) The Unhappy Marriage of Marxism and Feminism: Towards a More Progressive Union. *Capital and Class*, 8, Summer, 1-22.

Haug, F (1984) Morals Also Have Two Genders. *New Left Review*, 143, 51-67.

Healy, L M & Havens, C M (1987) Feminist Leadership Styles as a Force for Humanizing the Workplace. Paper presented at the Third International Interdisciplinary Congress on Women. Dublin.

Hearn, J et al (eds) (1989) *The Sexuality of Organization*. London: Sage.

Hearn, J & Parkin, W (1983) Gender and Organizations: A Selective Review and a Critique of a Neglected Area. *Organization Studies*, 4, 219-242.

Hearn, J & Parkin, W (1986/87) Women, Men and Leadership: A Critical Review of Assumptions, Practices and Change in the Industrialized Nations. In *International Studies of Management & Organization Studies*, 16, 3-4.

Hearn, J & Parkin, W (1987) *"Sex" at Work. The Power and Paradox of Organization Sexuality*. Brighton: Wheatsheaf.

Hemming, H (1987) Combining Psychology and Sociology of Women's Oppression. Paper presented at the Third International Interdisciplinary Congress on Women. Dublin.

Hennig, M & Jardim, A (1977) *The Managerial Woman*. New York: Anchor Press.

Hilmo, I (1983) An Analysis of Norwegian Textbooks in Science. Contributions to the II GASAT Conference. Oslo.

Hochschild, A (1983) *The Managed Heart*. Berkeley: University of California Press.

Hollander, J (1972) Sex Differences in Sources of Social Self-Esteem. *Journal of Consulting and Clinical Psychology*, 38, 343-358.

Holter, H (1984), Kjønnsroller, kjønnsidentifikation og autoritetsrelasjoner i yrkeslivet. *Tidsskrift for Samfunnsforskning*, 25, 347-358.

Homans, H (1987) Man-Made Myths: The Reality of Being a Woman Scientist in the NHS. In Spencer, A & Podmore, D (eds). *In A Man's World*. London: Tavistock.

Horner, M (1980) Learning to Read: Beyond Fear of Success. *Working Woman*. 5, 47-48.

Illich, I (1982) *Gender*. New York: Pantheon Books.

Izraeli, D (1986/87) Women's Movement into Management in Israel. *International Studies of Management & Organization*, 16, 3-4, 76-107.

Jick, T & Mitz, L (1985) Sex Differences in Work Stress. *Academy of Management Review*, 10, 408-420.

Johns, G (1983) *Organizational Behaviour*. Glenview: Scott, Foresman & Co.

Juristen & Økonomen (1981), 231-238.

Kanter, R M (1977) *Men and Women of the Corporation*. New York: Basic Books.

Keesing, R (1974) Theories of Culture. *Annual Review of Anthropology*, 3.

Keeton, K (1985) *Woman of Tomorrow*. New York: St. Martins's/Marck.

Keller, E F (1978) Gender and Science. *Psychoanalysis and Contemporary Thought*, 1, 409-433.

Kelly, A et al (1984) Girls into Science and Technology. Final Report. Manchester: Department of Sociology. University of Manchester.

Kerfoot, D & Knights, D (1993) Management, Masculinity and Manipulation: From Paternalism to Corporate Strategy in Financial Services in Britain. *Journal of Management Studies*, 30, 4.

Kirkham, L M & Loft, A (1993) Gender and the Construction of the Professional Accountant. *Accounting, Organizations and Society*. Forthcoming.

Knights, D & Morgan, G (1991) The Concept of Strategy in Sociology: A Note of Dissent. *Sociology*, 24, 3, 475-483.

Knights, D & Willmott, H (eds) (1986) *Gender and the Labour Process*. Aldershot: Gower.

Kotter, J (1982) What Effective Managers Really Do. *Harvard Business Review*, Nov-Dec, 156-167.

Kovalainen, A (1990) How do Male and Female Managers in Banking View their Work Roles and their Subordinates. *Scandinavian Journal of Management*, 6, 2, 143-159.

Lane, C (1992) Gender and the Labour Market in Europe: Britain, Germany and France Compared. Paper presented at a Gender Research Workshop, UMIST. Manchester.

Langer, S (1957) *Philosophy in a New Key*. Cambridge: Harvard University Press.

Laurent, A (1978) Managerial Subordinacy: A Neglected Aspect of Organizational Hierarchies. *Academy of Management Review*, 3, 2, 220-230.

Legge, K (1987) Women in Personnel Management: Uphill Climb or Downhill Slide? In Spencer, A & Podmore, D (eds). *In A Man's World*. London: Tavistock.

Lensink, M (1983) Girl's Physics and Technology in the Netherlands. The MENT-Project. *Contributions to the II GASAT Conference*. Oslo.

Lerner, G (1986) *The Creation of Patriarchy*. Oxford: Oxford University Press.

Lige nu (1988) *Nyt fra Ligestillingsrådet*, 26.

Lipman-Blumen, J (1976) Towards a Homosocial Theory of Sex Roles: An Explanation of the Sex Segregation of Social Institutions. In Blaxall, M and Reagan, B (eds). *Women and the Workplace*. Chicago: Chicago University Press.

Loden, M (1986) *Feminine Leadership or How to Succeed in Business Without Being one of the Boys*. New York: Times Books.

Loft, A (1992) Accountancy and the Gendered Division of Labour: A Review Essay. *Accounting, Organizations and Society*, 17, 3/4, 367-378.

Lowe, G S (1987) *The Feminization of Clerical Work: Women and the Administrative Revolution in Canada, 1901-31*. Cambridge: Polity Press.

Lukes, S (1978) Power and Authority. In Bottomore, T & Nisbet, R (eds). *A History of Sociological Analysis*. London: Heinemann.

Maccoby, E E & Jacklin, C N (1975) *The Psychology of Sex Differences*. Stanford: Stanford University Press.

Maegaard, B (1986) Kvinder i departementerne. *DJØF-bladet*, 17.

Magisterundersøgelsen (1986) Højtuddannet? – Ja. Ligestillet? Nej. Copenhagen.

Mann, M (1986) A Crisis in Stratification Theory? Persons, Households/Families/Lineages, Genders, Classes and Nations. In Crompton, R & Mann, M (eds). *Gender and Stratification*. Cambridge: Polity Press.

Marcuse, H (1964) *One-Dimensional Man*. Boston: Beacon Press.

Markens, M (1987) Women, Success and Civil Society. In Benhabib, S & Cornell, D (eds). *Feminism as Critique*. Cambridge: Polity Press.

Marshall, J (1984) *Women Managers. Travellers in a Male World*. Chichester: Wiley.

Marshall, C & Rossman, G B (1989) *Designing Qualitative Research*. Newbury Park: Sage.

Martin, J (1987) A Black Hole: Ambiguity in Organizational Culture. Paper presented at the SCOS Conference. Milan.

Martin, J & Meyerson, D (1988) Organizational Cultures and the Denial, Channeling and Acknowledgement of Ambiguity. In Pondy, L R et al (eds). *Managing Ambiguity and Change*, New York: Wiley.

Martin, P Y (1985) Group Sex Composition in Work Organizations: A Structural-Normative Model. *Research in the Sociology of Organizations*, 4, 311-349.

Marx, K (1947) *Das Kapital*. Berlin: JHW Dietz.

Melin, H (1990) Managers and Social Classes. In Clegg, S R (ed). *Organization Theory and Class Analysis. New Approaches and New Issues*. Berlin/New York: de Gruyter.

Meyer, J & Rowan, B (1977) Institutionalized Organizations: Formal Structure as Myth and Ceremony. *American Journal of Sociology*, 83, 340-363.

Miller, A (1981) *Det självutplånande barnet och sökandet efter en äkta identitet*. Stockholm: Wahlström & Widstrand.

Millett, K (1970) *Sexual Politics*. London: Abacus.

Mills, A J (1988) Organization, Gender and Culture. *Organization Studies*, 9, 351-370.

Mills, A J (1989) Gender, Sexuality and Organization Theory. In Hearn, J et al (eds). *The Sexuality of Organization*. London: Sage.

Mills, A J (1992) Sexuality and the Airline Industry: The Making of an Organizational Culture. Paper for Management Department session, University of Nijenrode.

Mills, A J & Murgatroyd, S J (1991) *Organizational Rules: A Framework for Understanding Organizations*. Milton Keynes: Open University Press.

Mills, A J & Tancred, P (eds) (1992) *Gendering Organizational Analysis*. London: Sage.

Mills, C W (1972) *The Sociological Imagination*. New York: Oxford University Press.

Mintzberg, H (1983) *Structure in Fives*. Englewood Cliffs: Prentice Hall.

Morgan, G (1980) Paradigms, Metaphors and Puzzle Solving in Organization Theory. *Administrative Science Quarterly*, 25, 605-622.

Morgan, G (ed) (1983) *Beyond Method*. Beverly Hills: Sage.

Morgan, G (1986) *Images of Organization*. Beverly Hills: Sage.

Morgan, G et al (1983) Organizational Symbolism. In Pondy, L R et al (eds). *Organizational symbolism*. Greenwich: J.A.I. Press.

Mumby, D & Stohl, C (1991) Power and Discourse in Organization Studies: Absence and the Dialectic of Control. *Discourse & Society*, 2, 313-332.

Mygind, A M & Humeniuk, J (1987) *Hvorfor avancerer kvinder ikke i banker og sparekasser?* Århus: Handelshøjskolen i Århus.

Nicholson, N & West, M A (1988) *Managerial Job Change: Men and Women in Transition*. Cambridge: Cambridge University Press.

Nieva, V & Gutek, B (1980) Sex Effects on Evaluation. *Academy of Management Review*, 5, 267-276.

Normann, R (1983) *Service Management*. Chichester: Wiley.

Ott, E M (1987) Effects of the Male-Female Ratio at Work: Policewomen and Male Nurses. Paper presented at the Third International Interdisciplinary Congress on Women. Dublin.

Peltonen, K (1987) Are Women Able to Change the Image and Content of Science and Technology? In *Contributions to the 4th Gender and Science Conference*. Ann Arbor.

Persson-Tanimura, I (1987) Kvinnors ekonomiska jämställdhet – nuläge och utvecklingstendenser. Working Paper. Lund: University of Lund.

Peters, T (1978) Symbols, Patterns and Settings: An Optimistic Case for Getting Things Done. *Organizational Dynamics*, 7, 2, 2-23.

Pfeffer, J (1977a) The Ambiguity of Leadership. *Academy of Management Review*, 2, 104-112.

Pfeffer, J (1977b) Toward an Examination of Stratification in Organizations. *Administrative Science Quarterly*, 22, 553-567.

Pfeffer, J (1981) Management as Symbolic Action. In Cummings, L & Staw, B (eds). *Research in Organizational Behaviour*. Vol 3. Greenwich: JAI Press.

Podmore, D & Spencer, A (1986) Gender in the Labour Process – the Case of Women and Men Lawyers. In Knights, D & Willmott H (eds). *Gender and the Labour Process*. Aldershot: Gower.

Powell, G N (1988) *Women & Men in Management*. Beverly Hills: Sage.

Powell, G N & Butterfield, D A (1979) The "Good Managers": Masculine or Androgynous? *Academy of Management Journal*, 22, 395-403.

Pringle, R (1989) *Secretaries Talk. Sexuality, Power and Work*. London: Verso.

Reif, W, Newstrom, J & Monczka, R (1975) Exploring Some Myths About Women Managers. *California Management Review*, 17, 4, 72-79.

Reskin, B. F (ed) (1984) *Sex Segregation in the Workplace. Trends, Explanations, Remedies*. Washington D.C.: National Academy Press.

Ressner, U (1986) Women and Group Organised Work in the Public Sector. In Fry, J (ed). *Towards a Democratic Rationality*. Aldershot: Gower.

Riger, S & Galligan, P (1980) Women in Management: An Exploration of Competing Paradigms. *American Psychologist*, 35, 10, 902-910.

Riley, P (1983) A Structurationist Account of Political Cultures. *Administrative Science Quarterly*, 28, 3, 414-437.

Rix, S E & Stone, A J (1984) Work. In Pritchard, S M (ed). *The Women's Annual*. Boston: G. K. Hall.

Rose, M & Fielder, S (1988) The Principle of Equity and the Labour Market Behaviour of Dual Earner Couples. Paper presented at the 6th Annual Aston/UMIST Conference on Organisation and Control of the Labour Process. Birmingham.

Rosen, B & Jerdee, T (1973) The Influence of Sex-Role Stereotypes on Evaluations of Male and Female Supervisory Behaviours. *Journal of Applied Psychology*, 57, 1, 44-48

Rosen, M (1988). You Asked for It: Christmas at the Bosses' Expense. *Journal of Management Studies*, 25, 463-480.

Rothwell, S (1985) The Nature of Management. Is Management a Masculine Role? *Management Education and Development*, 16, 79-98.

Salancik, G R & Pfeffer, J (1978) A Social Information Processing Approach to Job Attitudes and Task Design. *Administrative Science Quarterly*, 23, 224-253.

Schein, E H (1985) *Organizational Culture and Leadership*. San Francisco: Jossey-Bass.

Schein, V E (1973) The Relationship Between Sex Role Stereotypes and Requisite Management Characteristics. *Journal of Applied Psychology*, 57, 95-100.

Schein, V E (1975) Relationships Between Sex Role Stereotypes and Requisite Management Characteristics Among Female Managers. *Journal of Applied Psychology*, 60, 3, 340-344.

Schein, V E (1978) Sex Role Stereotyping, Ability and Performance: Prior Research and New Directions. *Personnel Psychology*, 31, 259-267.

Schmidt, E (1987) På vej til lederjob. In Haslebo, G et al (eds). *Magt og indflydelse – kvinder i job*. Copenhagen: Teknisk Forlag.

Scott, A M (1986) Industrialization, Gender Segregation and Stratification Theory. In Crompton, R & Mann, M (eds). *Gender and Stratification*. Cambridge: Polity Press.

Schneider, B (1980) Service Organizations: Climate is Crucial. *Organizational Dynamics*, Autumn, 52-65.

Shorter, E (1976) Women's Work: What Difference Did Capitalism Make? *Theory and Society*, 3, 513-527.

Shotter, J & Gergen, K (eds) (1989) *Texts of Identity*. London: Sage.

Silverman, D (1985) *Qualitative Methodology & Sociology*. Aldershot: Gower.

Skvoretz, J (1983) Salience, Heterogeneity and Consolidation of Parameters: Civilizing Blau's Primitive Theory. *American Sociological Review*, 48, 360-375.

Smircich, L (1983) Concepts of Culture and Organizational Analysis. *Administrative Science Quarterly*, 28, 3, 339-358.

Smircich, L (1985) Toward a Woman Centered Organization Theory. Paper presented at the Academy of Management Meetings. San Diego.

Smircich, L & Morgan, G (1982) Leadership: The Management of Meaning. *Journal of Applied Behavioral Science*, 18, 257-273.

Smith, D E (1987) *The Everyday World as Problematic. A Feminist Sociology*. Boston: Northeastern University Press.

South, et al (1982) Social Structure and Intergroup Interaction. *American Sociological Review*, 47, 587-599.

Spear, M G (1983) The Biasing Influence of Pupil Sex in a Science Marking Exercise. Research in Science and Technological Education. In *Girls and Science and Technology*. Contributions to the III GASAT Conference. London.

Statistical Informations (1991). Danmarks Statistik. Copenhagen: Danish Bureau of Statistics.

Statistisk årbog (1989). Danmarks Statistik. Copenhagen: Danish Bureau of Statistics.

Statistisk årbog (1990). Danmarks Statistik. Copenhagen: Danish Bureau of Statistics.

Steier, F (ed) (1991) *Research and Reflexivity*. London: Sage.

Symons, G L (1986) Coping with the Corporate Tribe. How Women in Different Cultures Experience the Managerial Role. *Journal of Management*, 12, 379-390.

Symons, G L (1986/1987) Women's Occupational Careers in Business: Managers and Entrepreneurs in France and in Canada. *International Studies of Management & Organization*, 16, 3-4, 61-76.

Terborg, J R & Ilgin, D R (1975) A Theoretical Approach to Sex Discrimination in Traditional Masculine Occupations. *Organizational Behaviour and Human Performance*, 13, 352-376.

The Equal Status Council (1990). Copenhagen: Ligestillingsrädet.

Thompson, P (1983) *The Nature of Work*. London: Macmillan.

Tkach, H (1980) The Female Executive. *Managing*, 1.

Tolson, A (1977) *The Limits of Masculinity*. London: Tavistock.

Van Maanen, J & Barley, S R (1984) Occupational Communities: Culture and Control in Organizations. In Staw, B & Cummings, L L (eds). *Research in Organizational Behavior*. Vol 6. Greenwich: JAI Press.

Wahl, A (1992) *Könsstrukturer i organisationer. Kvinnliga civilekonomers och civilingenjörers karriärutveckling*. Stockholm: EFI, Handelshögskolan.

Wallace, R A (ed) (1989) *Feminism and Sociological Theory*. London: Sage.

Walters, P A (1987) Servants of the Crown. In Spencer, A & Podmore, D (eds). *In a Man's World*. London: Tavistock.

Weinstein, H & Zappert, L (1980). Stress and the Working Woman. Paper presented at the Annual Meeting of the American Psychological Association. Montreal.

Weisbord, M (1987) *Productive Workplaces*. San Francisco: Jossey-Bass.

Whyte, J (1986) *Girls into Science and Technology. The Story of a Project*. London: Routledge & Kegan Paul.

Willmott, H & Knights, D (1982) The Problem of Freedom. Fromm's Contribution to a Critical Theory of Work Organization. *Praxis International*, 2, 204-225.